INSIDE THE NDP WAR ROOM

Inside the NDP War Room

Competing for Credibility
in a Federal Election

JAMES S. MCLEAN

McGill-Queen's University Press
Montreal & Kingston • London • Ithaca

ISBN 978-0-7735-4092-7 (cloth)
ISBN 978-0-7735-4093-4 (paper)

Legal deposit fourth quarter 2012
Bibliothèque nationale du Québec

Printed in Canada on acid-free paper that is 100% ancient forest free
(100% post-consumer recycled), processed chlorine free

This book has been published with the help of a grant from the Canadian
Federation for the Humanities and Social Sciences, through the Aid to
Scholarly Publications Program, using funds provided by the Social
Sciences and Humanities Research Council of Canada.

McGill-Queen's University Press acknowledges the support of the Canada
Council for the Arts for our publishing program. We also acknowledge
the financial support of the Government of Canada through the Canada
Book Fund for our publishing activities.

Library and Archives Canada Cataloguing in Publication

McLean, James S., 1956–
    Inside the NDP war room : competing for credibility in a federal election /
James S. McLean.

    Includes bibliographical references and index.
    ISBN 978-0-7735-4092-7 (bound). – ISBN 978-0-7735-4093-4 (pbk.)

    1. New Democratic Party – Case studies. 2. Canada. Parliament –
Elections, 2006 – Case studies. 3. Political campaigns – Canada –
Case studies. 4. Communication in politics – Canada – Case studies.
5. Campaign management – Canada – Case studies. 6. Public relations
and politics – Canada – Case studies. 7. Truthfulness and falsehood –
Political aspects – Canada – Case studies. I. Title.

JL197.N4M36 2012   324.27107   C2012-904235-8

This book was typeset by Interscript in 10.5/13 Sabon.

To Anna
From the first inkling to the final line your insights and experience
helped to make this book possible.

Contents

Acknowledgments

This book would not have been possible without the help and support of the individuals who made up the campaign team for the New Democratic Party in the election campaign of 2005–06. These dedicated and decent people often went out of their way to leave me with insights that would otherwise have been impossible to divine. I thank you all for your generosity. However, I would like to single out Brian Topp for special acknowledgment.

As campaign co-chair in the 2005–06 contest, Brian made it possible for me to obtain access to internal war room conversations that would normally have been out of bounds to a researcher. He was generous with his explanations about how the war room worked. He never ducked tough questions or tried to influence what I was writing. Even during his bid for the NDP leadership in 2011–12, when every waking minute of his day was taken up with winning that contest, he made himself available to me. For a chief strategist of a major Canadian political party to be this open is truly remarkable and comes, I believe, from his genuine desire that average people understand why politicians and political parties do what they do on the campaign trail and why the votes of everyday people are so important to the life of the nation. For all of this, my heartfelt thanks.

Finally, I would like to acknowledge the community of people – my colleagues and students, family and friends, the publishing professionals who encouraged me, supported me, and guided me back to the path when I wandered into the wilderness. Going in, I had no idea that it takes a village to publish a book. I know it now.

INSIDE THE NDP WAR ROOM

Introduction

As the Conservative government of Stephen Harper prepared for an election in the fall of 2008, word began to leak out of a massive self-contained media and operations complex in Ottawa's east end. This integrated partisan communication facility (including a professionally appointed television studio) was said to have a political "war room" the likes of which had never been seen in Canada. It was ready to launch into action the minute the election writ was dropped.[1] This centre devoted to the continuous application of strategic communication initiatives would provide the means to deliver the party's message directly to Conservative supporters, bypassing parliamentary reporters in the process. The Harper Conservatives, flush with money from their base, claimed to be on the verge of breaking the influence of the traditional journalistic model, an arrangement of more or less respectful adversarial oversight endowing journalists with the responsibility to oversee, question, and challenge the democratically conferred governing power of elected officials.

Journalists were invited to briefly visit this Conservative *über* war room at the beginning of the 2011 election campaign where, under tightly controlled circumstances, they were introduced to an election team with a single, stated purpose: to deliver the Conservatives a parliamentary majority.[2] Between the two campaigns, the war room had remained in action mode, part of the perpetual commitment to readiness of a party governing from minority status. When the Conservatives obtained their coveted majority in May 2011, it was thought that war-room tactics and strict communicative control might soften. Instead, the Harper Conservatives have shown little inclination to turn down the strategic heat. If anything, the fingerprints of the government's war-room operatives are more evident in the day-to-day communication of the governing party. Should this come as a surprise?

As Tom Flanagan, Stephen Harper's hagiographer and former campaign manager, has observed, the Conservative war room remains a part of a new general system of strategic planning and readiness: "A campaign manager reporting directly to the leader, not to a committee, is always in place. Voter identification linked to fundraising goes on 363 days a year (Christmas and Easter excepted)." The party has a "university" to train Conservative campaign workers. Money is spent to reach out to targeted ridings and ethnic groups. It is, as Flanagan has put it, a "formidable machine."[3]

To my knowledge, no journalist has been permitted to observe the 17,000-square-foot Conservative "message factory" in action. As in most political organizations devoted to crafting partisan speech, access is strictly controlled. This is not unexpected, given the growing premium placed on strategic secrecy by war rooms of all stripes, yet it does represent a shift from the original manifestation of the war room and a commensurate upping of the ante in the high-stakes game of strategic political communication.

That's because political war rooms were originally meant to lend a measure of transparency to the communicative processes involved in electoral politics. Instead of secret backroom deals made by anonymous party operatives, politics would be done in the open, in an organized space where the construction of messages could be witnessed by anyone willing to invest the time. Indeed, the original, self-declared war room was the subject of a documentary film, *The War Room*, about Bill Clinton's successful run for the presidency.[4] In the film, one of the central figures in Clinton's campaign, political organizer James Carville, openly states before a room full of volunteers that a fundamental purpose of the Clinton organization is to shine a light on the dirty tricks and underhanded tactics used by the Republican opposition. Transparency on the part of the Clinton organization is meant to show that the good guys, the defenders of democracy on Clinton's team, have nothing to hide, while the purveyors of the dark arts in the Republican camp prefer to operate in secret because they are interested only in power. It is a fine performance.

But before the transparency fairy steals the show, it is worth noting that *The War Room* was not released for public consumption until *after* Clinton had won the presidency. It is not difficult to argue that a significant part of this film is about political operatives using the "truth" of the documentary form and the reputational prestige of the filmmakers to support an agonistic declaration of selected assets, intentions, and objectives.[5] Behind the performance, then and now, are organizations that secretly compile information, use selected bits of biographical information to undermine reputations, engage in outrageous diversionary tactics, seek to suppress voter turnout when it suits them, and generally engage in cycles of spin that are relentless and perpetual. If the agonistic function of the Clinton war room was anything other than window dressing, it was mainly concerned with symbolic sabre-rattling in the often vicious competition for votes that characterizes US presidential races.

The Conservative war room that reporters in Canada were permitted to briefly glimpse in the lead-up to the 2011 election simply dispensed with the artifice. It was unapologetic in its purpose and intention: a massive state-of-the-art organization meant to intimidate not only political opponents but the journalists who would have to deal with its output. "We are going to be the government," said this formidable machine. "Be careful what you report and how you report it."

The very fact that journalists now routinely show up for controlled war-room tours and duly report their messages is proof enough that this political communication entity has evolved into an embedded part of our political culture. Parties with big, rich, "professional" war rooms are seen to deserve respect. Parties with war rooms that are considered poor, limited, or "amateur" are themselves considered poor, limited, and amateur. For the record, the New Democratic Party also performed a major makeover on its war room in preparation for the 2011 election and invited journalists in for a tour.[6] In many respects, then, the war room has become a serious metonymic measure for a party's commitment to govern – less important than the persona of the leader but more important than other party organizations such as riding associations. After all, the logic goes, if you can't organize the way your messages are crafted and disseminated, how can you possibly hope to run a country? Nevertheless, in spite of their name, Canadian war rooms have generally been reluctant to cross certain boundaries for fear of a public backlash. That reticence may no longer be the case, just as it is no longer the case that war rooms are ad hoc entities brought into being to win elections. Indeed, the war room, in the hands of government, appears to have morphed into an important but non-exclusive part of a larger system of institutionalized message manipulation and control.

Bit by bit, the flow of information from government to the people has been consolidated in fewer, partisan hands: the Prime Minister's Office (PMO), where *everything* from all arms of government is vetted by political operatives before public release; the hand-picked "communication officers," hired members of the party faithful, whose job it is to spin the government line (one of whom, Kory Teneycke, was hired, de-hired, and re-hired by Québecor to head up the Ottawa bureau for the right-wing cable channel Sun Television); the Conservative caucus where the prime minister rules with an iron fist and where elected members, including cabinet ministers, receive their marching orders; and, of course, the war room, where the often nasty and always manipulative strategies and tactics of election campaigns have been extended into the daily political life of the nation. It is fair to say that the public discussion in this country between the governors and the governed has never before been subjected to such a thorough and systematic attempt at control.[7]

Many journalists, notably columnists from major Canadian newspapers, have taken a stand against these controls. Reporters have produced stories about the latest tightening of the communicative screws. A recent feature-length story from two Canadian Press reporters outlined the systematic plotting behind staged political events: audiences with the prime minister where every question asked had been written beforehand and placed with a willing audience member.[8] In such cases, political operatives work the room following the staged event, heading off any reporter who dares to ask an "unapproved" question of the participants. The story garnered interest not because of the substance of the political event but because of the lengths that political operatives were willing to go to control information!

Still, even as such stories become commonplace, it is comparatively easy to find journalists working for big news organizations who have not considered the full extent of the management and control that has gone into the information in their stories. Often deadline pressures preclude such consideration. Sometimes it is a question of offending those who hold the power to release or withhold critical material. Editorial pressure may play a part: the expectation from "the desk" to match a competitor's story rather than pursue another angle, or to provide more than the surface "objective" detail provided in a news release and the "balanced" response from the opposition. Often all of these elements work in tandem. Sometimes reporters are just lazy or overwhelmed.

When I recently met with some of my former journalism students, one of them, now a valued reporter with the Canadian Press wire service, described his experience in covering Stéphane Dion during the 2008 federal election campaign as the Liberal leader crisscrossed the country. This reasonably seasoned CP reporter seemed amazed that his BlackBerry – standard issue for all reporters on the campaign trail – would start alerting him to messages from the Conservatives *before* Dion had finished delivering whatever campaign speech he was giving, regardless of where or when he was giving it. Invariably, said the reporter, a text would appear, "Ask him this ..." followed by "a really good question."

It was a conundrum, because every other reporter in the room was getting the same message. The intended effect was to set up a kind of psychological game of journalistic chicken. Every reporter *wanted* to ask the question, but most were reluctant because they knew the intent of the Conservative war room was not to enlighten their readership but to destabilize Dion, to undercut his message by co-opting a reporter into asking a question that would make Dion appear dumb or unprepared. Of course, the Conservatives could always claim that they were working in the public interest, but if this were the case, why did they need a reporter to pose their question? The situation was usually resolved when someone less aware of the machinations of the Conservative war room – a local reporter, for example – asked the question. Then everyone would breathe a sigh of relief and record Dion's response for their stories

If we dig a little deeper into the case of the questionable question, some subsumed motivations start to emerge. And they lie at the theoretical core of this book. While the questions offered by political war rooms to reporters may be legitimate to the public discussion, political strategists understand that journalists lend *credibility* to political speech and that the credibility of the journalist as a supposedly disinterested producer of meaning is central to the process of getting people to trust the truth claims in the message. The "rapid response" question that appears on all those BlackBerrys (now a standard tactical gambit in Canadian political culture) is intended to turn that disinterested (as in politically neutral) journalistic credibility to the advantage of partisan operators. Credibility conferred by the journalist remains the real prize in this complex communicative game.

But how might credibility be measured? How does one even begin to talk about it without opening a can of associative worms connected to terms that are themselves culturally grounded and subject to interpretation according to the filters that are deployed? Truth to a lawyer may have a much different meaning than to a scientist, even though both claim to base their respective truths on evidentiary facts. The standards of integrity are much different when applied to the marketplace than when used to choose a winner of the Nobel Prize. Yet these concepts, like credibility, form the basis for much of the give and take that makes modern (and postmodern) life possible. If we are to understand why credibility and related concepts are so meaningful to political operatives, we must take on the difficult task of developing a theory to explain credibility. This book undertakes such a theorization. It uses war-room practices to situate the value of credibility to political actors, while theorizing credibility as a means to explain the actions of war rooms. Even so, how does one go about studying the slippery concept of credibility as it pertains to an organization whose reason for being is the manufacture of partisan meaning?

The only way is to get inside the organization, to study it from the inside out – an especially sticky proposition when the organization in question is protective of its trade secrets, suspicious of outsiders, and preoccupied with the business of getting its candidates elected. It also isn't helpful when the organization is full of people who make their living spinning reality to their own advantage. Nevertheless, when the election drums began beating in the fall of 2005 around the core issue of Liberal integrity (centred on the so-called "sponsorship scandal"), I went hat in hand to the main political parties, asking if I could study their war rooms in action once the election was called. The Liberals and the Conservatives ignored me. The New Democrats returned my calls, or, rather, a fellow named Brian Topp returned my emails.

Topp and I had known each other from a distance for more than a decade. He had been a central behind-the-scenes figure in the Saskatchewan NDP government of Roy Romanow during Romanow's first two terms, occupying a position as deputy chief of staff. As the de facto political strategist for the Saskatchewan NDP, he had left the province when Romanow's third run at a majority sputtered and the party barely managed to cling to minority power. During Topp's time in Saskatchewan, I was employed as a current affairs producer for the CBC. This meant that Topp would be generally aware of any stories we were pursuing that involved the government, and we at the CBC were certainly aware of Brian Topp. For all of this, I did not meet him or even talk to him on the telephone until my wife went to work for the Saskatchewan government as a communications officer. She would eventually become Romanow's press secretary. Her boss was Brian Topp.

When the NDP withdrew its support and effectively pushed Paul Martin's minority government into an election in 2005, Topp was elevated to the position of co-chair for the NDP's national campaign. It occurred to me that he would be in a position to help me access the NDP war room. Thus began two months of negotiation that culminated in my proposal to work as a war-room volunteer. "Basically I think what we're going to do is take you up on your volunteering offer," wrote Topp. "What you write afterwards is up to you."

The offer was extraordinarily generous but also something of a mixed blessing. My proposal to study a political war room in action was originally intended to borrow from the model of a "workplace ethnography" used by researchers such as David Hogarth in his case study of CBC Newsworld, Barry Dornfeld in his study of public television in the United States, and, more recently, Georgina Born in her exhaustive examination of the BBC. John van Maanen's study of work practices at Disney and Ester Reiter's study of the culture of minimum wage work at Burger King also offered useful guides to this genre.[9] In each case, researchers were able to "embed" themselves within the work structure of the organizations and, in the manner of a traditional ethnography, grow into the social structures of the workplace as (mostly) accepted members of the localized culture. With relatively few constraints, they observed and recorded the practices of employees in order to take note of the relations at work in the management systems and corporate cultures of the places that employed them. This was my conceptual objective in proposing to study the NDP war room. However, it soon became clear that this approach, for reasons that are inherent to the organizational structure and purpose of a political war room at election time, simply would not work.

Most political war rooms in 2005 were still ad hoc organizations formed for the specific purpose of generating partisan political communication during an election campaign. For this reason, their lifespan was roughly commensurate with the dates of any given campaign. In the case of the 2005–06 general election, this was the fifty-six days from the drop of the election writ at the end of November until the day of the vote on 23 January 2006. Even though this was an unusually long campaign by Canadian standards, any "ethnography" involving such an organization would be impossible in the traditional sense because legislated time constraints limited the life of the organization being studied. There was simply not enough time to permit an observer's presence to become normalized.

The culture of the war room made a traditional approach even more problematic. Unlike its counterparts in the other federal parties, the NDP campaign team was made up of a collection of party workers taken from pools of New Democrat talent across the country. On any given day, party workers from Manitoba worked together with employees of the federal caucus. Communication specialists from British Columbia laboured side by side with their counterparts from Ontario, Saskatchewan, and Atlantic Canada. The Liberals and the Conservatives had adopted a more corporate approach to their war-room organizations – the Earnscliffe Strategy Group, for example, handled much of the "file" for the Liberal campaign in the 2005–06 election. The NDP, then and now, draws upon its grassroots talent, notably from provinces where it has actually formed a government. This is a unique arrangement within the Canadian political mosaic, and because the NDP talent pool is relatively small (and the war chest comparatively shallow), war-room workers tend to get called upon to work on successive campaigns, both provincially and federally, in a kind of lend-lease system that has grown up among political kin. They are a close-knit group and a bit wary of "outsiders."

The challenge, then, was to gain entry to an exclusive political "club" – anywhere from a dozen to about thirty people, depending on where the boundaries of the war room were drawn – with a limited lifespan, and then to make sense of its core communicative practices during the most intense period of the political cycle, a time when most of those involved considered the stakes to be particularly high and any distraction especially loathsome. And there was an unforeseen difficulty: I had envisioned a work environment where strategies and tactics were discussed in open space, where the banter of co-workers with a common purpose could be heard and remarked upon, but the reality was much different. The vast majority of communication among and between war-room workers was conducted behind an electronic wall. Most conversations happened on a secure list-serve developed specifically for campaign communication.

Fortunately I was a member of the team, at least on paper, and that permitted me on my first day on the job to get into line with a group of fellow campaign workers signing up to have their email addresses entered into the list-serve system. This access was no small gift. When I used the list-serve for the first time, the world of the NDP's election campaign literally appeared before my eyes. My address would eventually be scrubbed from the list-serve during a "spy sweep" conducted during a more paranoid phase of the campaign. But for more than a month, from the middle of November through the end of December, I was made privy, in writing, to the mid-level exchange of information among the party's political operatives. To my knowledge, such sweeping electronic access to a working political organization by an arm's-length researcher had never before been achieved and has not been achieved since.

These messages of record represent a body of communication distributed across a range of functional fields. By far the most numerous were daily news stories generated by newspapers and wire services, and "advisories" that flagged journalists on upcoming campaign events. These sources were normally taken verbatim from an electronically published source – notably CP but also the major dailies – and cut and pasted into emails sent out to all interested parties in the NDP campaign. Relevant reports by television and radio stations and networks were transcribed and circulated. Abstracts of long-form journal articles were sent around and, if the material was deemed to be critical, the full-length articles would be circulated. Some of these files ran to several thousand words.

Information from competing camps that might be of interest to the war room was also forwarded. This could include news releases posted on a competitor's website or statements made by a party leader from an obscure source such as an Internet weblog. Of the 1,200 emails that landed in my list-serve account, about two-thirds came from media sources. The remaining third literally recorded the way that war-room workers used media-generated and other information to develop and disseminate campaign strategies and tactics.

I was also able to observe the NDP election team in action. From my desk I could hear the party's press secretary delivering lines to the media, complaining about story treatments, or relaying requests.

Campaign workers would often stop by to chat with the war-room manager about developments in their own area of interest. I was never admitted to the morning meeting where the various campaign unit heads came together to plan the day and talk about successes and failures. I was never permitted to meet with the advertising team, a group that, in my opinion, produced the most original commercials of the campaign. But I was able to range freely through the organizational space, talk to people and observe small actions and reactions, feel the original giddy energy of the place turn to perseverance, and then to exhaustion. In short, while the list-serve provided documentation, my physical presence as a "volunteer" provided texture and reminded me that behind the bluff and bluster, the spin and speciousness of so much strategic political communication, are real people with real lives. Most would describe themselves thoughtfully as "progressives," dedicated to the leader, their party, and its objectives.

On the surface, those objectives were, of course, to get "ink and airtime" for the NDP, the beginning of a perceived causal chain that, if successful, would see public opinion shift in favour of the party. This book examines in some detail the first link in that chain: the campaign's strategic communication centre. However, observations of war-room practices would be largely meaningless, mere description, without some attempt to follow the messages produced by those practices through the interpretive and disseminative processes of journalistic production and into some notion of the public sphere. For this reason, I have added two further areas of discovery to the mix, journalism and publics.

While I was at work in the war room, I had arranged to collect three prominent English-language daily newspapers for each day of the election campaign: the *Globe and Mail*, the *National Post*, and the *Ottawa Citizen*. I referenced other newspapers from time to time, particularly when there was a local response to a national issue being reflected in the campaign, or I wanted a broader view of national interests, such as a viewpoint from Western Canada or Quebec.

I selected the *Globe and Mail* because it is a Toronto-based publication with a national reach and an editorial policy that tends to occupy the centre of the opinion spectrum. The *National Post* (then still owned by the Asper family's CanWest media group) remains a self-proclaimed national newspaper of the right and, therefore, offered a different editorial slant from the *Globe*. The *Ottawa Citizen* is a local newspaper with considerable influence in national affairs because it serves official Ottawa. (The Aspers also owned it at the time.) In each case, I analyzed daily news stories, opinion columns, and editorials to ascertain the level of response (or non-response) reporters and editors gave to matters pertaining to the NDP and, more specifically, the extent to which language developed in the NDP war room was reflected in the reporting of each publication.

I gave particular attention to the Canadian Press (CP) wire service. CP is a source of journalistic content and context for virtually every newspaper and broadcaster in Canada (CanWest subsequently opted out of its use-agreement with the wire service but was a full member of the CP subscriber "family" during the election of 2005–06). CP was also available to non-journalistic subscribers including the major political parties who used it as a source for tracking reports about themselves and competing campaigns. The NDP relied heavily on the wire service in order to track the main stories in circulation during the daily news cycle, to incorporate any reports that might offer a potential platform to develop war-room communication, and to gauge the extent of circulation of communication originating in the war room and in opposing camps. As such, CP wire stories became a record of the immediate journalistic response to political news. The information included in CP reporting was often taken as the factual basis for editorials and columns in subscriber papers. Therefore, I used CP as a kind of baseline communication resource, a reflection of what generally happens when the political and journalistic fields work from the same "script." Often I could track the exchanges between political actors and journalists as stories were haggled over and updated in the daily struggle to "own" an issue.

In addition, I have made limited use of certain journalistically situated Internet-based resources, notably weblogs and column postings generated by working journalists. In the case of Paul Wells and Andrew Coyne, genuine working weblogs offered me a daily informal account of the various political campaigns; the observations and opinions of these writers were often used to inform material circulated by political actors and other journalists.

Antonia Zerbisias of the *Toronto Star* played a different role. Her company-based weblog, *azerbic* (now defunct), offered a daily open forum for general discussion on matters pertaining to the media and the election campaign. Her thoughts, and those of her readers, were often cited on other weblogs, including two that have gained a measure of credibility in the realm of political commentary: *Conservative*

Party of Canada Pundit, operated out of Ottawa by Stephen Taylor and *calgarygrit*, operated during the 2005–06 campaign by Dan Arnold from Calgary. The work of both Arnold and Taylor was often indistinguishable from the daily production of so-called mainstream journalists; however, the two enlivened the debate during the campaign around specific issues because they were not constrained by many of the conditions that apply to traditional journalists such as production deadlines and traditional editorial oversight.

I also used the discussions that occurred on these two weblogs as a means to peek behind the curtain that normally conceals the dynamic exchange of opinion among interested publics. It is no secret that most political communication strategists aim to convey simple messages through heavy repetition. It is also no secret that they are greatly concerned about how their messages are perceived in public space. They might be surprised to learn how the public response areas offered on most blogs have opened up the discussion around matters of public concern, and just how sophisticated the discussion around those concerns can be.

Indeed, I develop in this book the crucial role of publics in the conferral of credibility, both journalistic and political, as a means of explaining how power and legitimacy are intertwined in the social, political, economic, and legal space of an election campaign. This book's subtitle, "Competing for Credibility in a Federal Election," gestures towards the distinct fields of action and expression that are thrown together during a unique constitutional moment. The challenge and the value of the book are that it looks to the inevitable interrelationships between these elements in order to attempt to comprehend the underlying and mostly unrevealed stakes in play. It seeks to level the playing field a bit for those who may not have realized just how complex and how manipulative the whole business of public political communication has become. In doing so it seeks to give practical expression to an often disregarded ideal: that the people with their own interests at heart – publics – have their own role to play in conferring credibility and, therefore, democratically obtained political power upon those who would govern.

Without knowing it at the time, I had been given a unique opportunity to witness the beginning of a political trajectory that would see the NDP struggle and grow through three campaigns, pick up a few seats here and there, gain a cherished beachhead in Quebec, try to position itself to take advantage of a slow-motion Liberal collapse, push back against Conservative inroads while trying to refine its own ideological stance in the face of world economic pressures that threatened this country's own stability and terrified those who were least able to cope. If such a trajectory begins with the election campaign of 2005–06, it concludes with the historic breakthrough in Quebec in May 2011, the rise of the NDP to official opposition status, and the tragedy of Jack Layton's death the following summer.

Throughout, the NDP war room has adapted and grown. As this book went to press the person who opened the war room to me in that pivotal election campaign of 2005–06, Brian Topp, had all but disappeared from public view, retreating into private life following his own failed campaign to lead the party. (He has since resurfaced to prepare the NDP in British Columbia for an anticipated provincial election in 2013.) The new leader of the federal party, Thomas Mulcair, is a man who could not be more different from Jack Layton in temperament and political style. He has already started to turn the page and take New Democrats into a new era, supported by dozens of MPs from Quebec, each bringing their own concerns to the caucus table and shifting the party culture as they do so.

In such an era of flux, the NDP's communicative brain trust, those in charge of crafting the narratives and constructing the messages to both ground the party and move it forward, have become increasingly important. Alas, many of the senior keepers of the residual strategic memory have departed in the face of Mulcair's leadership victory, leaving to the few who remain the vast responsibility of adapting the public face of the party to its new internal realities, even as it begins to prepare for the fight of its life in the next election campaign. They also face a shifting technological and journalistic landscape where tolerance for the darker side of war-room communication is wearing thin, and where publics are less reluctant than ever before to push back against perceived political manipulation and bully tactics. The way that political war rooms operate in this uncertain future, whether they are able to adapt to these new realities, is certain to leave an enduring mark on the competition for power and the practice of government in Canada.

1

Campaigning in Canada: The Credibility Quotient

It is late morning on a biting December day in the nation's capital. In a room full of cubicles in a nondescript building on a street lined with similar buildings, people emerge from their work spaces, drawn to a bank of television monitors on a rickety stand in one of the few common areas. None of the television sets match in size, make, or model, but one of the larger ones is tuned to CBC Newsworld (now CBC News Network), the all-news, English-language cable channel run by the national public broadcaster. The anchorperson, veteran journalist Nancy Wilson, reads a standard script promoting an upcoming round of leaders' debates to be carried on Newsworld in the coming days, then throws to a "live hit" in Regina, Saskatchewan. It is week 3 of the winter election campaign of 2005–06 and the New Democratic Party, represented by leader Jack Layton, has come to the birthplace of publicly funded medicare in Canada to invoke the spirit of T.C. "Tommy" Douglas in a bid to bolster its "ownership" of the issue of universally accessible, single-tier health care.

The people back in Ottawa, the ones who normally occupy the cubicles, are NDP campaign workers, and this staged event, carried live on national television, is a rare opportunity for them to join in a good old-fashioned stump speech, albeit from a few thousand kilometres away. This is because the real star of this show is not leader Layton but Shirley Douglas, daughter of the late T.C. She has become a fixture in successive NDP campaigns because of her background in theatre and acting and her consequent flair for galvanizing the faithful behind her father's health-care legacy. It is one of the few times that Jack Layton, after a brief declaration of intentions, seems content to stand in the background in support of this living connection to the party's social-democratic past. There is general quiet as Douglas begins to speak, nods of approval as she lashes out at "right-wing politicians like Stephen Harper and the prime minister." The mood in the room turns electric as Douglas, her trained voice rising dramatically, declares: "We will not permit the dismantling of Canada's single-payer health care system!" There are more nods. The group breaks into applause when Douglas attacks the Liberal government's plan to inject billions into health care and "just hope it gets to where it's needed!" The odd "Hallelujah!" would not be out of place, but nobody obliges.

The point is made. The climactic moment comes and goes. But Douglas continues to talk, extolling the virtues of equal, accessible health care for all. She begins to repeat herself. Those who are watching seem uncomfortable. A few quietly slip away, returning to their cubicles and the day's campaign responsibilities. The manager of the strategic communication unit, the "war room," mutters that the event has gone on too long, that Douglas is losing momentum, losing her audience. Layton, still in the televised crowd behind Douglas, claps and nods with each point made and remade, but his smile is beginning to look a bit forced. The war-room manager repeats his concern more loudly. This draws the attention of a senior party strategist. He crosses the room to ask if there is a problem. "She's going on too long," says the manager.

"She's on national TV live," responds the strategist. "This is *not* a problem!" Those who have stayed to watch Douglas are suddenly more attentive, more willing to clap when a major point is repeated, more willing to cheer on this firebrand link to a glorious past – because she is, after all, *their* firebrand. And if the spirit of Tommy Douglas, Baptist preacher turned cornerstone prairie socialist, isn't exactly in the room, with a little prompting his political inheritors can still be made to feel a touch of the spirit. Hallelujah indeed!

This episode from the NDP election campaign is characteristic of a great deal that drives contemporary election politics in Canada. There is an appeal to historic tradition, a reaffirmation of the party's commitment to its fundamental values, recalling the old-time politics of a previous age when things seemed less complicated, when it was easy to tell, as T.C. Douglas would have it, the black cats from the white cats from the mice.[1] But beneath the veneer of traditional sentiment lies a twenty-first century communication machine delivering sophisticated messages crafted for an overarching objective: to ensure that the NDP faithful remain faithful and that those from other political traditions who show the slightest drift toward temptation are enticed into the New Democrat tent, at least for as long as it takes to cast a ballot. The communication machine behind the NDP (or Conservative, or Liberal, or Bloc) campaign, the war room, is the voice behind a latter-day secular evangelism, part midway hawker and part prairie revival-meeting preacher, using any means available to convince voters that the promise of what lies behind the party curtain deserves their support. And for the party workers who labour at the rock face of electoral politics, it matters not at all that the Shirley Douglas stump speech may be taken on almost every level as pure dramatic fantasy, especially if, for a time, it reaches a national audience.

Indeed, the example of the technologically resurrected old-time stump speech is a reminder that political communication has always had a proselytizing aura about it, often lubricated with a generous dose of snake oil. As Randall Collins has noted, paraphrasing an observation from Talcott Parsons of more than a half-century ago: "Elections do not have to be involved in the real transfer of power or in rational decisions of issues for them to be socially effective. Elections instead are a ritual by which loyalty to the political system itself is mobilized and demonstrated."[2]

Scholars of media and democracy sometimes choose to downplay this side of political communication, preferring instead to dwell upon loftier matters such as free access to information and its role in the democratic process, usually intimating that free access is somehow under attack and, therefore, so is democracy. Indeed, by the time Nicholas Garnham published *Capitalism and Communication* in 1990, this intimation had become an assumption, or, as Garnham suggested, it had become "a commonplace" to insist that the very idea of a democratic nation-state rests upon universal open access to information and the "equal opportunities to participate in the debates from which political decisions rightly flow."[3] Similarly, for political theorists such as William Kaplan, the "right to know" is taken as virtually indistinguishable from the definition of a free citizen, because people who are prevented from fully participating in their community are also prevented from sharing equally in "the economic, political, and social bounty of their society."[4] Each author infers that citizens have somehow been excluded from the general discussion around important political decisions or that such exclusion is imminent. The usual suspects are powerful vested interests that see the control of information as the key to controlling an ever-greater share of society's bounty. Bare-knuckled partisan speech is seldom discussed except as a manipulative deviation from the ideal and, therefore, in need of correction.

These sentiments should not be discounted. However, it is becoming difficult to see how access to information can possibly be under threat, or even moderately restricted, in a mediascape that is increasingly wide open to anyone.[5] As Robert Jensen has argued, the relentless bombardment of information, the unceasing competition for eyes, ears, and minds among media practitioners, ensures that average people going about their daily business not only have unfettered access to vast amounts of political information but it is virtually impossible for them to avoid message overload. "There is more information than ever before," writes Jensen. "Even if one brackets out the huge amount that is about celebrities, entertainment, sports and other non-political topics, the quantity of political information available is staggering. Quantity, yes, but of what quality?"[6] For Jensen, the problem that confronts the average person is to distinguish between what is worthwhile and what is not while struggling to stay afloat in a vast, heaving ocean of communication dross.

Yet everyday evidence suggests that average people are quite capable of navigating this sea of messages. Citizens willingly pick up the telephone and participate in open-line radio programs or write letters to the editor of their local newspaper. They readily go online to post their opinions in chat rooms or the comment sections of online newspapers and weblogs. They participate in social media, controlling the depth and range of their own interests and the debates that arise from them. Some take up the challenges of citizen journalism. In short, they are able and willing to select topics and issues in circulation and either add their voices to the general discussion or start discussions of their own. They manage information dross and volume on their own terms and by doing so make a hearty contribution to "the debates from which political decisions rightly flow." Of course, in Jensen's view, they might well be contributing to the quantity of information overload. But if everyday people invested in their own democracy in such a manner merely contribute to a glut of meaningless information, who, then, decides what information is of an acceptable quality? Nicholas Garnham? William Kaplan? Robert Jensen? The political strategists who organize stump speeches during an election campaign? The journalists and editors at the CBC who carry such speeches live to a national audience?

It is time, perhaps, to start rethinking the power dynamics of the democratic form as it is practised in contemporary Canada and to question some of the assumptions that have grown up around practices associated with political communication, or, more precisely, the way that those practices have been simplistically framed as manifestly detrimental to a deliberative democratic model. There is no point in denying that certain aspects of strategic political communication are manipulative. Nor is it fruitful to deny the commonsense observation that certain elements in our society spend a great deal of time and money in the pursuit of communicative control. But valid questions certainly arise around whether that investment is as effective as those doing the investing would have us believe. The average person is indisputably confronted daily with a changeable sea of information, a "glut of occurrences" that can at times be extraordinarily difficult to manage.[7] But it is also indisputable that the people who consume information are willing and able to navigate information clutter and clamour with a degree of freely applied goodwill that often seems astounding to everyone except those doing the navigating.

One of the central observations from my time in the NDP war room is that strategic political communicators must compete with extraordinary intensity to make their messages resonate above the din of the daily glut. In this light, the emergence of the political war room as an organizational entity and its role in the contest for democratically conferred power may actually be taken as a response to an existential threat: the fear of being drowned out by the shouts and murmurs of contemporary communicative exchange. This concern about being heard is what informs the complex relationships between war-room operatives and journalists and among political strategists, journalists, and publics. It is particularly relevant in the context of the NDP, a political party that has always had to shout a little louder. It also raises the question about *what* is being heard. What is that key measure, the essential quality that generates an enthusiastic public embrace of some truth claims while consigning others to the information landfill? What lends *credibility* to certain ideas, proposals, positions, and statements, and, ultimately, how might we conceptualize the nature of credibility?

Admittedly, such an examination gestures toward a vast subfield of interests that straddle the crowded boundary between communication studies and political science. It ranges over fields and sub-fields as diverse as political advertising, polling, political rhetoric, issue framing, and communication strategy at election time.[8] Yet few of these areas of more-or-less discreet inquiry fully investigate the complexities of the relationships among political communication specialists, journalists, and publics, even if some notion of *the* public is always assumed. A reckoning is due – indeed, overdue.

Some studies, notably from the realm of political science, have attempted to take on the sticky realities of political messaging. In their 2008 assessment of "information campaigns," Richard Nadeau, Neil Nevitte, Elisabeth Gidengil, and André Blais conclude that a voter's willingness to shift politically is directly related to his or her knowledge-capabilities. Those who are better educated – those at the top of the "information ladder" – tend to be better informed because their knowledge reserve permits them to engage a more sophisticated assessment of campaign rhetoric. Those who are less educated – those at the bottom of the ladder – do not possess the knowledge to critically assess campaign information, and the messages therefore have little meaning to their daily lives.[9] This still leaves a considerable segment of the voting population with enough knowledge-capability to assimilate campaign information and, because they are also open to persuasion, apply it to their own worldview.

Not surprisingly, Nadeau and his colleagues conclude that the well educated and those with little education are generally "unresponsive to new information about issues."[10] Voters who occupy the great middle ground – those with enough education to remain open to campaign messages but not so much that they have established a solid political stance – are most likely to shift political support under the influence of partisan messages.

The idea that persuasion has particular resonance with the great middle ground of the voting public dovetails with some of Neil Nevitte's previous work. In a 1996 study Nevitte outlined a series of macro-indicators that appeared to signal significant shifts in the attitudes of Canadians toward established value perceptions. The study found that assumptions about resistance to change were generally untrue; Canadians were found in many instances to be more open to change than "most other publics." Furthermore, Canadians were becoming less attached to traditional institutions, with "publics becoming less parochial and more cosmopolitan."[11] Perhaps most intriguing from the viewpoint of political communication,

Nevitte reported that (in a 1990 survey) 91 per cent of Canadians agreed with the statement "Our government should be more open to the public."[12]

These and other studies flow from a body of work that continues to influence the wider critique of the Canadian democratic process. Contributors to this collection of critiques argue that an unholy alliance between powerful media and political interests has skewed power relations so dramatically that the public scarcely matters anymore. A case in point is the royal commission on electoral reform and party financing of 1991, the last comprehensive survey of political and media practices in this country. In their published findings for the royal commission, William O. Gilsdorf and Robert Bernier portray the opinions of citizens as absent from the process of choosing a government, suppressed by the manipulative processes of big media and big government. Conversely, journalists and political operatives are depicted as opposite sides of the same coin, acting in a near-conspiracy to position their own narrow objectives before a voting public that has been all but divested of its participatory rights:

> Electoral campaigns have become media events. Increasingly, the voter is removed and/or insulated from the practice and process of campaigns, forced to become a passive observer and consumer of prepackaged messages and news reports. Where once the site of the contest might have been in the mind of the voter, the first line of struggle has now shifted to the contest between the journalist and the candidate's advisers for control of the campaign agenda and the interpretation of events and statements. At best, the voter is left with a strategic decision of where to place his or her vote, based on the predigested information provided by the candidate or the journalist.[13]

With respect, Gilsdorf and Bernier's description of the flow of political and journalistic communication is greatly oversimplified. It assumes a "pipeline model" for complex communicative actions by reducing election-time communication to a basic transmission model common to systems of corporate or business communication. By doing so, it greatly diminishes the role of citizens who are portrayed as "passive observer[s] and consumer[s] of prepackaged messages and news reports" incapable of performing the intellectual work required to act in their own interests.[14]

Indeed, much of the scholarly work on electoral communication treats the news media as a pipeline and publics as passive receivers of information. Even Nadeau et al. skirt the issue of media source (radio, television, newspapers, Internet) as a factor in how campaign information is presented and received. They do address the matter of alignment: the practice by political strategists of crafting messages that confirm biases within a particular demographic in order to lead that group to identify with the values of the politician on offer. Unwittingly, perhaps, and without naming it directly, they touch on a campaign tactic, the push poll, now largely out of favour but once widely used by political operatives to speak directly to the "information poor" so as to exploit an extreme vulnerability to "new information if only that information were to reach them."[15] On a much cruder level, the mediated landscape of partisan political communication includes a host of possibilities – Conservative-oriented talk radio comes to mind – where the endless repetition of partisan themes is calculated to persuade, like the placement of political advertising, by sending "the right message to the right person."[16] The simple truth of the matter is that political communication operatives have been exploiting the gap between the information rich and poor for a long time.

Still, these observations from the realm of political science provide a valuable insight into the rise of political war rooms. It is no coincidence that political parties began to adopt war rooms at precisely the moment when Canadians overwhelmingly expressed a desire for more open government, when they said they were open to change, and when a royal commission declared that big media and political machines were using their influence to manipulate election outcomes. The political sphere saw an opportunity to get in front of a growing body of public opinion and took it, but did so with a deep-seated understanding of the volatility of the public reception of information and a far less sanguine regard for the journalist than proponents of the "pipeline model" would have us believe.

Anyone who has seen a political war room in action understands immediately that the work of political communicators and journalists is essentially meaningless without the continual validation of publics: basic configurations of individuals connected through the communication of shared interests or values. The age of the ubiquitous Internet enables such communication, and, as noted, has provided a platform for (among other practices) citizen journalism. This in turn has exposed the fundamental contradiction in the claim that citizens are marginalized in the processes of political decision-making while having access, simultaneously, to more political information than ever before.

Political discourse thrives with the warts and scars of its most outrageous practices exposed, as does journalism, because engaged publics have never surrendered an ounce of their real power to decide what is important to them. Publics are the ultimate arbiters of information currency in both meanings of the term: that which is current (or indicative of this time) and that which has a symbolic exchange value (in the manner of a coin of the realm, a currency). And information currency, with its necessary exchange of certain kinds of communication within the collective public mind, is deeply implicated in questions of confidence, trust, legitimacy, belief, and credibility.

The question, then, is how to bring the public, or publics, back into the scholarly debate around matters pertaining to contemporary journalism and politics. The first step is to recognize that journalists, political actors, and publics engage in a complex and ongoing set of negotiations that support an ever-evolving set of relations. The public cannot be excluded from the public's business because the public's business, the quotidian actions of people, is what motivates journalists and political actors to do what they do. It is the public, broadly considered as a collectivity of individual structural interdependences, sharing broadly communicated values, understandings, agreements, and methods of conduct, that lies at the core of the collective conferral of power by citizens on those who would seek to govern.

For political communicators, the construction of partisan messages is a wholly legitimate practice founded in the requirement to distinguish a partisan position within a milieu that perceives journalists as necessary adversaries. L. Ian MacDonald is the editor of *Policy Options*, an influential monthly publication published by the Montreal-based Institute for Research on Public Policy. He is also a journalist of long standing with columns on political affairs published regularly in Montreal's *Gazette* and a collection of national newspapers. He occupies a rare position in Canadian media circles because he has also worked as a high-level political communicator, as chief speechwriter for Prime Minister Brian Mulroney and, later, as the head of the public-affairs division at Canada's embassy in Washington. With credentials that straddle both sides of the political/journalistic divide, he is uniquely placed to comment on the recent history of the competition between political and journalistic actors. "What has really changed in the past twenty years," says MacDonald, "is the difficulty of controlling the message if you're on the inside. And there's always this constant struggle between the media and the parties for control of the agenda, getting the message out, staying on message."[17] According to MacDonald, the rise of organizations such as political war rooms is in direct response to a perceived increase in the competition for control of meaning – the struggle between political actors and journalists over the meaningful content of messages. The unnamed participant in this struggle is the public, or publics, the target receiver(s) of political communication that is, at its best, certainly from the political perspective, circulated without media "distortion."

Why is message control so important to strategic political communicators? Part of the answer lies in the conditions of "legitimation." As Hans-Peter Müller has proposed (following Habermas), political systems are made legitimate across three dimensions – the economic, the political, and the socio-cultural – by the performance of those in power.[18] A "legitimation crisis" occurs when the governing authority, singly or concurrently, fails to maintain economic equilibrium, fails to maintain "an agenda of important issues" that enables widespread political participation, and/or fails to maintain "active communication with the public." It is centrally important to the maintenance of legitimacy that political action around issues and policies is "factually accepted as binding by the people."[19] Legitimacy is therefore conferred through public confidence. From the political insider's point of view, public confidence is forever in danger of being undercut by journalists who, in the normalized practices of their daily work, compete to question, contextualize, and interpret the messages of elected officials or those who seek to be elected.

A second set of related conditions has had considerable influence on the emergence of strategic political communication and its preoccupation with message control. In MacDonald's words, since the late 1980s, Canada (and earlier, the United States) has seen "an explosion in the number of media platforms." This phenomenon began in 1989 with the appearance in Canada of Newsworld, the first twenty-four-hour television news service in this country. For MacDonald, wearing his political insider's hat, the movement toward a highly specialized sub-organization wholly devoted to crafting and disseminating political messages is in direct response to a dramatic increase in the volume of critical journalistic voices working across an ever-increasing number of outlets of transmission, which today include a potentially limitless number of Internet sites. Partisan political actors, therefore, regard themselves as underdogs in a struggle to remain distinct in the face of an ever-increasing fragmentation of the mediascape, a fragmentation that supports an increase in the distribution of competitive journalistic voices interpreting the debates from which political decisions flow. The political war room, then, may be viewed as an organizational response to a technologically motivated shift in the political economy of media. It is a response that has occurred hand in hand with the development of argument strategies directed at issues of message control mobilized in the competition to maintain distinction, credibility, and legitimacy.

There is general agreement that campaign war rooms came to the Canadian political stage after the concept was imported by the Liberal election machine following Bill Clinton's upset presidential election victory and the subsequent release of the film *The War Room* in 1993. Much of what is known about the internal workings of these organizations in Canada is anecdotal and comes from a single source: Warren Kinsella, a former "political aide" to Prime Minister Jean Chrétien. Kinsella's often blustery and self-serving account of his time in the Liberal Party's campaign war room, outlined in *Kicking Ass in Canadian Politics*, is unabashedly partisan. More recently, Tom Flanagan's account of Stephen Harper's rise to power makes thoughtful reference to the war room of the Conservative Party. However, Flanagan is more concerned with documenting the story of a prime minister's rise to power – and doing it from the ultimate insider's perch as, variously, chief of staff and political organizer to Stephen Harper – than with analyzing the day-to-day construction of political messages.[20] Having said this, both Kinsella and Flanagan have been widely read in their respective political and academic circles.

Of course, one can never be completely sure about the partisan intentions of former political operatives, especially those who have been involved in generating strategic political communication. And independent reflections are difficult to come by where war rooms are concerned. However, by examining a series of distinct strategic and tactical gambits deployed by the war room of the New Democratic Party, it is possible to examine at arm's length the connected, subsumed intentions of all the major players in the 2005–06 election campaign and situate those intentions within the complex and ongoing set of negotiations that continues to characterize the relationship between journalists, political actors, and publics.

From such a position, the unrepentant theatricality of the Shirley Douglas stump speech becomes something much more than a standard campaign event. As intended, it evokes a chain of symbolic associations connected to the memory of T.C. Douglas: his mythic status as a champion of the average person, his appeal to collective solutions, his commitment to individual and group agency, and – most importantly – his success as the leader of a home-grown political movement.[21] Arguably, these associations are more important that the words spoken by his daughter, a living connection to the "great man." Yet Shirley Douglas's stump speech was also intended to elicit a number of provocative possibilities that had little to do with the actual event. It is a fairly uncomplicated example of symbolic exchange in action, an expression of "the resources to re-enact and reproduce the symbols emotionally charged by participation in a history of past rituals."[22] This key concept permits us to begin to conceptualize what is at work within current strategic communication initiatives employed by war-room operatives.

Communication and influence are deeply intertwined here. As conceptualized by Heine Andersen, influence is a practice of purely symbolic exchange within a community founded on "a capacity to bring about desired decisions in the interest of collectivities through persuasion" where the ability to persuade is based on "position in a prestige hierarchy." Value commitments, on which the ability to persuade are ultimately founded, operate through a "general conviction of legitimacy of norms and moral values, and a readiness to implement them into moral action."[23] One way to make sense of strategic communication initiatives, then, is to imagine them as practices within a very broad, socially based democratic system wherein power, influence, and value commitments are considered as media of exchange in their own right; that is, they contain a measure of meaning in their communicative form.[24] This perspective helps to explain the evocative resonance of a contrived stump speech by the daughter of a long-dead political figure and the lengths to which political actors will go to gain an edge.

Each of these symbolic media of exchange is based on an assumption of trust. Each time we enter into a communicative exchange with another human being, we presume a degree of good faith, honest dealing, and accurate truth claims on the part of the person we

are involved with.[25] In the special case of the choice of a government, however, the expectations of trust are held to a higher standard. The requirement to obey and the power to coerce that are part
and parcel of the transfer of power demand serious consideration
simply because the individual and collective stakes are so much
higher.[26] Should we as citizens be concerned, then, that strategic
political communication, the work of war rooms, increasingly calcu-
lates influence and persuasion on the basis of intentionally distorted
appeals to the legitimacy of norms and values in order to obtain and
retain power? The Conservative Party's rage in early 2009 against a
possible Liberal-NDP-Bloc coalition (resulting in a questionable pro-
rogation of Parliament) had all the earmarks of a war-room strategy
and is but one example of crafted urgency, an appeal to moral panic,
disseminated as an emergency response (*a coup!*) to perceived threats
to the legitimate status quo. Few seem to consider the risk of the
permanent crisis of legitimacy that rises with the transfer, storage,
and reproduction of such manipulated symbols.

   At this point there is a risk of falling into the same trap that caught
Gilsdorf and Bernier. After all, the "interpretation of events and
statements" that is central to their position has a great deal in common with the contest to control the transferability, storability, and
reproduction of symbols. The key to avoiding this trap – a priori
capitulation to a structure of power that simply privileges political
and journalistic elites while excluding everyday people – lies in a re-
evaluation of the conditions of legitimacy or, rather, an evaluation of
the conditions under which legitimacy is itself legitimated. The role
of credibility lies at the heart of this conceptual evaluation.

   I would like to begin, then, with a basic truth claim of my own:
that an appeal to credibility, as a specifically theorized currency of
symbolic exchange, lies at the heart of every communicative practice
that engages political actors, journalists, and publics. Furthermore, I
would make the case that credibility is central to all concerns about
the way that power is conferred and maintained, accumulated and
dissipated in our democratic nation-state. Finally, I would argue that
to follow the flow of credibility in an election-time political war
room is to observe an entirely different facet of the political world,
one where the ability of political actors to obtain a measure of power
and influence is directly tied to a symbolic economy where credibility
is the coin of the realm. It is a complex world where actions always

contain an intention – often subsumed or concealed, but just as often transparently projected – that is somehow tied to credibility.

In this symbolic economy, communication specialists craft each moment of a political campaign with an eye to its credibility dividend. The campaign is a place where journalists have great influence because of their ability to extend or withdraw credibility based on endorsement, itself a form of symbolic exchange that is implicated in matters pertaining to legitimacy and public trust. Yet campaigns are also places where publics are much more independently in control of the credibility sweepstakes than we may have previously imagined, in spite of what political operatives would have us believe. The trick is to understand how these invested participants – politicians and their operatives, journalists, and publics – engage the ebb and flow of this complex form of symbolic capital and claim it for their own purposes. With this in mind, in the next chapter I employ the work of the French social and cultural critic Pierre Bourdieu as a starting point for discussing the nature of credibility, its influence on sociopolitical concerns, and the way those concerns are communicated.

2

Bourdieu's Fields and Capitals:
The Implications for Political Life

The social world is accumulated history, and if it is not to be reduced
to a discontinuous series of instantaneous mechanical equilibria between
agents who are treated as interchangeable particles, one must reintroduce
into it the notion of capital and, with it, accumulation and all its effects.

Pierre Bourdieu[1]

To attempt to excavate the conceptual heart of credibility calls for a
shift in the theoretical ground away from deterministic arguments
arising from debates about structural fundamentals to an orientation
more attuned to subsumed symbolic interaction. Pierre Bourdieu's
theoretical work on the forms of capital offers a richly developed
means to delve beneath the surface of complex concepts such as legitimation, the logic of argument strategies, prestige hierarchies, or the
transferability and storability of symbols. Bourdieu's proposition that
there are many different kinds of capital operating in social systems –
and that most of them are not of the economic variety – unzips a
universe of capital exchange that is uncanny in its ability to reflect the
actually existing communicative practices adopted and refined by
political war rooms and journalists in the competitive pursuit of
public legitimation.[2]

In addition, a related area of conceptual inquiry from the work of
Bourdieu may be used to enhance our understanding of the competitive differences that distinguish political from journalistic communication. The concept of fields – distinct areas of social practice
complete with their own hierarchies and rules – is directly on-point
for any examination of the attributes that make all formalized areas
of human endeavour distinct.[3] Bourdieu is particularly useful in discussions that centre on politics and journalism because he has specifically theorized these fields and their position in a third, more

abstract field: the field of power.[4] The theoretical relationships that exist *among* fields and capitals may therefore be superimposed upon the observed web of complex relationships that are seen to operate in the daily production of strategic political communication at election time, the response by journalistic practitioners, and the resonance of such communication among publics and in the field of power.

The epigraph for this chapter, the opening line from Bourdieu's 1983 essay "The Forms of Capital," presents a fundamental disagreement with the debates circulating at the time around issues of structure and agency. Boudieu's dismissal of the "mechanical equilibria between agents who are treated as interchangeable particles" is used here to herald a different regard for the social world, one that simultaneously critiques conditions of dominance while making room for the "dialectic of strategies" that, Bourdieu says, "allows for individual intervention against the model."[5] In this case the "model" may be taken as the entire functionalist paradigm with its overriding concern for dominant structural imperatives over human initiative. Bourdieu's concern is to "make explicit the power relations inscribed in social reality" by introducing those relations that operate as a result of "differences in position in the social hierarchy."[6] But he is also interested in human social practice as a "relationship of meaning" between individuals based on the recognition of a socially constructed connection between dominance and legitimacy.

From the outset, then, a relationship exists in Bourdieu's work between the communication of meaning and relations of power. He introduces a different grammar to expose legitimation as a key element of hegemony, achieved when a dominant group controls the communicative terms of rational justification and, therefore, controls the conditions of its own legitimacy.[7] He theorizes complex fields of human interaction where symbolic forms of capital are accumulated and exchanged in a competition for distinction, a competition that requires strategic acumen, an understanding of the rules of the social game, and a sense of the cultural and social resources that are available. These theoretical configurations (*habitus*, capitals, and fields, in Bourdieu's parlance) are especially useful for dissecting and examining the forces at play in complex spheres of social action and reaction such as journalism and politics. These configurations are also useful in situating these spheres in the much broader, much less contained realm of public space (as opposed to institutional structures).

In order to contextualize Bourdieu's vision of these specific and interrelated areas of theoretical concern, it is worth taking a brief side trip into the Anglo-American canon, specifically to Anthony Giddens's concept of structuration. Giddens's examination of individual action and its relationship to institutional power opens the door to a richer understanding of Bourdieu's theoretical creativity. "Action," according to Giddens, "depends upon the capability of the individual to 'make a difference' to a pre-existing state of affairs or course of events. An agent ceases to be such if he or she loses the capability to 'make a difference,' that is, to exercise some sort of power."[8] For Giddens, systems (reproduced practices) and institutions (reproduced rules and resources) cannot exist without human action. Similarly, institutional change (usually over time) is dependent on human action. This interrelationship is the central feature of stucturation.

But while human beings do "exercise some sort of power," for Giddens it is the routines of daily life that characterize social reality. "Ontological security" is founded on the autonomy of bodily control within predictable routines and encounters.[9] This "routinization," which Giddens describes as a "fundamental concept of structuration theory," is itself underpinned by the notion of "practical consciousness: all things that actors know about how to 'go on' in the contexts of social life" or the "taken for granted, common sense, naturalized way of thinking about things."[10] In such a world, the routines of daily life, the reproduced practices of social systems, are both enabled and constrained by rules and resources even as "tacitly enacted practices" gradually become the very "institutions or routines" in which the rules and resources reside.[11] For Giddens, this is a framework for theorizing how "the structural properties of social systems exist only in so far as forms of social conduct are reproduced chronically across time and space."[12]

Yet to accept Giddens's view of social reality is also to accept an inexorable drift away from the very freedom to act that is central to his definition of agency. It is difficult to reconcile routinized individuals acting within systems as agents capable of motivating organic changes to the application of rules and allocation of resources. In a social reality where elite actors – de Certeau's famously named "subjects with will and power" – possess exceptional control over the means of dispensing rewards and sanctions within administered systems (after all, they are the administrators), it is comparatively easy to envision how the power to act, the central characteristic of agency, may be diminished to the point of inconsequence.[13]

Bourdieu takes a different approach, one that is reflected, for example, in the relationships between political actors, journalists, and publics. In Bourdieu's sense of social reality, actors learn and internalize the "rules of the game" in an atmosphere of pitched competition. Social structures are not done away with so much as reconsidered in order to accommodate a range of relational forces that individuals use, consciously and unconsciously, to obtain status. Thus the rules and resources that characterize Giddens's institution give way to Bourdieu's field, "the site of actions and reactions performed by social agents endowed with permanent dispositions, partly acquired in their experience of these social fields."[14] Actors within fields inhabit a terrain characterized by relational thought and action "vis-à-vis others in an ongoing process that is enacted for the most part unconsciously" and bounded by its own rules and customs (the doxic "universe of presuppositions" that organize actions).[15] In this conceptual arrangement, the more-or-less free competition for distinction among actors within fields and the relations of power that arise from the competition for recognition within and among fields lie behind the "ongoing struggle that is society."[16]

For Bourdieu, then, the competition for recognition is "a fundamental dimension of social life." Competition as a basic building block for social interaction provides him with the means not only to distinguish his theoretical approach from contemporaries such as Giddens but to introduce a related concept: the permutations of capital, the *symbolic* resources available to those in competition within fields. "The forms of capital" is all about categories of capital that may work in tandem with the economic form but operate in a different kind of economy: a *social* economy. Actors use social capital, cultural capital, and symbolic capital in systems of accumulation and exchange.

Thus, certain actors may mobilize social capital, "the aggregate of the actual or potential resources which are linked to possession of a durable network of more or less institutionalized relationships of mutual acquaintance and recognition" – not what you know but who you know – to give them an edge in systems of established power.[17] Others may offset a deficit in social capital through the accumulation and exchange of cultural capital – not who you know but what you know – tied to the investment of time required to obtain educational qualifications, cultural knowledge, official certification, and other kinds of knowledge qualification. The result is a vision of the social world that accounts for the structures of power but establishes a means to think about change, even radical change, in terms of an individual's willingness to mobilize the symbolic resources at hand. Within this system of exchange, it is the idea of symbolic capital – prestige within a group – and its relationship to other forms of capital that provides the ground for theorizing the struggle for recognition that characterizes complex social relationships, relationships such as the one involving political actors, journalists, and publics.

The concept of symbolic capital possesses a certain heft, largely because of a provenance that is directly related to its origins (albeit obscure) in observed human practice, specifically the anthropological field studies conducted by Bourdieu among the Kabyle people of Algeria. Here he witnessed complex systems of capital exchange in a society where money and other forms of exchange property – economic capital – were generally subordinated to symbolic expression, the predominant means of validating power relations within the group. Bourdieu's *The Logic of Practice* devotes a great deal of space to the discussion of the intricacies of symbolic capital exchange among the Kabyle – the conversion of economic capital, usually in the form of gifts, into symbolic capital in the form of prestige – in order to propose a sociological point that the author suggests can be extended to social practice in general: "When one knows that symbolic capital is credit, but in the broadest sense, a kind of advance, a credence, that only the group's belief can grant those who give it the best symbolic and material guarantees, it can be seen that the exhibition of symbolic capital (which is always very expensive in material terms) is one of the mechanisms which (no doubt universally) make capital go to capital."[18]

The idea that capital can be converted from one form to another, sometimes with relative ease but more often at a considerable symbolic rate of exchange, is central to Bourdieu's vision of fields as actor-motivated relations of power. In a sense, fields turn the economic world on its head because they are both constructed by and serve to facilitate a specific space of mostly invisible relations, the ongoing rules of a particular "game" (such as politics and/or journalism) where all forms of capital, including economic capital, are used in "the accumulation of a particular form of capital, honour in the sense of reputation and prestige."[19]

The above set of relationships also contains an embedded concept that is key to *all* processes of social exchange: the idea of credence. To unpack the meaning of credence is to introduce a cascade of inter-related meanings – creed, credential, credit, credibility – all of which are tied to the connotative sense of a belief that something is true or to be trusted. In his later works, Bourdieu reflects upon notions of reputation and prestige and refines the predominant objective of all agents operating in all fields as the "struggle for the production and imposition of a *legitimate* vision of the social world."[20] It can be argued, therefore, that credibility is the symbolic capital that legiti-mates this "legitimate vision of the social world." And while Bourdieu never fully articulates the role of credibility as a specific force within his system of symbolic exchange, this discreet form of symbolic capital may be brought forward as the central motivator in the competition to define the social world. For this reason, an enhanced understanding of the nature of credibility is essential if we are to comprehend the work of those who deal in the truth claims that define democratic discourses: notably, political communicators, journalists, and publics.

If "symbolic capital is credit," then it is a kind of credit, according to Boudieu, that is based solely on the confidence of a group of actors who have an arranged collective stake in setting and maintaining the specific rules that govern a field. The group underwrites matters of cultural, symbolic, and economic repute when individuals in competi-tion for distinction make specific claims. In such an extended relation-ship, credibility comes into play in three senses: first, by extending symbolic credit to individuals with the understanding that they will fulfill their end of the bargain, thus paying a symbolic dividend through association with success to those who advanced the credit; second, in inducing a symbolic debt to be repaid (in the manner of a gift) after a suitable interval, an obligation of gratitude and support of greater consequence than the original debt that may be used stra-tegically by the "creditor" in the pursuit of prestige; and third, in sustaining the distinction of those with prestige and reputation and by doing so maintaining the legitimacy of the field in which all par-ticipating actors have a stake.[21] Symbolic credit may also be withheld or withdrawn if matters on offer are seen to be "inadequate" accord-ing to the immanent laws of the field. This form of symbolic violence (think of someone in power who no longer returns your phone calls) is manifestly concerned with a refusal to confer credibility. In all of these examples, credibility, as a distinct category of symbolic capital, acts as a central motivating force, possessing a quality that is directly related to the nature of a particular field.

Those who practice within fields of strong autonomy (Bourdieu uses academic disciplines as examples) obtain prestige in a formal yet still complex and competitive system of capital acquisition. In Bourdieu's view, strong autonomy is a function of a field's control over its own social, cultural, and symbolic capital and its independent ability to resist incursions from the economic sphere. Such "homologous" fields administer their own "immanent laws" of capital exchange and conversion. Thus, in a chain of practice that might extend over a lifetime, individuals acquire credentials such as degrees (accumulated cultural capital). They seek ways to convert cultural capital into a measure of symbolic capital (status) in order to gain entry to successive levels of prestige within the field. Those who succeed embark on a program of ever-greater status acquisition – perhaps by undertaking research and publishing books – until, through the continued accumulation of symbolic capital, they may be elevated by the group to representative status, a level of empowerment dependent on the ability of the subject to continually, through force of reputation and prestige, "reproduce and reinforce the power relations which constitute the social structure of the social space."[22] Of course, any individuals may be denied advancement in the field at any step along the way if their capital resources are deemed by the group to be inadequate or illegitimate according to the immanent rules of the field.

Each conversion of capital in the chain is underwritten by symbolic credit advanced by the group. Credentials are deemed to be legitimate according to the standards of the field as endorsed by those who practise in it (peer review is a good example of this). Credence is extended to practices intended to obtain status based on a legitimate expectation of the fulfillment of a promise, a fiduciary claim. Representative status with its connection to the naming of the "legitimate vision of the social world" is obtained through the recognition by those of considerable status of the extraordinary accumulation of creditable symbolic capital (and power) by a peer. In fields of strong autonomy, therefore, credibility is behind virtually all processes of capital acquisition and conversion.

As Bourdieu has pointed out, this is essentially a description of change based on the elevation of one individual or group over another through extended competition within a field. This competition amounts to an exchange of dominance. Fields, as more or less bounded areas of specific practice, provide for a significant measure of individual action, an ability to legitimately persuade that is tied directly to the belief that a certain vision of the social world is to be trusted relationally. It is a vision based on the possibility of an exchange of non-economic capital in a formal assessment of reality that is itself contingent on the communication of a credible critique of the status quo. Credibility, therefore, is a central relational force in fields, one that is deeply implicated in a legitimate exercise of action in support of change.

Yet it is the circulation of credibility in fields of *weak* autonomy that is most salient to the discussion of politics, journalism, and publics and their part in the processes of democracy. For Bourdieu and his adaptors, notably Patrick Champagne, political actors and journalists are both subject to forces, especially economic influences, that lie outside the field. For example, in his polemic *On Television*, Bourdieu attacks what he describes as a decade-long trend toward commercial, popular, mass-market journalism in France arising out of the deregulation of broadcasting (particularly pertaining to news programming) and the commercialization of public air space where a state monopoly had previously existed. He characterizes this process largely as a conspiracy between the market and the state. Similarly, Champagne portrays journalism as a field of unstable autonomy that must always be "re-won because it is always threatened" by the "social, especially political and economic conditions in which it is organized."[23] In short, the political economy of the media sets up conditions that journalists must constantly struggle to overcome in order to fulfill the obligations of cultural capital that accrue to their field. Among these conditions is a concern for the free flow and exchange of information that foregrounds the practice of meaningful democracy, Garnham's "equal opportunities to participate in the debates from which political decisions rightly flow."

Champagne theorizes a media landscape where journalism is practised along a continuum bounded by economic capital on one side and cultural capital on the other. The changing face of journalism in France (echoed in similar quarters in Canada, the United States, the

United Kingdom, and elsewhere) is attributed to a shift by deregu-
lated (or reregulated) media organizations toward the economic
pole. For Bourdieu, this shift is reflected in an obsessive pursuit of
advertising revenues and profits that "favours those cultural producers most susceptible to the seduction of economic and political powers at the expense of those intent on defending the principles and
values of their professions."[24] The unrelenting pursuit of economic
gain means that cultural producers are themselves made into com-
modities, their value determined by the popularity they generate as
measured by ratings. Bourdieu regards this commodification of cultural producers as an abandonment and betrayal of the very life of
the culture through the corruption of those in a special position to
shape and form the vision of the social world. For this reason, as
Champagne puts it without apparent irony, "the press is too serious
a matter to be left to journalists."[25]

This theorization of the political economy of weak autonomy
deserves reconsideration. For Bourdieu and Champagne to clinch
their case, it must be assumed that the influence of economic capital
is great enough to compromise the autonomy of vast swaths of the
field of journalism (and politics). But Bourdieu's own theorization of
capitals provides for, indeed requires, exceptions to the status quo.
In the field of journalism, as in the field of politics, specialized individuals and groups continue to operate in a system of capital
exchange where the influence of the marketplace is largely offset by
the *practice* of symbolic capital: that is, the dissemination of ideas,
critiques, and commentary that is grounded in an accumulated body
of cultural and symbolic capital that resists market pressures to conform. To use the journalistic field as an example, it can be seen that
certain practitioners have accumulated representative status both
within the field and within their area of specialization. In such cases,
what matters is not so much the position of a newspaper or broadcaster in relation to its commitment to cultural or economic capital
as the relationship of journalists with representative status to the
field in general. Journalists with strong autonomy do exist, indeed
flourish, within a field that to a greater or lesser extent is weakly
autonomous. How is this possible?

According to Bourdieu, the influence of the journalistic field and
the political field is directly related to the position that each occupies
within the *field of power.*[26] If there is competition among agents
within fields for the "claim to the legitimate vision of the social

world," then there is also competition among fields for ascendance within the field of power. For Bourdieu, the fields of journalism and politics occupy elevated positions in the field of power that derive from the assumed power to consecrate certain views of the social world and reify them on behalf of society in general. In each case, in ways that are different yet related, politics and journalism exercise inordinate influence over the acceptance or rejection of claims to legitimacy of every other field except the field of power.

An act of public communication must take place in order for these consecrated views to be widely known. If, as Bourdieu proposes, fields are weakly autonomous when they admit influence from the economic sphere, is it not also possible that weakly autonomous fields such as journalism and politics are equally open to non-economic influences, cultural influences, that originate in the field of power and guide the acts of consecration? If the field of power is theorized as the space of "symbolic struggle for the production of common sense," it is entirely possible, indeed necessary, to include the common sense that arises from a wider social formation among the influences that inform these influential fields.[27] Consecrated views must, after all, resonate somewhere.

Furthermore, while it may be true that actors are greatly influenced, even habituated or routinized by the conditions of competition in a particular field, it does not follow that their entire life-world is a function of the field. Factors such as gender, ethnicity, and language (elements that Bourdieu would agree contribute to *habitus*) have significant influence on the way that individuals support or reject visions of the social world, even visions that may be endorsed by highly credible and influential individuals of representative status. Actors have home lives: they go to church, they belong to clubs; they participate in what Raymond Williams identifies as primary areas of social communication.[28] Opinions, ideas, the accumulation of mundane and important thoughts and actions that form the texture of everyday life – all of the concerns that are held and reproduced in this manner – lie, in large part, beyond the direct influence of the relational forces at work in fields. They are circulated through various forms of discourse in public space or discussed in the private space of the home. Some actors may risk their status within the field, motivated by factors such as a sense of justice or a particular moral or ideological stance to take a position that appears contrary to their own interests. Whistleblowers are an example: they may sacrifice cultural, symbolic, and even economic capital within their field to gain public credibility for a moral position, in effect exercising "some sort of power" to affect change for the greater good. Often their actions are confirmed and endorsed, and credibility is publicly conferred by like-minded people who are drawn to the symbolic content in this exercise of personal power.

The factors that operate both within fields and external to them reflect a power formation of great complexity and consequence, a formation that mirrors the pursuit of distinction within fields but is played out in a much wider, public domain. In this domain, the broadest *societal* sense of credence contributes to a social formation that self-constructs around the resonance of credibility produced by a process of selection within a wide distribution of discourses. How does this self-construction take place?

I would like here to import a concept from the work of Michael Warner. Among the many critical attempts to explain the implications for contemporary public life of Jürgen Habermas's ideal public sphere, Warner's notion of publics and counterpublics or, more specifically, how these entities form and how they act, speaks directly to the notion of self-constructing publics operating in a field of power.[29]

It is Warner's position that a public "is constituted through mere attention." He writes: "Public discourse craves attention like a child. Texts clamor at us. Images solicit our gaze. Look here! Listen! Hey! In doing so they by no means render us passive. Quite the contrary. The modern system of publics creates a demanding social phenomenology. Our willingness to process a passing appeal determines which publics we belong to and performs their extension."[30] This passage embraces several related lines of inquiry and presents an articulated model of constantly shifting public space imbued with uneven power relations and the appellative energy of the constant cry for attention and recognition. Our *willingness* to process a passing appeal places the power of free choice with the individual. Based on personal and private motivations, we select the publics we belong to and give them attention according to our own measure of their worth. At this point we may claim a public as our own and do nothing more. But if we choose to recognize the goals of that public as worthy of greater symbolic investment, then we may *actively* perform the extension of those goals within discursive space; that is, we may invest our own appellative energy and enter into the competition for attention and recognition on behalf of that public.

Warner's assertion, like that of Bourdieu, is that the social world is competitively dynamic. The notion of the passing appeal paints discursive space as a raucous and continuous assault on the senses, a marketplace of competing truth claims of all stripes communicated through speech acts, textual and pictorial representations, and, notably, mass media. In such a world, individuals are not confined to membership in one public; they may choose to invest symbolically (and materially) in a plethora of publics, engaging each to a greater or lesser extent. Similarly, they may choose to divest themselves of membership in one public, should the passing appeal of another resonate more credibly.

This freedom to choose is the crux of the dynamic behind the willingness to process a passing appeal. Such a willful extension of the self (with its resonances of goodwill and trust) connects individual belief to the extended offer of a group claim to a legitimate, credible vision of the social world. Publics, like fields, are spaces of internal and external competition for symbolic capital; however, unlike fields, they lack the structure of immanent laws. They are more nascent forms, drawing upon claims to legitimacy, forming and dispersing according to an appellative energy that derives principally from the rational and critical extension of symbolic credit. They represent a moment of formation, reified decision-making of the most basic kind, and in their success or failure manifest a collective will that is fundamentally important to the practice of democracy. This is the space where the ground is decided for the opening gambits of a much larger game. It is also the space where all other forms of social and (especially) political organization must return for the renewal and reaffirmation of their credibility, expressed through the constant competition for attention.

Our central concern at this point is to refine the field of power, theorized by Bourdieu as a place of struggle among fields, to include individual agency of a kind that recognizes everyday people engaged in a natural communicative dynamic. It is people, average and anonymous people, not fields, who freely decide whether passing appeals are worthy of extension. The conceptual underpinnings of the field of power must therefore be made to admit the basic mechanisms of consensus formation and deliberative democracy that are themselves expressed through this basic communicative act.

This is uncomfortable territory for Bourdieu. He is more at ease with formal systems of capital exchange within fields of struggle, or the sociology of closed cultural practices such as those of the Kabyle. Yet if we retain his basic map of the field of power and import the idea of multiple publics, forming and dispersing around certain discourses according to the perceived credibility of the matters at hand, it becomes possible to put forward a concept of a field of power as a space where the "imposition of the vision of the social world" is made legitimate not just by competition among fields but also (and predominantly) by the willingness of publics to deem the vision to be credible. In this theoretical configuration, the field of power is, first and foremost, a field of publics.

If the fields of journalism and politics, then, are seen to occupy elevated positions in the field of power (expressed by publics), it is because actors within these weakly autonomous fields have a special relationship with the structures of communication that enable them to give priority to certain visions of the social world and elevate them in the competition for attention. Bourdieu is quite correct in pointing out that a great deal of influence has accrued to media organizations and journalistic agents who are motivated primarily by economic capital. But it would be wrong to conclude that the accumulation of economic capital, even with all of the incentives for organizational compliance that it is able to exercise, acts as a commensurate measure of credibility within the field of power. On the contrary, where actors in the journalistic and political fields are concerned, the ability to circulate messages, to lend serious credence to visions of the social world based on economic means, is greatly tempered by the cultural considerations that constantly inform the flow of debates in circulation within this wholly autonomous field.

We are faced then with a system of shifting and competing tensions and forces that shape practice in the fields of journalism and politics. On one hand are all the conversions of capital, material and symbolic, that occur *inside* these fields and that permit actors to accumulate reputation and prestige (credibility), impose a legitimate vision of the social world within the field, and reproduce and reinforce the relations of power that make up the structure of the social space.[31] On the other hand, the validating function of publics, independent of fields, constrains the conferral of power by ensuring that the extension of credence from the group at large is well invested in any vision of the social world that is put into public circulation.

If journalism and politics are viewed as a fields where autonomy must always be re-won because of the social, political, and economic conditions in which they are organized, this is not least because the credence that is extended or withheld by publics confirms or destabilizes the processes of autonomous practice at every instance. This is as it should be: actors within the fields of journalism and politics rightly compete for credibility in the field of power because that is where they are held to account by the publics that operate there. The organizations that employ journalists or underwrite politicians may have significant influence at an economic level, but as individuals accumulate credibility within the field, the less these organizations are able to impose structural compliance and the more these actors are judged independently in the field of power.

Veteran political reporters, notably members of the Parliamentary Press Gallery, spend decades observing and reporting on the manoeuvrings of diverse players in the political field. Top political reporters may have professional lives that outstrip by decades those of their political counterparts: at the time of this writing, for example, Craig Oliver, CTV's chief political correspondent on Parliament Hill, has been employed as a journalist for more than fifty years, more than forty of them as a political reporter. To achieve this kind of tenure, these people must become intimately familiar with the public record and equally familiar with the internal and external forces that motivate individuals and political organizations to act. They cultivate long-term sources in political parties. They have friends and colleagues in the academy. They have detailed knowledge about the circuits of power in the bureaucracy. Armed with knowledge of the public record *and* a version of the internal collective history of political organizations, they are formidable forces. They have accumulated enormous social, cultural, and, in some cases, considerable economic capital. On a day-to-day practical level, they are also well aware of the critical importance of symbolic capital, of credibility.

Chantal Hébert has been a journalist for more than three decades. From her start as a reporter at the Ontario Legislature in the late 1970s, she now occupies a position as a lead columnist on political matters, commenting on federal politics for the *Toronto Star*. Hébert is also a regular contributor to political discussion panels on the CBC's *The National*, Radio-Canada, and the French-language RDI network. I asked her (in an exchange of email messages) how she decides whether a particular politician, political party, or political position is credible. Her reply: "A track record in government and the relationship between actions and promises undoubtedly helps to shore up or undermine credibility. A capacity to continue to make a case in the face of adversity and to do so on the basis of solid arguments. A demonstrated capacity to own an issue on the basis of facts."[32]

Each of these deciding factors is directly related to an exchange of some form of non-economic capital. The "relationship between action and promises" directly reflects that between the journalist's belief in the "credence" of a position, a promise (acting on behalf of some understanding of the public good), and the material fulfillment of that promise. These relationships form the basis for a "track record in government," the accumulation of a body of fulfilled expectations. To use solid arguments to continue to "make a case in the face of adversity" speaks to matters of commitment, an investment in the symbolic value of a position arrived at through critical thought, itself a basis for "solid arguments" and requiring the investment of cultural capital as a means to form those arguments. Commitment to a position may also be regarded as a reasoned expectation that the investment of cultural capital will convert to symbolic capital – prestige – if the position or argument prevails. Finally, the demonstration of a capacity to "own an issue" based on "facts" reflects both the symbolic (credibility) value of the issue (since it is worth "owning" in the first place) and the need to continually reinforce its credibility value through substantive reinvestment of cultural capital (facts). It is worth noting that this exchange makes no reference, either directly or obliquely, to money or any other form of economic influence.

Hébert also cited a reliance on facts and a solid track record as factors when I asked what contributes to her own credibility as a journalist. She included two other factors, each addressing (albeit indirectly) matters pertaining to her relationship with some sense of public awareness or responsibility: "The perception that I am independent and non-partisan. Avoidance as much as possible of the 'preacher syndrome' or to be clear, the temptation to tell others how they should think rather than what they might consider on their way to formulating their own opinion."[33]

The *perception* of independence and non-partisanship is directly concerned with reputation. This perception certainly carries weight among Hébert's peers: the immanent laws of the journalistic field call for credibility to be withdrawn should a practitioner be deemed to speak for partisan reasons. This process is largely an exercise in reinforcing the value of independence and non-partisanship as conditions for validation within the field of power and publics. Hébert's reading and viewing publics expect her to weigh the facts and arguments in circulation in the political field, to sift and consider them through the filter of her own investment in cultural capital, and to present them in a manner that is the best reflection of a rational-critical assessment in the public good. In return, the publics who turn to Hébert's columns for information on the political life of their community confer, restore, and maintain her symbolic capital, her credibility, on the basis of an assessment of the truth-value that is extracted from her work. It is not the lure of the marketplace that rewards a journalist such as Chantal Hébert, but the prestige that accrues from the relationship she has developed with her publics. So valuable is this relationship that the temptation to proselytize – "the preacher syndrome" – is excluded from the terms of communication in order to maintain the perception of a commitment to fact-based reason.

Candidates for political office are engaged in their own accumulation and conversion of the various forms of capital. Significantly, the process of capital accumulation is parallel to the one undertaken by journalists. With rare exception, political actors must build a portfolio of community service and demonstrate an aptitude for building consensus (accumulate social and cultural capital), be elected to a local or regional political position (exchange cultural capital for symbolic capital), raise money to finance their campaigns (obtain economic capital), and so forth. They must develop written and spoken communication skills to a level that permits them to compete with political opponents *and* convince an often sceptical electorate (usually via journalists) that they are best suited for the position they hope to attain. Over time, the accumulation and exchange of capitals may permit those political actors who manage to get elected to acquire enough reputation and prestige, enough credibility, to assume a certain formal and literal representative status. This acquisition of status is, of course, apparent in institutional forms of government with their infused regard for rank: prime minister, cabinet minister, leader of the opposition, committee chair, member of parliament, etc. This institutional conferral of representative status, complete with control over certain significant rules and resources on behalf of "the public," significantly raises the stakes in the relationship between the journalistic and political fields and their agents.

To speak with senior practising journalists such as Tom Parry of CBC Radio is to be made aware of the extent to which *social* capital foregrounds the relationship between politicians and journalists. Parry has been a member of the Parliamentary Press Gallery for more than a decade. He has reported from Parliament Hill on a daily basis and has covered three federal election campaigns. For such reporters who daily cover federal politics, there is a direct connection between social capital and credibility, in this case arising from the relationships that form over time between a politician and a reporter. Says Parry, "Credibility comes in part from personal relationships. Over time working on Parliament Hill, I've come to trust certain MPs on certain issues. I'll go to them for a comment because I think what they will say will be intelligent and relevant."[34]

The cultural capital of the reporter, his or her experience as a working journalist, together with the social capital engendered through a long association of professional and personal trust with certain political actors, creates conditions where an act of communication, the dissemination of "relevant and intelligent" information to the public, results in the accumulation of prestige for both parties. Once again, there is no exchange of economic capital in this relationship. It is based entirely on the exchange of social and cultural capital, and the accumulation of symbolic capital for political and journalistic actors. This system of accumulation and exchange, according to Parry, characterizes the normal course of journalistic practice for most of the political cycle. However, once an election is called, the relationship changes.

An election campaign in a democratic nation state such as Canada shifts the rules of the game by levelling the field of politics and vaulting journalists into positions of prominence. Political actors are relieved of their institutionally conferred power and forced to return to the field of power (to use Bourdieu's parlance) in order to have their record, their contribution to the legitimate vision of the social world, confirmed or reaffirmed by publics. They must spend their accumulated social, cultural, symbolic, and economic capital in order to remain literally "in power." In a very real sense, credibility (the form of symbolic capital at the crux of all capital exchanges) is extended and expended in the exchange of favourable public opinion for votes and a majority of votes for institutional power. The central objective of political actors, then, is the accumulation of as much credibility as possible and its conversion in the field of power, through publics, into the currency of power.

Political actors engaged in an election campaign have an array of communication vehicles at their disposal. They may attempt to "speak directly" to the public through advertising campaigns; they may hold town-hall meetings and political rallies; they may hand out flyers as they make their way door-to-door through their constituencies. Mass electronic "mail-outs" via the Internet have become the norm, as have Internet sites that outline virtually every aspect of a party's campaign position. However, the most coveted channel for campaign communication remains so-called "earned media."[35]

It is well recognized that a word of support from a prominent political journalist such as Chantal Hébert, Tom Parry, Andrew Coyne of the *National Post*, CTV's Craig Oliver, the CBC's Don Newman (now retired but still highly influential), André Pratt of *La Presse*, Don Martin of CTV's political discussion program *Powerplay* (formerly with the *National Post* and the *Calgary Herald*), or Jane Taber of the *Globe and Mail* (to name a few) is perceived to carry much more weight than many full-blown advertising campaigns. But access to these people and their colleagues (those with representative status in the field of journalism) is limited and, for the reasons discussed above, often symbolically dangerous. A nod of agreement may be extraordinarily valuable because of the credibility that transfers and accrues to the political position, but a shake of the head may mean that an entire line of political strategy must be severely modified or abandoned altogether.

In large part, political war rooms have been functionally inserted between politicians and journalists in an attempt to maximize positive earned media and avoid communication disasters. But on a significant level, war rooms are also there to leverage social, cultural, and symbolic capital away from political opponents: that is, to negatively influence their ability to acquire various forms of capital and exchange it for the symbolic form, the form that permits a credible case for a partisan position to be made in the field of power and publics.

For this reason, operatives who practise strategic political communication regard journalists as resources for partisan use. Social capital – access – is severely restricted as political operatives, their eye on message control, set aside the normal relationships of accumulated trust between journalists and politicians-turned-candidates. The political strategist's function is not to report the news of the day or to be overly concerned with relevant and intelligent commentary on matters of public concern but to acquire credibility for the party line and strip it from their opponents. To achieve this end, war rooms import strategies and tactics from election campaigns in other countries; they watch rival domestic campaigns for opportunities to appropriate creative techniques; and, significantly, they borrow from the world of corporate communication. This commitment to a singular purpose is reflected in the way that political war rooms promote themselves to reporters as information-*service* organizations.

These organizations, according to CBC's Tom Parry, have cleverly inserted themselves into the traditional heart of the field of journalism: the newsroom's editorial nerve centre, known in journalistic parlance as "the desk." "On a practical level," says Parry, "the war room has changed the way journalists work on the campaign by eliminating the middleman: the desk. It used to be that if you wanted to know what the other campaigns were saying about an issue, you'd have to phone Toronto and speak to an editor who'd spoken to the reporters traveling with the other leaders. Now the talking lines are sent directly to your BlackBerry."[36]

Parry is quick to note that this kind of information is useful only as a stock response to claims made by competing campaigns, permitting "reporters to offer slightly more balanced stories on very tight deadline." The immanent rules of the field of journalism still apply to war-room truth claims, those circulated by strategic communicators as a matter of fact when they are, in fact, partisan positions. They are still subject to the most basic journalistic test of newsworthiness: "Check if it's true. Judge whether it's relevant to your story. Then decide whether to use it."[37]

These two varieties of communicative practice can be used as a general bracket to delineate the "working space" of the political war room. One side of the bracket handles responses to journalists that contextualize a party's position vis-à-vis a generalized political discourse around an issue. The other floats truth claims as fact. And because war-room operatives know that such information will be checked, judged, and decided upon by journalists, it is often accompanied by "inside" information provided to selected journalists (as a "scoop") that includes bits of research from the public record not immediately available to other journalists.

This is where the real game of strategic political communication starts: with the attempt to slip partisan positions into the public debate by developing journalists as surrogates. To scratch the surface of such practices is to expose the true stakes in play: the intent to manipulate public opinion in a party's favour by presenting a truth claim that garners wide acceptance by being pushed through the journalistic credibility filter. In short, the central objective – and a significant part of the grand strategy of political actors – is to affect the transfer of journalistic credibility to partisan truth claims. By tracking the strategic objectives and the tactical measures employed by war rooms, all aimed at making this transfer of credibility happen, by sifting through the symbolic objectives of the war-room apparatus with respect to the manipulation of various exchanges of non-economic capital, it is possible to bring to light practices that have remained largely hidden from public view.

So how do strategic political communicators – the people who work in war rooms – go about *practically* influencing the exchange of meaning in the field of power? One way to investigate the practical aspects of their work is to examine it through the lens of Habermas's theory of communicative action.

This central concept from Habermas's later work holds that human beings are invested, at the heart of active communication, in reaching agreement or consensus.[38] In its most direct sense, communicative action with its central concern for a priori goodwill is an uneasy prospect for Bourdieu, largely because he found communicative action to be severely wanting in its attempt to bracket out embedded and underlying strategic objectives, the "feel for the game" grounded in conditions of *habitus* that "account for the practical elaboration of strategies without having recourse to some specific strategic calculation."[39] Yet the discussion *around* the concept of communicative action, as with so many critiques of Habermasian thought, is what really matters. For this reason, and as a means to flesh out an approach to actual war-room practices, I would like to introduce some final and connected concepts, including the idea of the register, S.N. Eisenstadt's notion of the institutional entrepreneur, and Stanley Deetz's adaptation of Habermas's theory of communicative action.

The concept of registers (also called argument strategies) may be employed here to illustrate how war rooms use universal thematic categories of moral concern to appeal simultaneously to broad swaths of a generalized "public" and, simultaneously, to clusters of individuals who are predisposed to react to a specific set of circumstances because of a community and/or cultural investment.[40] These thematic categories usually correspond to areas and treatments of political action claimed by a party and often frame the party's platform during an election campaign.

During election campaigns the New Democratic Party's list of "official" registers is actually posted on its website under the category of "issues." A visitor to the site during the 2005–06 campaign would see such offerings as "Better Health Care," "Clean Air," "Economic Security," "Accessible Education," "Equality for Women," and so forth. Such an appeal to the integrity of a particular stance creates a kind of safe zone, a legitimized boundary around an issue that provides the space in which a debate can take place over the partisan details of how the particular issue should be handled. It is the basic bounded ground for message control. Political war rooms have become increasingly concerned with discovering ways to move these boundaries, to increase control over claimed bits of communicative space (and the votes that reside within that space). This is where the notion of the institutional entrepreneur comes into play.

Eisenstadt's institutional entrepreneurs are "small groups of individuals who crystallize broad symbolic orientations, articulate specific and innovative goals, establish new normative and organizational frameworks for the pursuit of those goals, and mobilize resources necessary to achieve them."[41] Institutional entrepreneurs are precisely what characterize political war rooms as organizational entities.

If we add to Eisenstadt's list the time constraints that are built into every election campaign, the motivation to act quickly, the reputations that are made and lost, and the overarching drive to succeed, the aims and objectives of war rooms come into clearer focus. War rooms do not just practise the "crystallization" of broad symbolic orientations: they *implement* specific symbolic transfers within a window of opportunity that closes quickly and firmly once the election ends. Their purpose is not just to articulate "specific and innovative goals" but to put them forward in a contest for real power, often as a reactive response to a competitive gambit. War rooms invent and reinvent themselves daily in order to better achieve the strategic objectives that have been self-identified as important. They are the resources – human, economic, and symbolic – that have been mobilized to achieve political goals.

If we connect registers and institutional entrepreneurs and apply this articulation to the various strategic and tactical practices outlined by Deetz in his conceptualization (by way of Habermas) of systematically distorted communication, a picture emerges of the basic strategic tool put to use by war rooms. Indeed, systematically distorted communication – "the latent strategic *reproduction* of meaning rather than participatory production of it," and its similarity to "strategic manipulation, but without overt awareness" – is fundamentally what war rooms do.[42] However, they also participate in strategic manipulation *with* overt awareness, a communicative practice that opportunistically mobilizes the symbolic resources available to meet strategic objectives.

How does this opportunistic mobilization work? To get a sense of what's at stake, the following chapter looks into an "overtly aware" strategic communication gambit. It examines some specific public truth claims made by an influential politician, former British Prime Minister Tony Blair, the reaction to those truth claims by a well-regarded media voice, and the response of a reading public to the equivalent of a communicative donnybrook. By doing so, it prepares the ground for a deeper understanding of the pitched competition that characterizes contemporary election campaigns and explores how institutional entrepreneurs, the strategic communicators that run political war rooms, have pushed the basic bounded ground of partisan communication toward the production of systematically distorted messages.

3

The War Room

The reality is that as a result of the changing context in which
21st Century communications operates, the media are facing a hugely
more intense form of competition than anything they have ever experienced before. They are not the masters of this change but its victims. The
result is a media that increasingly and to a dangerous degree is driven by
"impact." Impact is what matters. It is all that can distinguish, can rise
above the clamour, can get noticed. Impact gives competitive edge. Of
course the accuracy of a story counts. But it is secondary to impact.

Tony Blair[1]

The above assessment of the hyper-competitive British news media is
lifted from the final speech in a series of eight on the future of the
United Kingdom delivered by outgoing Prime Minister Tony Blair.
The speech was posted in its entirety on the official web page for
Number 10 Downing Street. The excerpt is revealing for several reasons. First, it represents a timely view of the shifting terrain of journalism from the point of view of an experienced political actor of
considerable international repute. Second, it does so with only passing acknowledgment of the role of political-strategic communication in the generation of the "impact" that Blair considers so
deleterious to communication in public life and, in a related point,
makes no mention of the complicity of "New Labour" in the estab-
lishment of an internal organization devoted to strategic and tactical
communication. The omissions were immediately seized upon by
most of the British dailies, including *The Guardian*, in an editorial
entitled "Right Sermon, Wrong Preacher": "It is pretty rich to be
lectured on such matters by this prime minister who, more than any
other, has marginalised Parliament through a combination of sofa
government, selective leaking and sophisticated media manipulation.
His 'complicity' in such methods was not simply – as he implied – a
feature of early New Labour. It has been a consistent pattern –

witness recent terror briefings to the Sunday papers. Truly, he helped feed the animal he now wants to chain."[2]

Finally, Blair's speech/essay is very much a political document. It claims to step back deliberately from blaming anyone, while in reality laying blame squarely on the shoulders of journalists and the organizations that employ them. In other words, it is a bit of well-timed political manipulation. And it was almost certainly constructed for Prime Minister Blair in the Downing Street equivalent of a war room.

It is of special interest that Blair's message was crafted for release in the final days of his mandate. The date of his widely anticipated departure from Number 10 Downing had, by this time, been announced for 27 June 2007. Yet here we have an example of strategic political communication at work in the attempt to create a legacy for a prime minister increasingly marginalized by criticism of his stances on both domestic and foreign policy – notably, the abrogation of civil liberties at home as a response to threats of terrorism and Britain's continued involvement in the war in Iraq. It is also worth noting that the release of Blair's speech, on the official website of the Prime Minister's Office and residence, is intended to deliver his message directly to the world, to bypass the news media he so richly criticizes, all the while knowing that his words will be picked up, circulated, and critiqued by that same media. The strategies of political communication deployed in the early electoral successes of New Labour and maintained as daily working strategies through successive parliaments are here employed to construct the image of a thoughtful, caring, and concerned political leader about to leave the world stage, while simultaneously levelling a last rhetorical broadside at his media adversaries.

Blair's communication machine, like that of the White House of George W. Bush and Bill (and Hillary) Clinton before him, was adapted from an electoral organization and applied to the daily dissemination of partisan political communication.[3] Upon the ascension of the Clintons to the White House, Hillary Clinton, who was closely involved in the presidential campaign, is quoted as saying, "I think you have to run a campaign for policy just like you do for elections."[4] Recent observations about the Harper government's management of communication – strict control of all political communication through the Prime Minister's Office, attempts to coerce and control the Parliamentary Press Gallery, the muzzling of most ministers – suggest that the current government in Canada is familiar

with the models of communication control that have been applied in
the United States and the United Kingdom.[5] For this reason, it is
imperative that we understand as much as possible about how this
kind of political communication works and about the internal party
organizations that generate it. These organizations are almost impossible to study once they become embedded in the internal routines of
a political apparatus that holds power. They are secretive, fiercely
protective of both the strategies and tactics of daily political communication and the aura of power they are charged with enhancing
and upholding on behalf of the party leadership. Still, since they are
modelled on political war rooms, they are not entirely opaque. By
studying a war room in action, both in its functional and symbolic
sense, it is possible to anticipate the shifting shape of political
communication in Canada.

The war room of the New Democratic Party, like its counterparts
in opposing political camps, is a place and a space. As a *place* in the
leadup to the 2005 election call, it occupied coordinates on a city
map: an address corresponding to the third floor of the three-storey
building on the northeast corner of Bank and Laurier Streets in
downtown Ottawa. As a *space* the war room was (and is) a transient
organizational phenomenon, claiming a symbolic position in the firmament of competing interests that characterize a federal election
while communicating the party's point of view in the heavily mediated
space of public political discourse.

In the case of the NDP, place and space, the physicality of surround-
ings and the communicative purpose that emits from them at election
time, were (and remain) tightly interwoven. The place that housed
the war room for the 2005–06 campaign houses the NDP's business
offices when the party is not on an election footing. It is the site where
everyday activities happen, everything from paying bills to ordering
stationery to communicating with stakeholders. While government
is in session, political work mainly takes place in the opposition and
caucus offices on Parliament Hill. At the drop of the election writ,
however, everything changes: the *place* shifts in functional purpose –
the political actors move downtown from the Hill – and the *space* is
utterly transformed. It becomes the campaign headquarters.

Anyone out for a stroll in downtown Ottawa can open a street-
level door at 279 Laurier Street and walk up a few steps to a nondescript foyer. Against a wall are four Canadian flags hanging languidly
from short poles jammed into portable stands. It is unclear whether

they are there as decoration or because of a shortage of storage space. More likely, they are kept handy in case an impromptu news conference requires a colourful and patriotic backdrop for the television cameras. In 2005, when I entered the war room, the only direct hint that this was the business headquarters for a major federal political party was the understated party logo on the building directory. NDP? Third floor. Less obvious but much more informative was the etched-glass plaque hanging on the wall directly across from the rickety elevator that still carries visitors to the upper levels. On it were listed the names of forty Canadian unions and labour organizations, together with a short statement informing the reader that "working people" contributed the cash to buy this building for the New Democratic Party. The powerful Canadian Auto Workers' union, the CAW, headed the list, a bit of alphabetical synchronicity that predated a very public falling-out over the antics of union president Buzz Hargrove. Union politics aside, the NDP was and remains the owner and landlord of this prime piece of urban real estate in the heart of the nation's capital.

Once the elevator made it to the third floor (a seemingly onerous task in pre-renovation 2005), the doors opened onto a typical reception desk fronting a thoroughly bland warren of cubicles upholstered in neutral federal gray. This was where the daily grind of running a political party took place. Executive offices lined the perimeter of this nondescript workspace. There was a fairly elegant "boardroom" with a transparent glass wall. Small reminders of the party's history appeared from time to time, mostly printed artifacts from provincial and federal election campaigns that were hung, framed and unframed, on the few common walls. During my time at election headquarters, the real treasure trove of the party's electoral memory leaned haphazardly against the walls of a corridor leading to the washrooms: posters from T.C. Douglas's CCF victories of the 1940s and '50s and campaign material from the Ed Broadbent years through to the leadership of Jack Layton. Nobody seemed to pay these traces of history much attention. Telephones rang. Party workers went about their daily routines.

Certain changes began to happen at the party offices as the NDP ramped up its pressure on the Martin minority government, trying to extract every ounce of political capital from its pivotal position as the only party remaining in support of the Liberals. Security tightened. The elevator suddenly required a swipe card to access the third floor.

Party workers began to wear photo identification cards on cords around their necks. Political workers from the caucus offices on Parliament Hill showed up more frequently. By the first week of November, when it became clear that the government would fall on its refusal to guarantee the NDP demand that no public money flow to private health services, senior campaign coordinators left their day jobs in cities across Canada to take up residence in an Ottawa hotel. Strategic planning began in earnest. These were mainly experienced political communicators who worked in provinces where NDP governments have held power – British Columbia, Saskatchewan, Manitoba, Ontario, and more recently, Nova Scotia – or in areas where there were significant seats in play, such as southwestern Ontario.

For all of this, most of the people who undertook the normal routines of daily party life were not involved in the war room per se at election time. Campaign headquarters comprised many more or less discreet organizational "units" involved with logistics and campaign administration. This work included tour planning for the leader and his entourage: chartering the party's airplane; reserving hotel rooms; booking special events such as specific news conferences and appearances for the leader and other party spokespeople on various media offerings (a spot on *Music Plus* in Montreal was a big hit, as was one on *Politics*, fronted by Don Newman on CBC Newsworld); administering support in the ridings through budgets for party literature and lawn signs; and maintaining links between local candidates and the central party apparatus. In short, most election workers were involved with keeping the system up and running. However, there were (and are) two specialized units that stand apart from the others: the research department and the rapid-response team. Together they formed the backbone of the war room, a separate organizational unit concerned specifically with strategic communication.[6]

The research department continues to be responsible for facts and figures and has two main functions. First, it is the keeper of the party's political memory. When a candidate or political operative says something publicly, any past position adopted by the party is taken into account. This practice is intended to provide continuity for the party's point of view but is also meant to give candidates – from the leader to incumbents to first-time candidates – a body of considered and adopted organizational history to draw upon. In this respect, the political memory of the party also acts as an inoculation against attacks by political opponents who have their own easily accessed databases of statements and positions made by competitors, including the NDP.

The second function of the research department, opposition research, or "oppo," is the flip side of research in support of the party memory.[7] It deals in information, from mundane facts to complex statistics, about political opponents. The New Democrats and other political parties spend time during the normal political cycle compiling information about the Conservatives, Liberals, Bloc Québécois, and other political entities. The research may extend to the provincial organizations for each party and even to municipal players, particularly in large urban centres. The idea is to amass as much information as possible, mainly from public sources. Public sources are creditable; that is, they leave a trace in the public domain that can be referenced. *Hansard* is a valuable resource for this kind of research, since it is the official record of everything said in both the House of Commons and Senate. Position statements by members of opposing political parties are also lifted from the minutes of committee meetings. This kind of information may be especially valuable to political operatives since it represents a succinct record of policy stances but is largely unknown to average Canadians since parliamentary committees in Canada generally go about their business with little or no media attention.

Statements made by politicians and disseminated by mass media are another important source of opposition research. Newspapers and magazine articles, radio programs, television news and public affairs offerings are scoured for quotes from political leaders, MPs, those who might wish to make the jump from municipal or provincial political office to Parliament Hill, workers in various political campaigns – indeed, anyone in the public record who has an opinion about anything. It is a wide net that, increasingly, includes statements made on various partisan and non-partisan sites on the Internet.[8]

The Internet has become a valuable resource in another sense. Websites dedicated to political campaigns of all stripes publicize constituency meetings, planning sessions, and other political gatherings that are unlikely to be covered by traditional media. Political opponents regularly send "observers" to such meetings to record the "grassroots" discussions and the positions adopted by those seeking political office. Such information may be held for years, to be released at precisely the moment when it will cause the greatest damage to the credibility of an opponent. Increasingly, however, political operatives are branching out. On 26 January 2006, two days after election night, a self-identified Conservative Party supporter named Stephen Taylor – the hand and mind behind the website *Conservative Party of Canada Pundit* – speculated, somewhat tongue in cheek, that leaks that had plagued the Liberal campaign were in part attributable to the proximity of Conservative and Liberal war rooms to a specific coffee outlet in downtown Ottawa. Posted Taylor, "On the corner of Metcalf and Slater is a Starbucks, which was often frequented by Liberal war-room staffers in need of some java and by their Conservative counterparts who liked to sit around and 'read' the newspaper (while eavesdropping on the competition). Granted, it was a good place for bloggers to pick up tips too."[9] If this is true (and let's keep in mind that Taylor is a political partisan and therefore not above spinning his own brand of strategic communication), opposition research has pushed the boundaries of the public record to accommodate elements of amateur espionage.

This vast reserve of information about political opponents, collected and stored in the opposition research department's data banks, is the "ammunition" available to the rapid-response team. When asked about the function of the rapid-response team, one war-room participant who wished to remain anonymous said, "It's about using opportunistic information on opponents – undermining your opponent by going on an immediate attack and trying to make dirt stick." It should be noted and underlined that such opportunism is *not* concerned with inventing the "dirt" that is intended to "stick." All information used against political opponents is factual inasmuch as it can be confirmed by a reference to the public record. The real power of rapid response lies in its ability to present a contrary point of view to an opponent's truth claims as quickly as possible, in some cases even before the questions and answers posed by the news media on a position announcement by a competing camp have ended. Indeed, a large part of the objective of rapid response is to prompt reporters to ask questions that have been generated in the war room or to use war-room material as factually based information to round out their reports.[10] Opposition research and rapid response are therefore generated specifically to provide a competing point of view to challenge the truth claims of opponents, to undermine their credibility and, by so doing, to garner credibility for the home team.

In order for opposition research and rapid response to work effectively, however, the war room requires two other elements:

an individual or team to coordinate and direct the strategic-communication resources, and a person or team to monitor what the opposing political camps are doing at any given time during the campaign. A group of experienced political communicators, a specialized organization within the larger party operation, decides the strategic and tactical priorities on any given campaign day and how those priorities will be communicated. During the campaign, this group is mainly based in the party offices in downtown Ottawa, although a significant and influential element of the organization travels with the leader. In the campaign of 2005–06, the on-the-road contingent was led by the NDP's then director of communications and long-time political activist, Jamey Heath. This travelling group of advisors was instrumental in conveying the concerns of the political leadership back to those in Ottawa, dealing with matters as they arose on the ground, and generally advising colleagues at campaign headquarters how communication strategies were being received across the country.

As co-chair of the campaign, Brian Topp directed campaign strategy from Ottawa. His team included Brad Lavigne, then a strategic communication specialist, and Raymond Guardia, recruited from ACTRA (the Alliance of Canadian Cinema, Television and Radio Artists) and charged with managing the daily operations of the war room. Press secretary Ian Capstick, a full-time caucus employee, was the party's media contact, charged with handling reporters' requests (including requests to tour the war room), ensuring that perceived inaccuracies in media reports were clarified, and communicating general information about the campaign, such as the leader's schedule, to media sources and others.

The final element in the organizational structure of the NDP war room was perhaps the most critical and the least recognized. Two regular party workers were assigned to monitor and report on the daily news cycle. This was no small task. It involved disseminating a daily synopsis of the political reporting in all of Canada's big daily newspapers; monitoring radio sources such as CBC/Radio Canada for reports on opposition campaigns; monitoring CBC Newsworld and RDI for similar material, including live reports of announcements and other campaign related material; monitoring similar offerings on CTV, Global Television, and CSPAN, the all-politics cable channel; reporting on the content of national newscasts from all network television sources; and keeping a close watch on the Canadian

Press (CP) news service for breaking information about the NDP campaign and those of its rivals. This last task was particularly important, because CP was (and is) regarded as the agenda-setter for political news of the day.

From a general and purely functional point of view, the war room instituted a strategic-information campaign on two fronts. It promoted and disseminated the daily position of the party on issues dealing with the ideological position of the organization, and, conversely, it attacked and attempted to undermine the position of competing parties. Within these offensive and defensive modes, the war room was responsible, as much as possible, for anticipating attacks by competitors and responding to them. When a competitor scored a surprise "hit," it was the responsibility of the war room to deflect the damage. Various tactics were employed in these circumstances, from stony silence to traditional "spin" to full frontal assault. The objective in all cases was to gain credible ownership of the issues of greatest importance to voters and to enter into a series of parallel conversions. All parties sought to convert cultural capital to symbolic capital and garner the credibility, as Bourdieu would put it, to impose a legitimate vision of the social world. This outcome was practically obtained by attempting to control the flow of information to the complicated collectivity that makes up voting publics, the collectivity that, everyone understood, must be convinced to embrace a particular vision and manifest it in the votes that elect members of Parliament.

All political war rooms have taken a page from a series of classic studies and theoretical positions on the way that journalists frame reality. Todd Gitlin's use of Goffman's theories on strips and frames is particularly useful. In Gitlin's view, frames are "persistent patterns of cognition, interpretation, and presentation, of selection, emphasis and exclusion, by which symbol-handlers routinely organize discourse."[11] It is Gitlin's position – adopted and adapted to specific areas of study such as the journalistic treatment of political communication and electoral reportage – that the media, as symbol-handlers, are complicit in ensuring that discourse is constructed and organized in a manner that favours the state. Gaye Tuchman, also borrowing from Goffman, posits that media organizations have significant influence over "strips" – the slices of defining reality chosen by intelligent observers from a "seemingly infinite number of concrete occurrences" – and the ideological conditions that frame them.[12] According to Tuchman, those ideological conditions, embedded in the organizational structure of newsrooms and the culture of news work, ensure that the "legitimized institutional view" predominates in news accounts.[13] Michael Parenti extends Tuchman's critique by contending that personality trumps issues, events are favoured over content, official positions are considered more important than popular grievances, and the atypical and sensational is considered "more interesting" than the everyday because news organizations make a conscious choice "to withhold the informational and ideological tools" that citizens need to question elite constructions of reality.[14] Finally the media, especially television, are specifically credited with framing election campaigns "as war, as a game, as drama, but rarely as a competition between alternate visions."[15]

All of the cited studies and theoretical positions that arise out of Goffman's work on frame analysis are focused on the news media. All allude to journalists as agents of limited free expression, overtly or indirectly influenced by the ideological (and economic) limits imposed by the companies that employ them.[16] Yet by focusing on the media, these critiques fail to address a lacuna in the relationship between journalists and political actors. If the game is so fixed along the ideological lines that favour elite consensus, how are political parties such as the NDP – parties that stand in openly stated ideological opposition to the corporate aims and objectives of media companies – able to garner any coverage at all?

Part of the answer lies in Canadian law and electoral policy, particularly the sections of the Elections and Broadcasting Acts enforced by the CRTC, that specify coverage on an "equitable basis to all accredited political parties and rival candidates."[17] Another part of the answer lies in journalistic convention, the institutionally normalized "rule" that eschews one-sided or partisan reporting in favour of stories representing competing views, a convention that is itself open to criticism because of the often arbitrary decisions – usually made by editors – about which competing views will have merit and which will be excluded from journalistic representation.[18] The upshot is that war rooms have become adept at using law and policy, together with knowledge about journalistic convention, to justify the often seamless insertion into news stories of opposition research through rapid-response techniques and, by doing so, to generate credible messages.

Furthermore, it is not enough to say, as Matthew Mendelsohn suggested in his study of the 1988 federal election "horse race," that "the frames used will be negotiated between parties and the media, but will never be allowed to challenge the elite consensus and dominant ideology."[19] The competition for credibility is *all about* challenging the dominant ideology. It is put into practice at the very level where the bits and pieces of everyday reality, worked upon by the rules and resources of law, policy, and convention, are assembled into a representation, a construction of credible understanding, *a legitimate vision of the social world*, that seeks to resonate with a public or publics to motivate democratic expression precisely aimed at shifting elite consensus and dominant ideology. The question is whether the means justify the ends.

With the struggle to construct and inject a "legitimate vision of the social world" now embraced by all political war rooms at the most basic level of message control, concerns about the rapid deployment and strategic placement of opposition research and the possibilities for manipulation and systematic distortion are of utmost importance. Does the opportunistic insertion of opposition research at this fundamental level, often without regard for context, remove the very possibility for reasoned debate on matters of public concern? The fact that political war rooms have constructed a layer of myth to insulate and conceal their core communicative practices is indicative of a general reluctance to openly engage this core question.

The act of concealment lies within the symbolic identity of the war room, the *space* of political communication that extends beyond the *place* where the party organization constructs its daily offerings. This symbolic extension of the space – an omnipresent force "out there" that must be reckoned with – creates the impression that the place is something greater than the sum of its parts while simultaneously shielding its most closely held practices from public view. As the social geographer David Harvey observes, "concepts of space and time affect the way we understand the world to be"; they are therefore deeply implicated in how we construct meaning around the concept of "place." The layering of meanings around and within places is, as Harvey points out, powerfully normative. Such meanings contribute to the creation of dominating conventions that "operate with the full force of objective facts to which all individuals and institutions necessarily respond."[20] War rooms of all stripes are deeply invested in the creation of dominating conventions, layers of meaning that shield their purely functional aspects. These meanings are intentionally constructed to represent the beating election-time heart of the party organization, enabling the *idea* of the war room to transcend its physical place, to become normalized as a powerful metonym in Canadian party politics. It is at once the transparent public heart of the party (inasmuch as the leader is its face) and a supra-organizational entity that stands in for the functional entity: its hip, postmodern, alter-representation that diverts scrutiny from the nuts-and-bolts practice of manipulating communication to obtain and hold political power.

This concern for the war room as an organization that is simultaneously transparent and secretive is addressed on a significant level in the work on meta-imaging undertaken by Shawn and Trevor Parry-Giles. The two examined the documentary film *The War Room*, by Chris Hegedus and D.A. Pennebaker, a film based on an "insider's view" of the presidential campaign of Bill Clinton and promoted as a "revealing, behind-the-scenes journey to the White House."[21] The authors contend that the film is a "political-rhetorical genre wherein campaign outsiders attempt to 'get inside' presidential campaigns to unmask the image" and reveal the "real" candidate, but are thwarted by campaign operatives who turn the documentary into a device to promote a highly controlled image of the candidate and campaign.[22] In this view, the credibility of the documentary film genre, with its emphasis on capturing "reality in as pure a manner as possible," is appropriated by political operatives in order to construct and project an image of the political candidate in keeping with the communication strategies of the campaign.[23]

However, *The War Room* differs from other examples of "behind the scenes" documentary reportage. Its principle subject is supposed to be Bill Clinton and his political campaign for the presidency, but as the film unfolds, the subject shifts to James Carville and George Stephanopoulos, the people responsible for running Clinton's war room and, therefore, responsible for controlling the flow of access and information to the filmmakers. The political strategists behind the Clinton campaign become the representational foreground for the politician. Their war room – the term was coined, according to Stephanopoulos, by Hillary Clinton – becomes a metonym for the entire campaign. Parry-Giles and Parry-Giles rightfully point out that the *film* is an example of meta-imaging, "the communicative act in which political campaigns and their chroniclers publicly display and foreground the art and practice of political image construction."[24] It is also worth noting that the war room itself is a meta-*language* signifier.[25] This symbolic role for the war room, constructed by grafting a functional purpose onto the mythic/historic language of organized hostility, is the idea that has been refined, adapted, and imported into the Canadian political context.

This idea of the war room has been constructed in part by the insertion of its metonymic presence by political actors into daily news and information cycles. Invitations to journalists to visit a party's war room are about more than colour commentary. For example, the *Globe and Mail* of 30 November 2005, published a day after the federal election call, devoted a half-page to a "behind the scenes" look at the war rooms of the competing political parties. The story arose from a request (that I observed while in the war room) from various media organizations for access to competing party war rooms, a request that the NDP capitalized on by permitting a general media tour. For a brief period, camera crews from CTV, the CBC/Radio Canada, and Global Television were given more or less free rein to collect images. Reporters from various publications wandered through the place, taking notes about ambience and asking superficial questions about organizational structure. The result for the NDP was a small "earned media" coup. A photograph of the NDP war room was published in the prominent centre space of the *Globe and Mail* story. The image represented a literal picture of party openness and media accessibility, with a descriptive line that read: "Cameramen film the NDP war room in Ottawa yesterday, after the kickoff of the federal election campaign." Surrounding the photograph were the names and abbreviated political pedigrees of the senior strategists for the Liberals, Conservatives, NDP, and Bloc Québécois, outlined in the starkest detail by *Globe* reporters. A sub-headline reads: "Think it's the leaders who mastermind the campaigns? Think again. Meet the men and women who are really in charge."[26]

Yet the story provides no detail about the daily functional grind of strategic political communication. There is no description of opposition research or rapid response. There is no sense of the way that communication priorities are set, followed, adapted, or abandoned. The *Globe* report purports to reveal the secret workings of the war room by breathlessly uncovering "the men and women who are really in charge," but it never tells us exactly what they are in charge of. Instead, the war room is pictorially portrayed as a transparently normal part of daily life, a part of political life that just happens to house the "masterminds behind the campaigns." As a physical place, the war room becomes normalized, through its mediated representation, as the symbolic space of political grand strategy, a postmodern Olympus where the singular pronouncements of the masterminds represent the Zeus-like voice of the party while concealing the intimate inner workings of the organization.

The extent to which the war room protects its functional side may be glimpsed in a short episode that occurred about two weeks after the publication of the *Globe and Mail* story. A reporter from an unknown news organization contacted the NDP press secretary, Ian Capstick, to request access to the war room in order to write an "in-depth" story about party strategy. This conversation took place in the common space of the war room where it was overheard by numerous people including myself. While the NDP was willing to accommodate the reporter's request, there were definite limits. For example, in response to a presumed question about attending the morning war-room "strategy meeting," the press secretary told the reporter, "No, no, that would be like my asking to come to your story meeting." The response was referring to the standard morning news meetings held among reporters and editors in every newsroom across the country. The fact that most news organizations would likely be willing to accommodate a representative of the NDP, or any member of the public, is immaterial. By turning the question of accessibility back onto an assumed inaccessibility on the part of the reporter's own newsroom, Capstick was able to effectively constrain access by a journalist. The effect was to protect the symbolic space of the war room while heading off the process of demystification that may have come about by the dissemination of a story about the nuts and bolts of strategic political communication. The reporter dropped the request.

This small anecdote demonstrates the level of control over reflexive communication practised by the war room. It is indicative of the constraints placed upon any "outsider" (including myself) intent on examining the inner workings of the organization. However, these organizational constraints and the tactics used to implement them are also markers or signposts that direct the way to the communicative control mechanisms used to conceal the practices of strategic political communication. Nothing piques curiosity like a locked door. The challenge of unravelling the practice of strategic political communication often lies in avoiding the tactical diversions that, for example, led to the quashing of a perfectly legitimate request by a reporter for access to the party's communication apparatus, a request for transparency that would certainly have been in the interests of any number of publics.

A further example, this time from the 5 December 2005 edition of the *Ottawa Citizen*, illustrates how a certain form of meta-imaging has become commonplace. The story, by *Citizen* reporter Doug Fischer, is entitled "Media focus on lobbyists in the war room." Its photo and text take up more than a half-page. The gist of Fischer's story is that firms of lobbyists – the Earnscliffe Group and its close ties with the Paul Martin campaign is specifically profiled – are no longer able to work behind the scenes because of a higher expectation of transparency on behalf of the public (attributed to the work of the Gomery Commission in exposing questionable practices by the previous Liberal government). A sub-headline for the story sums up Fischer's thesis: "The people who help politicians win elections no longer do so without public scrutiny."[27] Fischer goes on to detail the cozy and sometimes murky world of alliances between professional lobbyists who change hats, seemingly at will, to become senior strategists for political parties and, once the job is done, return to their lobbying work. The writer raises concerns about valuable information on policy being passed to corporate clients from inside the political campaign, about the possibility of serious conflicts of interest, of ethical misdeeds in pursuit of profit.

While all of this is certainly worthy of journalistic scrutiny, the true value in Fischer's account lies in the tactics of justification and diversion that the story unwittingly brings to light. The response to Fischer from those being profiled is a veritable primer in communication strategy. Political operators point out that Prime Minister MacKenzie King used "advisers drawn from high-powered outside firms" as early as the 1920s. The reporter reveals that party strategists had been anticipating media questions about the role of lobbyists and, in anticipation, the Liberal Party's national director, Steven MacKinnon, was assigned the task of responding. His defence of the practice pretty much sums up the alpha and omega of political tactics: "Look, there's nothing wrong with using people from the private sector on campaigns. This is not policy-making – this is the work of getting a political party elected and I would submit to you that the day people cannot participate in the democratic process will be a dark day for the country."[28]

MacKinnon's tactic is to push the issue into a safe register, deploying an "argument strategy" around matters of "democratic rights" or "democratic inclusion." Democracy itself will be undone, a pall will be cast over the land, if certain people are denied their right to participate in the democratic process just because they work in the private sector! Tactically, MacKinnon first attacks the very premise of Fischer's inquiry, implying that the reporter does not know the difference between making policy and working on an election campaign. He diverts attention by refusing to discuss the possibility of inside knowledge of policy or personal connections with powerful politicians being used to generate future profits, instead pointing out that nothing illegal is taking place. To top it all off, the story layout gives prominent place to a photo of the principals of the Earnscliffe Group, gathered around a smiling Prime Minister Paul Martin. In what is obviously a staged event, this group of happy, *normal* people, casually attired, perhaps a bit sheepish over all the fuss, grin for the television cameras. The Earnscliffe Group, the core of Paul Martin's campaign war room, is therefore portrayed in text and image as a group of reasonable, everyday people with nothing to hide. They just happen to have a devoted interest in the exercise of democracy. Not once is the question of what these people actually *do* (or how they do it) asked or answered. The strategic and tactical practices of the war-room operatives are employed to construct a meta-image of the war room, which is itself employed to divert attention from and conceal the true strategic and tactical practices being used. And it is all done in plain sight.

One way to penetrate this protective shield is to recognize from the beginning that not all political war rooms are created equal. As Ian MacDonald points out, they all perform essentially the same *functions*; they all engage in opposition research and rapid response; they all generate lines around issues for their political "clients" to use in the daily struggle for distinction; they are all concerned with message control.[29] But each is also an organization with its own internal culture. The war room of the New Democratic Party bore no resemblance to the *Citizen's* description of the Earnscliffe Group. Where the Liberal war room was, by its own description, connected to private-sector lobbyists and a coterie of political and communication professionals, the NDP organization was made up of union activists and administrators, and (mostly) young people brought in from the party's provincial offices. Whereas the group photograph of the Earnscliffe strategists published in the *Citizen* shows a collection of mainly white, middle-aged males, the NDP war room was the picture of diversity. While it is true that the senior strategists in the NDP organization were "pale and male," I also observed that women outnumbered men across the board, sexual preference was not an issue, nobody paid attention when the Muslim campaign workers stopped for prayers, and the place was profoundly colour blind.

Issues of "corporate" power and hierarchy were also in keeping with what one might expect from an "NDP" organizational culture. I observed a workplace where people spoke their minds, but also listened to the reasoned arguments of others – a place where passionate positions were often laid out in open space at fairly high-decibel levels. The very existence of an organizational hierarchy became apparent only when one outspoken war-room worker complained about the power relations that "everyone had agreed needed to be dealt with." She was referring to a group decision that had been made at some point prior to my arrival to "flatten" the organizational structure, to disperse the decision-making and power patterns of the war room over its workforce. The resolution may have caused the application of some daily strategic decisions to move more slowly than "management" would have liked – some meetings were quite lengthy because everybody felt they had a stake in discussing the matters at hand – but in general the rapid responses of the NDP war room were as fast as anyone else's and the institutional entrepreneurship of the group was always in evidence. Everyone understood the objectives. Everyone understood the resources, both human and material, that were available to make the objectives possible.

Indeed, in many respects it was the institutional "fit" of the war room that seemed to be at odds with the political culture of many of the people who worked in it. The kind of organizational discipline portrayed in the film *The War Room*, with its commitment to winning at any cost, did not appeal to the value commitments of many people in the NDP war room who were volunteering for a political party that at times seemed to be ignoring its own press. I have no proof of this assertion, merely a set of passive observations. Some war-room workers would become unusually quiet when certain tactical gambits were put in play, notably practices aimed at discrediting rivals rather than engaging core issues. Some would roll their eyes. Others would leave the room. Conversely, there was anger and outrage when tactics were employed against the NDP. In such cases the sentiment was openly voiced that the opposition was not "playing fair." The greatest approval for strategic and tactical measures came when the party's position was well represented by journalists as a reasonable alternative to the ones on offer from competing camps – that is, when the credibility of an NDP position was given its due.

However, as the campaign moved forward and the election drew closer, the practices of war-room operatives seemed to become more programmatic, more inclined to rely on the tactical playbook than on a keen desire to engage a rational-critical debate, even on issues such as publicly funded health care that lie at the core of the NDP identity. This was partly because the NDP was simply outgunned by the "communication professionals" employed by the Liberals and the Conservatives (the Bloc, of course, was concerned only with Quebec where the NDP in 2005–06 was a marginal presence). As a result, the NDP war room felt pressure to respond in kind, to conform to the tactics and strategies being deployed against it. This response often put the party out on a limb with journalists who, using their own experience and understanding of Canadian political history (their cultural capital), were able to ask uncomfortable questions to which the party, usually represented by Jack Layton, often appeared ill prepared to respond. On more than one occasion, the NDP undermined its own credibility, expended its own symbolic capital for no return, because it was unable to support its own truth claims.

This is not an indictment of the way the NDP conducted itself in the 2005–06 general election campaign as much as an observation on the way that political war rooms in their symbolic representation, in their own meta-imaging, can become a prescriptive solution for the very people who work in them. It is an observation on how the war room, having established itself as its own objective fact across the Canadian political firmament, has come to command the response of the individuals engaged in its own structurated *being*, largely in response to the competition among different variants of the same organizational structure. For the NDP this might have resulted in an electoral disaster; the party all but disappeared from the media spotlight in the second half of the campaign, relegated in the main to providing reaction quotes to "balance" stories being generated in other political camps. Yet voters did move to the New Democrats. The party did pick up seats on election day. There was resonance in the field of power among publics in support of the NDP as an alternative to the dominant political options. Why? And why, given the sound and fury of partisan political communication, the expenditure of considerable economic capital, the constant positioning and tactical challenge over matters of credibility that characterized the 2005–06 election campaign, did Canadian publics choose a minority government?

The following chapter assesses these and other questions as it begins the process of unravelling war room practices from the inside. It illustrates how the tactics and the responses they generate can overshadow larger strategic concerns. In many ways it is a lesson on just how ruthless Canadian politics can be and how committed the people who play in the field are to its *illusio*. But it is also an exploration of some of the inherent weaknesses of war-room communication practices, of how strategic political communicators can find their own strategies and tactics coming back to bite them. Above all, we begin to see how credibility lies behind every communicative exchange engaged by competing war rooms and journalists, and the lengths, symbolic and otherwise, that those in competition for power will employ to obtain this important species of symbolic capital.

The War Room in Action: Tactics

Buzz Hargrove, president of the Canadian Auto Workers Union, has been found in a very public embrace with Prime Minister Paul Martin and the feathers are flying.

Alan Ferguson[1]

On Friday, 2 December 2005, five days before Alan Ferguson's column in the *Vancouver Province* hit the streets, workers at the NDP campaign headquarters in Ottawa gathered in the media-viewing area of the war room. Word had spread that something was up. All eyes were on CBC Newsworld's live broadcast from the floor of the Canadian Auto Workers (CAW) annual convention in Toronto. CAW president Buzz Hargrove had taken the stage to ask delegates to support "strategic voting" in the upcoming election, something the NDP considered to be utterly contrary to its own interests. By Hargrove's logic, confirmed NDP voters could stop Conservative candidates in their tracks by switching their votes to the Liberal candidate in ridings where New Democrats had no chance of winning. This would stop the "common enemy" from winning in ridings where the vote was split on the left and centre. By the NDP's logic, however, the Liberals were *also* the enemy, perhaps even the greater of the evils confronting them in the campaign. In the war-room's view, Hargrove was asking committed New Democrats to endorse a hare-brained scheme doomed to backfire at their candidates' expense.

Hargrove's initial speculation on this "strategy" had been met with a certain amount of incredulity in NDP circles, but nobody anticipated the spectacle that had been engineered for the Toronto convention. Waiting in the wings was Prime Minister Paul Martin and, on cue, he walked out before the assembled representatives of the largest union in the country, embraced its president, and accepted a bomber jacket emblazoned with the CAW crest as a symbol of solidarity with the workers on the convention (and shop) floor. The symbolism was unmistakable. It was certainly not lost on the campaign workers watching from the NDP war room. Stunned silence gradually gave way to epithets about Hargrove's sanity and character. The shock and sense of betrayal – after all, a great many New Democrats, especially in Central Canada, see the party as a political extension of the union movement – were assuaged somewhat by a telephone call from a campaign worker at the convention. The caller pointed out that a large numbers of delegates were sitting on their hands, refusing to endorse Hargrove's new deal with Martin, a scene that was confirmed by the CBC cameras. For all of this, the prevailing sentiment among party workers was anger and dismay over what was universally regarded as an act of out-and-out treason.

Then something interesting happened. The war room communication machine kicked into high gear. Strategists met briefly and in very short order the war room issued a series of "lines" to be used in response to the inevitable questions that journalists would ask. These lines, along with a synopsis of the issue at hand, were immediately conveyed on the internal list-serve to all candidates and political operatives who might be approached for a comment:

BACKGROUND

At the CAW national conference in Toronto today, CAW President Buzz Hargrove endorsed Liberals in ridings in which "NDP has no chance in hell" and said he wanted increased Liberal representation in Parliament. Said minority should have continued because it was getting good stuff done.

LINES

Parliament was getting things done because NDP got results people. Just look at majority Liberal record.

Mr. Hargrove's entitled to his opinion. What's important to remember is if you want to vote NDP chances are very good your neighbours do too. That's why a vote for the ndp [sic] elects an NDP MP.

Working people need pension protection, better training, E.I. [employment insurance] that's there for them and Liberals haven't delivered. In this Parliament alone, the Liberals opposed a ban on scab labour in areas of federal jurisdiction.[2]

This classic "spin" is a common response in political communication circles, used to counter unforeseen circumstances that might be seen to negatively affect the party's fortunes. The idea is to reframe the issue by attempting to direct attention away from its perceived negative substance to matters more favourable to the party. But under the circumstances – a perceived betrayal by a key member of the NDP "family" coupled with a strike by the Liberals into the very heart of NDP territory – these lines had a secondary purpose: to maintain discipline by constraining everyone in the party, coast to coast, to the same set of responses.

As tempting as it would have been to launch a frontal attack on Hargrove's credibility, to hit back at a perceived betrayal, the media lines were intended to take issue with the union president's *position* without alienating the *person*. Political strategists recognized that, disagreeable political bedfellows aside, Hargrove was still in a position to influence a great number of voters in ridings where support for the NDP remained strong. Driving a wedge between voters and their union boss in a public showdown would do no good and might do a lot of harm.

After all, Paul Martin had reached out to Hargrove because the Liberals were convinced he could deliver NDP votes. The NDP was not interested in lending further aid to Martin's cause. A reasonable and respectful tone, reminding CAW members (and other union voters) of the New Democratic Party's record in Parliament, of the need for solidarity among "neighbours," of the party's values vis-à-vis its support for programs to benefit workers and, most significantly, of the mistrust that working people should hold for the Liberals based on their record in government, would paint Hargrove's plan for strategic voting as ill considered and out of step with the larger community of working people. Furthermore, the very act of suggesting that "Mr. Hargrove's entitled to his opinion" planted a seed of doubt about whether strategic voting had originated solely with Buzz Hargrove. The Liberals (then embroiled in the "sponsorship scandal" inquiry and questions over the possibility of illegal dissemination of insider knowledge on income trusts) were master manipulators, inferred the NDP, and not above leading Hargrove astray. As their record showed, they were not to be trusted.

For reporters working for national news organizations, the NDP response could not hold a candle to the spectacle of the mutual embrace of Martin and Hargrove. Keith Leslie of the Canadian Press, reporting from the convention, proposed in his introductory paragraph (lede) on the story (and seemed to confirm a measure of NDP suspicions) that this was an ingrained Liberal manoeuvre. "The time-honoured Liberal tactic of poaching New Democrat support got an early start Friday as Paul Martin warned Canada's largest union that only he and Steven Harper stand a chance of becoming prime minister," wrote Leslie.[3] His report quotes at length Martin's speech to the CAW delegates but makes no mention of the NDP position in the lines being circulated to party spokespeople. A followup story by CP's Gary Norris, filed an hour later, shifts to quoting Hargrove's position rather than that of Martin and seems to reflect an attempt by the union boss to step back slightly from his previous position: "A Liberal minority government with the balance of power held by the New Democratic Party," writes Norris, "would be the best outcome in the federal election, Canadian Auto Workers president Buzz Hargrove said Friday."[4]

Norris is also among the first to quote NDP Leader Jack Layton in response to Hargrove's actions. Layton's words are adapted directly from the lines issued by the war room: "'Mr. Hargrove is well known for having his opinions and expressing them and *he's entitled to them* in terms of how the house should be composed,' said NDP Leader Jack Layton. 'Our view and my job as the leader of the New Democratic Party, which is *the party most clearly associated with getting results for workers*, is to get as many New Democrats elected as possible.'"[5]

The *Globe and Mail* picked up on the drama of the Hargrove/Martin embrace in its Saturday edition, the day after the event, playing the story prominently under the front page headline "Liberals touted by CAW leader." A lead-in line in less prominent print follows – "Hargrove's endorsement bitter pill for NDP to swallow" – setting up the lede: "Autoworkers union boss Buzz Hargrove cut the legs from under the NDP's election message when he delivered a qualified endorsement of Paul Martin's Liberals yesterday."[6] The NDP reaction is reserved for the story "jump" on page 6 under a secondary headline: "Merely one person's view, NDP says." The words divide the remaining text of the story from a prominent photograph of the Hargrove/Martin public embrace. Layton's response, once again taken from the war room lines, attempts to underscore the personal nature of Hargrove's position while attacking the Liberal record (and simultaneously underscoring the NDP position): "Our view is that the Liberals don't deserve people's support. What have they done in the 12 years they've been in power to improve the lives of working people?"[7] The *National Post* and the *Ottawa Citizen,* both owned by CanWest, published stories on the Hargrove/ Martin clinch in their Saturday editions. Each plays down Layton's response. Indeed, the *Citizen* story (published at the bottom of page 3) contains no mention of the NDP leader.

The real stakes here are, of course, votes: the currency of exchange at election time that, theoretically, permits one vision of the social world to predominate. The *Globe and Mail* story contains an inkling of the overall NDP strategy and gestures toward an underlying reason for the party's very real concern over Liberal attempts to poach votes: "In places like Hamilton, Oshawa and Saskatchewan, where the NDP narrowly lost in 2004, Mr. Layton has been attempting to polarize the vote between the New Democrats and the Conservatives. 'Don't waste your vote on the Liberals,' he said yesterday morning in Regina."[8] The NDP strategy was underscored by comments from then Saskatchewan Premier Lorne Calvert who opined in a somewhat confused joint news conference with Layton that "he would be happy with a minority Liberal or NDP government." As Calvert put it in his inimitable style, "This election again I think there will be a building of New Democratic Party fortunes – not to put us into government this election, but I think positioning this party very well for a government not so far down the future."[9]

The objective for the NDP, then, was not necessarily to form government but to obtain enough seats to permit the party to once again hold the balance of power in a minority *Liberal* government (although the party would always take the public position that its intention is to form government). Hargrove's foray into federal election politics, therefore, was not necessarily off base with the overall election strategy of the New Democrats, but his *tactics* were highly problematic. On a significant level this was a turf war over who would decide which marginal ridings the party had a hope of gaining or retaining and how "NDP votes" should be dispersed in order to influence the outcome. It was also a dispute over the scope of Hargrove's vision. Whereas the union leader bore responsibility for the rank and file of the CAW, the NDP was, and is, a national political party and, as such, was concerned with the way that Hargrove's "strategy" would play out in places far beyond the scope of his influence, for example, in ridings such as Algoma–Manitoulin–Kapuskasing.

The Algoma–Manitoulin–Kapuskasing constituency takes in a huge swath of Northern Ontario. It is a riding long held by the Liberals. In recent years the economy has shifted from the traditional (and still strong) resource sector to tourist-related and other service industries, often seen as growth opportunities by organized labour. In the election of 2004, the NDP came within 3,225 votes of overturning Liberal incumbent Brent St. Denis. Recent history holds that candidates of the right tend to come in a distant third on election night in Algoma–Manitoulin–Kapuskasing.[10] Within days of Hargrove's call for "strategic voting" and his (by then) notorious embrace of Paul Martin, the Liberal candidate's communication team issued a news release to say how happy he and other Liberals were to have the labour leader's support.[11] However, St. Denis's contribution to the discussion was to ignore the issue of strategic voting and selectively claim Hargrove's endorsement for entire swaths of unrelated Liberal policy. "Mr. Hargrove's statement," wrote St. Denis, "shows that our government's focus on a strong economy and a balanced approach to investment in social programs, tax cuts and debt reduction is the best approach for Canadians, particularly those who depend on labour-related sectors of our economy such as forestry."[12]

Clearly, this is not what Hargrove or anyone else on the political left was actually saying. An exchange of messages in the NDP war room outlined the concern and framed the response:

To: War Room
Date: Dec 5, 2005 5:58 PM
Subject: NDP FIGHTS BACK LIBERAL NONSENSE
IN NORTHERN ONT

Not sure if there's any use for this, but here's an example of how Liberals who really face no competition from Conservatives are using Hargrove's comments to defeat New Democrats.

---

pretty rich given that St. Denis voted: against federal anti-scab legislation (22 Oct 2003) against allowing his OWN employees to benefit from federal labour laws including the right to collectively bargain (3 June 2003).[13]

This example of opposition research at work illustrates a wider concern. While the war room was ready and able to challenge St. Denis on his perceived distortion of Hargrove's position – the opposition research provided is intended for use by the NDP candidate to undercut the Liberals' position based on his own record – the response also conveys a sense that the limited resources of the war room could have been put to better use. If part of the overall Liberal strategy in the Hargrove affair was to disrupt the NDP in its own back yard, forcing it to use resources to put out brush fires in ridings such as Algoma–Manitoulin–Kapuskasing, it had succeeded. Following his "news release" of 5 December, St. Denis seems to have dropped this line of attack, possibly because of push-back from the NDP. But the love fest between Paul Martin and Buzz Hargrove was not over.

On 9 December, precisely one week after the Hargrove/Martin convention-floor embrace, the NDP war room received a message from a campaign worker headed: "Hargrove with PM in Windsor???" The message was based on an exchange on CTV's all-news channel, Newsnet, between Rosemary Thompson, the reporter traveling with the NDP leader's entourage, and Ravi Baichwal, the anchor on the network's morning news program. Editorial staff at CTV had heard a rumour that Hargrove was headed for Windsor to link up again with Martin, this time on a campaign swing through several disputed ridings in the area. Thompson was unable to confirm that possibility, preferring to discuss how weather conditions had grounded the NDP campaign jet the night before, preventing Jack Layton from making his own planned campaign stop in Windsor. The New Democrats were unaware of Hargrove's plans but justifiably concerned about a Liberal tour de force at Layton's expense, even the bizarre possibility, posited by CTV, of a media coup by the Liberals. "It would be very interesting," said Baichwal, "to see if Buzz Hargrove finds a way to get close to Jack Layton and link some arms and show some symbolism that way as well."[14] All the NDP war room could do at this point was to plaintively ask "Can someone look into this and confirm/deny???"[15]

Confirmation arrived via Broadcast News (BN), the radio arm of the Canadian Press, with a story filed early in the afternoon and circulated by the war room:

Dec 09 2005 13:34:00 – Source: BN
National Audio 1:45 p.m. ET 09 12 05

114 – (FedElxn-Liberals-Hargrove)
WINDSOR, ONTARIO. X–10S. It was a strange sight at the
Chrysler announcement this morning. Canadian Auto Workers
President Buzz Hargrove was on stage with Prime Minister Paul
Martin during his campaign visit in Windsor.
That, despite the fact N-D-P Leader **>Jack Layton<** will be
in the city today as well. During his speech Hargrove made a
joke out of his support.
("… hug you today." – laughs fade) (SOURCE: CHYR) (145p)
TAG: Hargrove says he supports the two N-D-P candidates in
Windsor, but he supports Liberal Susan Whelan in the county
because according to Hargrove, the Essex N-D-P candidate
doesn't have a chance to win.[16]

The injury to the NDP continued with an announcement later that
day of federal and provincial support for upgrades to two automotive
plants in Windsor and Brampton, Ontario. The provincial Liberal
government of Dalton McGuinty would contribute almost $76 million
and the federal government $46 million. Hargrove joined McGuinty,
Martin, and company executives on stage at Windsor's Daimler-
Chrysler plant to join in the announcement and, presumably, deliver
on his quid pro quo of support for the Liberals. Furthermore, as
quoted by CP, Hargrove was now on a first-name basis with the prime
minister: "I've been forewarned, though, Paul," Hargrove said, "we
have two NDP members of Parliament in this city, and I've been
instructed ahead of time not to hug you today, even though I feel like
hugging you based on this wonderful announcement."[17]
Layton, who had finally arrived in Windsor, was left to make a
tepid announcement before a student audience at the University of
Windsor on his party's support for enhancing the system at border
crossings (a big issue in Windsor) and, belatedly, the NDP's position
on support for the auto industry. He ducked the inevitable "reaction"
questions from journalists when asked his opinion on Hargrove's
latest gambit.
Canada's major newspapers carried the story of the automotive
plant upgrades the following day, though none placed it on the front
page. The Globe and Mail, National Post, Ottawa Citizen, and the
Saturday Star each homed in on the new "relationship" between
Hargrove and Martin, pointing out that this was the second time in

as many weeks the CAW boss and the prime minister had joined forces at the NDP's expense. Both the *Post* and the *Globe* ran their stories below a wire-service photograph showing Hargrove beaming with goodwill as he grasps Martin's hand. In each case, the growing rift between the New Democratic Party and the union chief was played up.

Reaction from the NDP was more muted in these reports than it had been the previous week. While Layton was cited in the stories, mainly with respect to his campaign stop at the University of Windsor the previous day, the on-point reaction to Hargrove was handed over to Joe Comartin, an NDP MP in Windsor. Comartin's response to Hargrove's actions was direct and widely quoted. The *National Post* report is typical: "Joe Comartin, NDP MP for Windsor-Tecumseh criticized Mr. Hargrove for 'going off on a tangent' and confusing CAW members. 'The reaction from the membership in Windsor and Essex County has been very negative to that position. Just overwhelmingly, 'What's he doing? That's not our traditional position.'"[18] Comartin goes on to ask why Buzz Hargrove is campaigning with the prime minister and not with an NDP candidate. In one of the least ingenuous responses of the entire campaign, Hargrove was quoted as saying he was not prompted by the Liberals to attend the Daimler-Chrysler event and that he was not campaigning for the NDP because nobody had asked him to. "I was invited here by Daimler-Chrysler," said Hargrove, "not the prime minister."[19]

The two Hargrove events, a week apart, exemplify offensive and defensive party war-room strategies. Clearly, the Liberal strategy was to reach into NDP territory and reach out to union members in the hope that they would support the Liberals in certain contested ridings. This was precisely the strategy the Liberals had used in the previous election when Paul Martin had made last-minute entreaties to NDP voters in a bid to shore up the Liberal vote. That the Liberals managed to leverage the credibility of Hargrove and his position as the CAW boss to their advantage was nothing short of a coup. The relative silence of the NDP with respect to Hargrove and the literal silence of Layton during the second episode spoke to the level of damage to its own credibility that the party sensed in Hargrove's actions. When, later in the campaign, the CAW president tried to extend his "strategic voting" initiative to Quebec, suggesting that NDP voters should support Bloc candidates to defeat Conservatives,

NDP campaign co-chair Brian Topp again advised measured silence: "I don't favor doing anything that puts hargrove back in the news. He's being relatively quiet let's try to keep it that way."[20]

Indeed, it was journalists and Conservative strategists who went on the offensive over Hargrove's plan for Quebec by asking disquieting questions about the wisdom of attempting to align a federalist party with one that favours sovereignty. When Hargrove, on a mid-January campaign swing through southwestern Ontario with Martin, accused Conservative Leader Stephen Harper of holding separatist views and urged Quebec voters to support the Bloc because "anything is better than the Tories," it ignited a small storm of incredulity and put Martin (who had repeatedly and forcefully declared his federalist credentials) in a very awkward position.[21] Shortly thereafter, the Liberals quietly deserted Hargrove. The NDP maintained its silence throughout, neither condemning Hargrove nor coming to his defence.

It is important to keep in mind that the Hargrove "affair" was just one moderately high-profile set of political incidents that took place within a complex web of competing campaign issues. For a short time it overshadowed the highly controlled daily roll-out of the NDP's position on a handful of major campaign issues – publicly funded medicare, child care, gun control, support for workers and senior citizens, the environment – that the party and its opponents were jockeying to frame as vote-winning issues. While Hargrove's actions were likely of little help to the NDP, they must be taken contextually. The surprise Hargrove/Martin hug of 2 December may have made the front page of the following day's *Globe and Mail*, but the story found itself in fierce competition with the announcement-a-day strategy of the Conservatives who at this time were presenting their GST tax-cut plan and their controversial child-care program. Indeed, the *Globe and Mail* of 3 December gives substantially more space to stories about these Conservative initiatives than to either the Liberals or the NDP.

There is also a difference in the texture of the coverage. Once again, the *Globe and Mail* of 3 December is generally indicative of that day's print coverage: a soft and speculative piece about Liberal campaign strategy, followed by a hard-edged report on Stephen Harper's promise to force provinces to reduce hospital wait-times.[22] The report on Hargrove's embrace of Martin was juxtaposed with a quantitative analysis of Harper's announcement earlier in the week of planned cuts to the Goods and Services Tax.[23]

Planned events, however important in the eyes of the planners, also get knocked off the news agenda. The staged event of 9 December, with Hargrove and Martin reprising their CAW convention act at Daimler-Chrysler, was an obvious Liberal tactic intended to keep the NDP off balance and the new Hargrove/Martin alliance in the public eye. The occasion was widely reported. But just two days later, the Liberal director of communications, Scott Reid, made his now infamous "beer and popcorn" comment on national television. Reid, representing the Liberals on a panel discussion on CBC Television, said of the Conservative child-care plan (inaccurately as it turns out): "It's going to give people 25 bucks a day, they [parents] can spend it on videos. Don't give people 25 bucks a day to blow on beer and popcorn."[24]

The remarks provided an opening for the NDP, through Jack Layton, to attack both the Liberals and the Conservatives on their respective child-care plans. "And as wrong as Mr. Harper's plan is," said Layton, "it's also wrong for Liberals to attack parents and suggest somehow [that] parents would take the money for beer and popcorn. The Liberals' mask on child care came down for a minute there and showed their real point of view."[25] Layton went on to outline the NDP's multi-billion dollar child-care proposal, a proposal in stark contrast to the Conservative plan and made all the more distinct by the self-inflicted discomfort of the Liberals. As one NDP wag put it in a general message to the war room, "Memo to Scott Reid and popcorn: The worst time to shoot yourself in the foot is when it's in your mouth."[26]

The point here is that the daily grind of war-room strategies and tactics is regularly thrown into an incomprehensible muddle by the unintended consequences of human actions. The negative consequences of launching a full frontal assault on Buzz Hargrove were not lost on the NDP: the party could scarce afford to lose those voters tempted to buy into Hargrove's strategic voting scheme as well as those who would vote with their feet *and* their ballots if they concluded that the party was unfairly beating up on their duly elected union brother. On the other hand, beer and popcorn became a generous unintended gift for the NDP delivered in a neat, thoroughly exploitable, nationally resonant media package. It was precisely the kind of relief from "the buzz about Buzz" that the party needed.

On any given day of the campaign, two streams of "media" releases would appear on the NDP's official website.[27] News releases formed one information stream, presented as an ever-growing list of hyperlinks, while rapid responses, presented in a similar manner, formed the other. News releases, in general, offered the "good news" about the party's position on core election concerns as identified and promoted by the NDP: protection for health care, support for seniors, and other traditional concerns "owned" by the NDP. Rapid responses were attempts to challenge the position on any issue that had been put into circulation by a competing party or to "hit back" at claims of competitors by "setting the record straight." Rapid responses were also used to signal the party's intentions on issues of core concern – to attempt to place the NDP in a position of control over a specific important agenda item. For example, in the lead up to the first French-language debate held in Vancouver on the evening of 15 December 2005, the NDP circulated the following rapid-response item to journalists:

> NDP Rapid Response: Paul Martin's Child Care Promises:
> Paul Martin claims to have kept his promise on creating a
> national Child Care program.
> Here's the promise: "In each year following a year of 3%
> economic growth, a liberal government will create 50,000 new
> child care spaces to a total of 150,000."
> *The Red Book, Creating Opportunity,* 1993, p. 40
>
> Economic growth of more than 3% occurred 6 out of 7 years
> between 1993 and 2000, no national child care program.
>   Why did it take 12 years to get going on this priority?
>   Jack Layton pointed out that the government only got going
> on childcare once it lost its majority, and found itself forced to
> work with the NDP.[28]

This rapid response item is a bit unusual because it *anticipated* a point of contention that was almost certain to be dealt with both in the French-language debate and, one day later, the English-language version. It also came at a time when the Liberals were still smarting over the "beer and popcorn" episode. Indeed, the timing of this posting served several tactical purposes. It telegraphed the NDP position and laid claim to the issue for all voters who were unlikely to support the Conservative plan; it put the Liberals on the defensive by suggesting that, as government, they only moved on universal child care when forced to do so by the New Democrats; and it challenged the veracity of Paul Martin's promises and priorities by citing statistics that appeared to show an unwillingness to act even when conditions supported action. According to the war room, the public record showed that Paul Martin was not to be trusted, whereas Jack Layton was indeed trustworthy. Layton used the essential points outlined in the rapid-response posting during the French-language debate.

The Liberal war room, clearly annoyed with the NDP attack, responded the following morning with a detailed rapid response of its own:

Layton Misrepresents Support for Child Care Plan
December 16, 2005
During the first French language debate Mr. Layton claimed, "it was only when he [Paul Martin] was in a minority government situation with N.D.P. Members that we were able to make progress on this issue [early leaning and child care]."
FACT
In Budget 2004, the Liberal Government delivered on its promise to create a national early learning and childcare system.

The Liberal government allocated $5 billion over five years to deliver on that promise and that money will begin to flow next year in 2006.

Since Budget 2004, the Liberal government has signed agreements with all 10 provinces – 3 final agreements and 7 agreements in principle – to put a national early learning and childcare system in place.

Mr. Layton voted against Budget 2004 and the $5 billion for early learning and childcare. When Mr. Layton had the opportunity to highlight the issue, in his proposed budget additions, there was no request for further childcare funds. It was Paul Martin's Liberal government that achieved this important evolution in our social foundation, not Jack Layton and not the NDP.[29]

This response also provided a platform to restate and clarify the Liberal party position on childcare.

Most major newspapers made mention of the child-care issue in their coverage of the French-language debate. Greg Weston, at the time a syndicated columnist with the Sun Media group and Susan Riley of the *Ottawa Citizen* went further, each providing a breakdown of each party's child-care offerings.[30] On balance the NDP's message tactic on child care permitted its position to circulate prior to and during the debate. Its full platform plank on child-care, together with reportage on the NDP position, was picked up by most major newspapers and analyzed in detail by two well-regarded columnists. And as a communication bonus, the party position was reiterated in the defensive Liberal rapid response to Layton's debate performance, all in anticipation of the English-language debate, which would itself be widely reported.

This kind of rapid-response duelling among parties was common during the course of the campaign; indeed, the thrust and parry of low level, rapid-response tactical communication has become characteristic of the day-to-day life of Canadian electoral politics. On any given day, the NDP would disseminate as many as five or six rapid responses depending on the claims being made by the competition. Journalists would normally ignore this background squabbling over the minutiae of "who said what when" or use the material as a prompt to develop their own stories or analyses, as in the case of Weston and Riley. But once in a while the war room would score a "pit hit," a situation where information gathered by the war room and crafted into a partisan message was picked up by reporters and disseminated virtually unchanged. One such situation occurred when Paul Martin attempted to spread around some Liberal largesse in Newfoundland.

The story begins innocuously enough with a standard posting on the CP wire of Paul Martin's upcoming itinerary, a "lookahead" to the following week's schedule for the Liberal campaign: "ST. JOHN'S, N.L. (5:39 p.m.) – Prime Minister Paul Martin speech to St. John's Board of Trade. (12 p.m. at St. John's Convention Centre)."[31]

The date and time are relevant. At this point, the NDP war room was still reeling over the Hargrove/Martin embrace at the CAW convention in Toronto, a story that would dominate news coverage through the night and into the following day. CP also advised that no campaigning by the Liberals was planned for the weekend of 3 and 4 December. Nobody knew what Martin planned to say to the St John's Board of Trade the following Monday, but any opportunity to make the Liberals pay for the Hargrove affair would be greatly welcomed by the NDP campaign team. The opportunity came at 9:23 on Monday morning:

ST. JOHN'S, N.L. (CP) Prime Minister Paul Martin says Newfoundland and Labrador should become a centre for the study of weather and issues such as the impact of global warming. Martin kicked off Week 2 of the federal election campaign with a brief appearance on a St. John's radio station (VOCM), where he was asked what the federal government would do to increase its presence in the province. He said with the cold war a thing of the past, CFB Goose Bay would not be seeing more military, but suggested the base could be used to study the effects of global warming on climate and fisheries.[32]

The story was picked up by CP's national radio service, Broadcast News, and circulated widely in several rewritten versions meant to serve radio listeners tuning in as the country woke up across multiple time zones. Clearly, the Liberal intention in releasing this information without prior notice, on a morning radio program in St John's, was to take the campaign initiative in a widening circle of exposure: first in Newfoundland and Labrador, then in Atlantic Canada and, as a secondary consideration, in the big Quebec and Ontario media markets where the story would have less resonance but still provide a measure of exposure.

At 11 AM (all times are EST) a campaign worker in the NDP's Ottawa office mentioned a possible weakness in the Martin announcement and sent an inquiry to the war room on the internal list-serve:

To: War Room
Date: Dec 5, 2005 11:00 AM
Subject: Martin in NL

Hi- Martin is claiming NL should become a centre for the study of weather and global warming ...
    I'd fact check this – BUT I believe the Liberals closed the Gander weather station – Newfoundland sitting in the North Atlantic now gets all its weather from Halifax.[33]

The opposition-research group rushed to confirm the facts and handed the information to the rapid-response team. The information was turned around and sent out immediately to the BlackBerrys of reporters across the country, among them those covering the

Liberal campaign on its stop in Newfoundland and assignment editors at all the major news organizations including the Canadian Press. Twenty-three minutes later, CP/BN released a story that included the information provided by the war room:

> FedElxn Roundup
> Source: The Canadian Press – Broadcast wire
> Dec 5, 2005 11:23
> (Liberals)
>
> Prime Minister Martin says Newfoundland and Labrador could serve as home for a centre to study weather and the impact of global warming.
>   He told a St. John's audience that with the Cold War over, C-F-B Goose Bay could be used to study the effects of global warming on climate and fisheries.
>   The N-D-P notes it was Martin's government that moved most of the jobs at the Newfoundland Weather Centre in 2004 to Nova Scotia and Quebec.[34]

The CP/BN story was then picked up and recirculated on the war-room list-serve as a means to advise all involved that the national news media were running with the NDP "story." The message bore a simple subject heading: "War Room, Media Monitoring Date: Dec 5, 2005 12:27 PM Subject: PIT HIT: PM weather station."[35]

War-room workers, tipped off by the list-serve acknowledgment, began to gather in the media area. Everyone was eager to see what would happen next. But the minutes ticked by, and there was no further mention of the CP/BN story with the "new" angle provided by the war room. This should not have been surprising. Journalists on the ground with the Martin campaign were preparing to cover his speech before the St John's Board of Trade, due to begin in a half-hour. The story appeared to disappear from the national news agenda. But it had been a fairly good run for a rapid-response "fact" inserted like a burr under the Liberal saddle. With any luck it had wrecked Paul Martin's Monday morning and stripped his promise of a weather-research station of all credibility, at least in Newfoundland and Labrador.

Later that afternoon as war-room operatives again gathered around the televisions in the media area, a roar of approval went up among the assembled. The afternoon roundup from journalists on the various campaigns had yielded another "pit hit."

The CBC's Susan Bonner, travelling with the Martin campaign, had included the NDP-supplied "fact" on the closure of the Gander weather station in her Newsworld report. The NDP's rapid-response "information" had obtained a second lease on life, at least for the moment. In fact, the flagship nightly CBC *National News* would make no mention of Newfoundland except in passing. Like other electronic media, its main story of the day would focus on the Harper campaign's announcement of a plan to give child-care dollars to parents (and reaction from the other parties). Coverage of the NDP campaign would deal briefly with a promise, made earlier in the day, not to raise personal taxes and, in more depth, with the leader's weekend admission that he would not ban private health clinics.[36] The following day's national newspapers made no mention of the Liberal plan for weather research in Newfoundland or the NDP's position.

Clearly, attempting to generate credibility through tactical gambits is a fickle game. And sometimes planned media events turn into self-inflicted wounds.

Talk around the war room on the afternoon of 6 December centred on a planned appearance by Jack Layton in Montreal the following day. The war room had scheduled a news conference at the Guy-Favreau Complex, an island of federal-government buildings in the city's downtown. News releases had been prepared indicating that Layton was going to seize the initiative on the "unity file," code for the relationship between the federal government, Quebec, and the rest of Canada. There was also some verbal joking in the war room (though not too loud) about the need to clarify the NDP position on clarity. This was a reference to Layton's declaration during the election campaign of 2004 that the Clarity Act of 2000, the federal act outlining the terms of any future referendum on secession for Quebec, should be repealed because "it only aggravates Quebec and accentuates division in our country."[37] Layton's comment had been widely viewed as a gaffe, drawing support from the sovereignty-supporting Bloc Québécois and condemnation from just about everyone else.

Layton's plan to clarify Clarity was developed as a tactic to address a number of strategic concerns. First, it was thought that it would resituate the NDP as a federalist option for Quebec voters. The New Democrats, without a seat in the province, were desperate to elect a

Quebec candidate. Without an MP from Quebec, the party could not claim legitimacy as a truly national political voice. Second, the NDP was seeking to poach votes from Paul Martin's Liberals in much the same way that Martin had attempted to steal votes from the NDP in the previous week's Hargrove affair. The Liberals, engineers of the Clarity Act, owned the federalist position in Quebec and were not above using the emotion of the sovereigntist/federalist debate to obtain support. Finally, the NDP saw a news conference on clarity as a means to "cut through," to present a dramatic moment for the media that would garner some positive "airtime and ink" for the party. The conference would address the party's underlying concerns that both the Liberals and Conservatives were getting more attention from reporters than the NDP. Layton's plans presented an opportunity to do some field work. I caught the bus to Montreal.

The morning of 7 December dawned cold in the city with the mercury dipping toward minus 17. A brisk breeze made it feel much colder. Members of the NDP's media entourage, print and radio reporters, television journalists with their technical crews, and at least one researcher (me) grumbled through the maze of interlocking spaces on the ground floor of the Guy-Favreau complex, looking for the site where Layton was scheduled to hold his news conference. They navigated around information booths set up by dozens of organizations (some private but most representing various arms of government), overflow from the United Nations Conference on Climate Change being held at Montreal's main conference centre a few blocks away. Paul Martin would be visiting that venue just hours later to state his party's position on climate change, exhort Canadians to produce lower greenhouse-gas emissions, and charge the Bush administration with a failure of leadership on the issue. He would then jet off to Toronto for an announcement on handguns planned for the following day.

The NDP advance team had been out the night before, plastering light poles around the complex with election signs. Posted directly across the street from the small, exterior courtyard where Layton would make his announcement, they were in line to be picked up by the television cameras, should they have reason to point in that direction. However, the main visual backdrop to the announcement was a large poster, several metres long, attached to the building directly behind the courtyard. Its prominent text (underscoring a photo of the earth taken from space) read: "Un monde de/A world of Solutions."

This poster had been put up by the UN climate-change conference organizers to convey a meaning that certainly had nothing to do with the NDP's position on the Clarity Act. Opportunistic party workers had simply appropriated the sentiment of the poster for their own purposes, setting up the microphone for Layton's use so as to bring the poster into frame for the TV cameras and print photographers. It was a clever consideration; those viewers who made the connection with the climate-change conference would have a visual reference to a key NDP campaign register (the environment), even if the substance of Layton's announcement had nothing to do with the climate. Viewers who did not make the connection would simply accept the poster's message as a reflection of the party's general sentiment. Few of the thirty-five national, regional, and local journalists who assembled in the courtyard remarked on the poster's position, though some of the photographers positioned themselves to capture Layton in profile, thus cutting it out of the shot.

As reporters stamped their feet and joked among themselves about the frigid weather, a technician rolled out an extension cord, carried out two large ground-level electric heaters, pointed them towards the general area where Layton would stand, switched them on, and left. By the time Layton made his entrance a short time later, the heater elements were red hot, blasting out a comfort zone for the leader to stand in. Waves of heat could be seen cutting through the cold and dispersing, kissing that climate change poster, wafting away on the December wind, and thoroughly discrediting any NDP claim to environmental stewardship. Camera operators quietly moved back into position, gently jockeying to get the heaters, the poster, and Layton in the same shot. Layton's announcement on the Clarity Act, in reality a flip-flop on the party's previous position, elicited a few questions from reporters about motive and timing. Journalists seemed slightly incredulous when Layton claimed the act now had "broad support" in Quebec but generally let him have his say. Only one reporter, Terry Milewski of the CBC, asked Layton about the heaters. This was done in a semi-joking tone, framed as a half-serious inquiry about why reporters had to freeze while the leader stayed warm. Layton shrugged off the question, finished the news conference, walked to his chauffeured limousine (engine running), and departed for the next event. The journalists packed up, climbed on the campaign bus, and followed.

The staff-written story from the Canadian Press on Layton's "cut through" announcement hit the newswire within minutes. It made no reference to heaters or climate change but pulled no punches on the NDP flip-flop:

> MONTREAL (CP) – Jack Layton says he now backs the Clarity Act setting out rules for future Quebec votes on independence.
>
> The statement is a reversal for the NDP leader who annoyed his own caucus in the 2004 election campaign when he said he would get rid of the law if the opportunity arose.
>
> Back then Layton said the law only accentuates division in Canada.
>
> Layton says he now supports the act because the Supreme Court of Canada set out many of the same rules.
>
> He also says the law is now accepted by a broad range of people, including former sovereignist leader Lucien Bouchard.[38]

Wire-service accounts for the remainder of the day made no reference to the heater gaffe.

Montreal's *Gazette* and the *Ottawa Citizen* (which ran a large photograph) made reference to the heaters the following day. A story filed by Rosemary Thompson of CTV for the Newsnet service and an election-roundup piece by Eric Sorensen produced for CBC Newsworld's *Politics* played with the imagery of the heaters. The effect was to poke fun at the seeming hypocrisy of the NDP on its climate change claims while pointing out the apparent flip-flop in the party's position on Clarity. The person monitoring the television networks in the NDP war room recorded a point-form description of the stories in question and posted it to the list-serve. Note the comment on the tone of the Thompson report:

> To: War Room, Media Monitoring
> Date: Dec 7, 2005 9:31 PM
> Subject: Afternoon broadcast scan, 3:00 – 8:00 Dec 7
> CTV Newsnet, 3:00 – 4:30
>
> Thompson: NDP ethics package; by-election proposal for floor-crossers: mentioned Martin, Brison and Stronach; "warm and

fuzzy message" from Layton on unity; Laytons' support of
Clarity Act, Layton says Clarity Act has broad support in QC;
prediction: Layton will be commenting on income trusts, NDP
asked for investigation and got things going on this; Layton
nothing to say on Harper's small business tax cuts.
   Tone: whining about Jack having heaters while making
announcement in −16 degrees; scoffed at idea of Clarity Act
having broad support in QC.

Politics with Don Newman, CBC Newsworld, 4:30 – 6:00
Sorenson: PM has advantage of being prime minister during
campaign: can appear at UN Conference and deliver campaign
msg; PM slammed by opp for hypocrisy re: Canada's environmental record; referenced Layton "heating up the sidewalk" in
Montreal; clipped Layton on poor record of Canada – worse
than US, clipped Harris.
Standup: Martin seemed to acknowledge criticism, saying
Canada's record is far from perfect.
   Tone: second reference to heaters used by Layton – didn't go
over well.[39]

Later that evening, Terry Milewski, reporting for the CBC National
News, would use pictures of Layton and the heaters in the setup to
his report on the NDP flip-flop on the Clarity Act.

Clearly the day-to-day life of the campaign challenged political
parties to be constantly vigilant, constantly aware of the strategic
intentions of their opponents, and constantly in touch with their own
symbolic resources in order to mount their own tactical initiatives
and parry those of the competition. Sometimes, as in the case of Buzz
Hargrove's relationship to the Liberals, a tactical coup in the service
of broad strategy (poaching NDP votes) was simply unanswerable
because of the perceived unpredictability of the individual involved
and the potential downside to alienating him. Often, as in the case of
the Newfoundland weather-research centre announcement, a simple
reminder about past actions, and possible hypocrisy, could have
widely dispersed (if limited) consequences. Once in a while, as in the
case of the announcement on the Clarity Act, the best-laid plans are
undermined when practicalities meet up with symbols, especially
when the symbols happen to belong to someone else.

Each of these instances demonstrates how tactical circumstances can turn on a dime. The finest calculations in the competition for credibility, the jealously guarded accumulation of the symbolic capital to be exchanged for votes and power, can easily come to naught in the aftermath of a thoughtless utterance about beer and popcorn. But it is worthwhile to keep in mind that both unforeseen circumstances and best-laid plans are played out against the backdrop of larger strategic issues.

The election campaign of 2005–06 is especially revealing in this respect because each small daily battle was fought out against the backdrop of one overriding strategic issue: integrity, specifically Liberal integrity in the wake of the sponsorship scandal. And if credibility is a specialized form of symbolic capital, integrity may be viewed as a specialized form of credibility. In very real terms, the NDP (along with the Conservatives and the Bloc Québécois) set out to effectively prevent the Liberal campaign, in spite of clever tactical coups, from accumulating enough credibility to win the day. The NDP did so by relentlessly exploiting a manufactured link between the sponsorship scandal and a single incident that was transformed by political strategists into a meta-language signifier for corruption – an incident that has become known as the income-trust scandal.

The War Room at Work: Strategies

OTTAWA (CP) – On the eve of an anticipated federal election, the governing Liberals announced new tax guidelines Wednesday that make dividends more attractive for investors but leave tax policy on income trusts unchanged.[1]

OTTAWA (CP) – Federal Conservatives kept up the corruption allegations against the Liberals over the weekend, claiming that insiders benefited from last week's announcement on income trusts. Deputy house leader Jason Kenney says there must have been a leak of the decision because of heavy trading on the Toronto stock market before Finance Minister Ralph Goodale's announcement on Wednesday.[2]

For the Liberal government of Paul Martin, the much-anticipated decision on income trusts – an obscure but lucrative way for companies to avoid paying corporate taxes by passing on more of their profits to investors – must have seemed a small (if calculated) godsend on the eve of an election call. By deciding to leave income trusts alone and cut regular taxes for investors, Martin's minister of finance, Ralph Goodale, had inoculated the government (and the party) from a potentially nasty backlash. Indeed, not only had a backlash been avoided but it was hoped that small and large investors of all stripes would now be predisposed to view the Liberals favourably. Cynics might say that the Liberals were engaging in the time-honoured strategy of vote buying, a practice that would pay particularly high dividends in this case because tax breaks would accrue to people from all points on the political spectrum as long as they had money in the markets. Such a strategy would be deemed particularly successful if Conservative investors could be enticed to vote their self-interest by putting Liberals into Conservative seats in the House of Commons. Then rumours of a leak turned into questions about insider-trading, strategy came face to face with ongoing suspicions about

Liberal integrity, and the Liberal train began slowly and inexorably to go off the rails.

There are literally hundreds of published reports about income trusts in the time leading up to, during, and following the election of 2005–06. They fall into two categories: those about companies who announced that they were converting or thinking about converting to income trusts, and stories about the politics of income trusts and what would eventually develop into the income trust "scandal." The two categories are obviously related.

The Finance Department's 23 November announcement of support for income trusts began a cascade of movement within corporate Canada toward these lucrative tax structures, a movement that brought high-profile players such as Bell Canada Enterprises and Air Canada into the income-trust fold and carried tens of thousands of investors along for the ride. At times during the election campaign the Canadian Press carried a story every other day about yet another company considering the move to income trusts. There is no question that Ralph Goodale let a genie out of the bottle on 23 November or, rather, two genies. One took corporate Canada by the hand and trumpeted what amounted to a government-sanctioned tax dodge; the other opened the door into a darker place of unintended consequences where many Liberals, scarred by the Gomery Inquiry, surely feared to tread.

The true, head-shaking irony of the income-trust scandal is that, on paper, it had few if any downsides for the Liberals. It could have been played as a simple ruling that favoured investors, necessarily decided on the eve of an election as a bit of required government housekeeping, a way to leave a pressing matter well managed while the election was underway. Indeed, the bald politics of income trusts aroused little opposition criticism. Later in the campaign, when the Liberals were virtually assured of an election-night loss, the Conservatives under Stephen Harper felt obliged to make the point that they *would not change* Ralph Goodale's 23 November decision. Months later, having formed a minority government, the Conservatives would renege on that promise. But during the election campaign the question of whether income trusts were good public policy never became an issue.

Instead, it was the appearance of wrongdoing, of leaked information, and the possibility that Liberal friends in the business world would benefit that dogged Goodale, the Liberal Party, and, by association, Paul Martin. This effect was directly linked to lingering suspicions over the former Liberal government's role in diverting money into party coffers from its discredited sponsorship program. These suspicions had swirled around the prime minister, who just happened to be the former federal minister of finance and Quebec lieutenant for the Liberals under Jean Chrétien. Martin claimed no knowledge of a government program that had been all but looted in his own backyard – the Gomery Inquiry had concluded that most of the sponsorship irregularities had occurred in Quebec and involved advertising agencies with Liberal connections – but the question that continued to float in the ether as the country went to the polls was: How could Martin *not* have known? The mere suggestion of income-trust wrongdoing, the very possibility of using the public trust invested in a department of the Crown to benefit a few cozy insiders, was thus like setting a match to gasoline. It is not too great a claim to suggest that the income-trust scandal, played out in the full light of the election campaign, was instrumental in turning the tide of public support away from the Liberals, giving the Conservatives enough of an edge to form the government.

The problem is that the income trust "scandal" was largely manufactured. It was constructed to deal in a minimum of fact and a maximum of nuance for stakes that were largely about using forms of symbolic violence to undermine the Liberals. Indeed, the income-trust tale framed the defining strategic battle of the campaign, one in which opposition war rooms showed the most dogged persistence in symbolically battling it out among themselves for ownership of the self-legitimized right to define Liberal credibility. The NDP war room, along with the party's finance critic, Judy Wasylycia-Leis, was a central player in this strategic push.

By 27 November, four days after Goodale's income-trust announcement and two days after the first published rumblings about an apparent spike in trading having preceded the income-trust announcement, both the Conservatives and New Democrats were calling for an investigation into insider trading. Both parties would ask the Ontario Securities Commission (OSC), the body that regulates trading on the Toronto Stock Exchange, to conduct an inquiry. But the NDP would go a step further and call for an investigation by the Royal Canadian Mounted Police.[3] By its nature this would be a criminal investigation.

The New Democratic Party was, through connotation, accusing the minister of finance (and the Liberal government of which he was a part) of criminal wrongdoing while in office. Finance critic Wasylycia-Leis was designated to be the point person on this major strategic file. She would later confide to Paul Wells of *Maclean's* magazine that she did not expect the call for a criminal investigation to yield a response, because the RCMP had *never* responded to such NDP requests in the past.[4] In other words, her actions were pure political posturing intended to attach the taint of criminality to the Liberals through an as yet uninitiated, even unacknowledged, association with Canada's national police force.

Yet the Conservatives and the NDP were mistaken if they expected the Liberals simply to swallow allegations of wrongdoing. On 28 November, following the official defeat of the government of which he was a part, Ralph Goodale rounded on the opposition:

> OTTAWA (CP) – Finance Minister Ralph Goodale accused opposition MPs on Monday of trying to smear his reputation on the eve of an election campaign with their demands for a probe of the way new tax policy announcements were made.
>
> Financial markets surged last Wednesday in late trading shortly before Goodale made an unexpectedly early announcement on new tax policies related to income trusts...
>
> "What we saw today was a baseless, very nasty personal attack," Goodale said outside the Commons, shortly before his minority Liberal government faced a non-confidence motion triggering an election campaign.
>
> "I have made inquiries within my office and within the department and I'm satisfied that all of the proper rules were followed appropriately."[5]

The Liberal communication strategy was quite remarkable and, as it turns out, quite effective. Goodale, whose squeaky-clean reputation had been profiled in news reports since he took over the "cleanup" of key ministries in the wake of the sponsorship scandal, effectively charged his opponents with stooping to character assassination rather than substantiating the claims against his department's handling of the income-trust announcement.

Both the NDP and the Conservatives were forced to back off. In the absence of hard evidence of wrongdoing (neither the OSC nor the RCMP were involved in the matter at this point), the opposition parties were in a tight spot. By stepping outside the House of

Commons to make his announcement, Goodale had effectively raised the stakes by setting the issue beyond the bounds of parliamentary privilege. This was libel territory. The last thing the Conservatives or NDP needed during an election campaign was to be forced into court to respond to a statement of claim for libel, especially if it originated with the minister of finance.

At this point (the beginning days of the election campaign) the Liberals were close to scotching any controversy over income trusts and insider trading. Without a smoking gun, the NDP, Conservatives, and later, the Bloc were forced to keep their own counsel on the matter. But the list-serve communications within the NDP war room indicate that the issue was not dead. Indeed, even as journalists gradually shifted away from an initial surge of reporting on the optics of the income-trust announcement of 23 November, the war room began to roll out a tactical gambit based on the release of information aimed at pressuring a regulatory or investigative body to assume responsibility for the income-trust issue. In the absence of any direct evidence unearthed by the party, the aim of the war room vis-à-vis income trusts shifted from directly exposing the possibility of wrongdoing to convincing an institutional player with investigative credibility to get involved.

It is worth noting that any investigation by the OSC or the RCMP would, at the very least, take months to complete. By then the election would be long over. Therefore, it is reasonable to assume that the overarching objective of the strategic minds in the war room was to continue to chip away at the issue of Liberal credibility and integrity: that is, to draw the public's attention to the possibility that a breach in the public trust had occurred. Proof could come later.

In the meantime, media players such as CTV were keeping close watch on the OSC and RCMP in the event that one or the other (or both) would announce that an investigation was in order, or even if an investigation into the *need* for an investigation should take place. On 30 November, just two days after Goodale had faced down his political opponents, CTV.*ca* (the web-based arm of CTV News) reported that the RCMP was indeed reviewing the income-trust matter. The report was framed as a follow-up to the NDP's call for an investigation and quoted a stock response by an RCMP spokesperson about the inappropriateness of commenting on the situation. But it also went a step further by quoting a guest on a popular political interview program hosted by CTV's then chief political journalist (and now Conservative senator), Mike Duffy:

RCMP Reviewing Complaint on Income Trusts
CTV.ca News Staff

The RCMP have begun a review of reported heavier-than-usual trading in income trusts and dividend-paying stocks ahead of an announcement last week that the federal government was increasing the tax credit on corporate dividends. "The RCMP will review the information provided to determine if there is a basis to proceed with a criminal investigation," Marsh said. "It would be inappropriate to speculate what action may or may not be taken." A forensic accountant told CTV Newsnet's Mike Duffy Live that he thinks the probability there was insider trading is between 75 and 85 per cent. Either "someone had tremendous good luck ... or there's a leak," said Al Rosen.[6]

In addition, buried within the CTV.ca story are quotes lifted from a market analyst interviewed by the Globe and Mail, Doug Maybee, a spokesperson for an organization called Market Regulation Services Inc., an arm of the Ontario Securities Commission. Maybee acknowledges that there was heightened market activity prior to the announcement on income trusts: "The markets did move prior to Mr. Goodale's announcement, there's no denying of that," he said. "What caused the markets to move, that's something we're still looking into."[7] The report then paraphrases Goodale's position on the matter, his denial that any information was leaked in advance coupled with a claim that no one should have been surprised at a surge in the stock market in anticipation of his announcement simply because the government's decision had been a matter of investor speculation for months. At this point a member of the NDP war room's rapid-response team seized on Goodale's position, paraphrased within the CTV.ca story, as possible fodder for a short but direct release of a tactical response:

Date: Nov 30, 2005 6:52 PM
Subject: RC to keep pushing income trusts?
To: War Room

Perhaps a couple of line release saying "maybe Ralph Goodale should let the RCMP decide based on the paraphrases. It's a sad day for democracy for Canadians when a minister of the Crown is speculating about an ongoing investigation. And it's more example of how the Liberals are stubborn arrogant and don't deserve your vote."

... and if he keeps up his "there's nothing to see here" in a couple of days I think we can think about asking him to step aside during the investigation.[8]

The rapid-response suggestion would never come to pass. However, the list-serve inquiry about whether such a release would be advantageous speaks to the growing resonance of the income-trust file within the war room. Of particular interest is the revelation of a strategic aim or goal not yet expressed by any of the competing political camps: that a time was fast approaching when the next blow to Goodale would be in order, that his continued denials would lead the NDP to (inevitably) demand that he "step aside" during the investigation – an investigation that at this point was still nonexistent. Effectively, the NDP was warming up to a demand that, if followed, would take Goodale out of the election campaign and possibly end his political career.

However, the following day, 1 December, brought the first indication that the Ontario Securities Commission was unlikely to cooperate with the New Democrats. A message from the OSC and an internal response was circulated on the war-room list-serve:

Date: Dec 1, 2005 11:03 AM
Subject: RE: ON regulator – no need to investigate income trust situation MORE TO COME
To: War Room

At this point, we should be careful not to let them [the Liberals] spin this as an exoneration.

The OSC has a bad track record on cracking down on corporate crime – which is why Judy WL referred the matter to the RCMP.

I'm not advising we smear the OSC (necessarily) but we cannot say that this ends the matter. It doesn't.[9]

The initial concern of NDP campaign strategists was to keep an eye on the Liberals to ensure that they did not attempt to portray the OSC non-involvement in the case as "exoneration." The second response was to question the credibility of the OSC by claiming a "bad track record on cracking down on corporate crime." This claim was made without reference to any substantiating evidence and likely for this reason the line was drawn at "smearing" the osc "(necessarily)." That final, somewhat cryptic comment foreshadows a game of formal requests and responses between the NDP and the osc that would continue throughout the first half of the election campaign.

For their part, the Liberals continued to defend their position (while making no direct reference to the osc matter) by reinforcing the minister's initial claims and alluding simultaneously to what amounts to a factual negative. The finance minister's general position, that nothing untoward occurred with respect to the income-trust announcement, was juxtaposed with a bit of information that was essentially empty of meaning. It was a sly conceit, inferring that that there was nothing to investigate because those who would conduct an investigation had not been in contact. Therefore, went the logic, there must be nothing *to* investigate:

> OTTAWA (CP) – Finance Minister Ralph Goodale is continuing to brush off allegations his department may have crossed ethical and even legal lines in the way it handled the release of new tax policies related to income trusts.
>
> Neither the RCMP nor the Ontario Securities Commission have contacted him concerning the issue, Goodale said Friday in an interview from London, England where he was at meetings of the Group of Seven finance ministers.[10]

It was an advantage to the Liberal position that Goodale was quoted as he attended a prestigious international conference with his peers in the Group of Seven. This was a reminder that he still held the position of minister of finance for Canada and, as such, retained the symbolic capital that comes with the job title. Goodale's defining vision of the social world was, at this point, consumed with convincing voters that nothing questionable had happened on his watch. With no indication of impending action by the RCMP or the osc, the income-trust issue was effectively pushed into the background. It was likely of great help to the Liberal position that Goodale was out of the country for a few days and directly unavailable to reporters. When he returned to Canada, however, he faced a bombshell dropped by CTV News.

A report on the CTV *National News* of 6 December by journalist Kathy Tomlinson (now employed by the CBC) and later posted on her CTV weblog, "Whistleblower," suggested for the first time that there was documentation, an electronic "paper trail," pointing to insider knowledge of the content of the income-trust announcement:

> More important, perhaps, CTV discovered evidence, in writing, that seems to suggest some people had advance knowledge of exactly what the finance minister was going to say.
> That evidence is in public bulletin board postings on a popular investor's internet site called "Stockhouse." The first posting – at 11:14 that morning – came from someone who wrote: "Skuttlebutt is that he (Goodale) will soon announce a reduction on dividend taxation to 'even the playing field'." This information was posted a full seven hours before the minister's press conference, and possibly viewed by many potential investors before the markets closed. The finance minister used very similar wording when he made his announcement two hours later.
> "We're going to help to level up the playing field as between corporations and trusts and we're going to be doing that by ending double taxation on dividends," said Goodale in his media conference that evening.[11]

For the NDP war room this was like rain in a parched land. Previously unable to make much mileage out of what they saw as an opportunity to undercut Liberal integrity, war-room strategists all but appropriated Tomlinson's report in a peculiar kind of combined news/rapid response release entitled, "In Case You Missed It," a treatment that permitted the war room to assume the appearance of participation in bringing the story to light without actually having done anything:

From: NDP Communications
Date: Dec 7, 2005 9:06 AM
Subject: IN CASE YOU MISSED IT: More Evidence of Alleged Goodale Leak

Last night, CTV reported that insiders were posting news of Ralph Goodale's November 23, 2005 income trust announcement hours before he made it:
Reporter [Kathy Tomlinson]: We found evidence in writing that some people seem to have advance knowledge of exactly what the finance minister was going to announce.[12]

But it was another CTV story, released in a standard thumbnail treatment on the network's daily advisory to the Canadian Press, that returned the income-trust matter to the front ranks of campaign communication concerns. The report involved a little-known investors' group known as CARP, the Canada association for those over fifty years in age:

> TORONTO – Advisor to Finance Minister Ralph Goodale alleged to have tipped someone off about upcoming announcement on income trusts; a representative for CARP, a powerful seniors' group, says the group was tipped off in the morning about an announcement coming that afternoon, although he was given no details; Goodale says it does not appear that there was any untoward conversation that revealed either the nature or the timing of the announcement.[13]

The problem, as CARP would explain in a news release the following day, was that CTV's information was inaccurate. The group distributed a clarification on the afternoon of 8 December via the widely received Canada News Wire service stating unequivocally that it had *not* been tipped off by anyone in the Department of Finance. The clarification was received and circulated on the NDP war room list-serve:

> Date: Dec 8, 2005 2:40 PM
> Subject: RE: NEWS: CARP Income Trust Announcement
> To: War Room
>
> CARP in the Dark About Income Trust Announcement
> Toronto, Dec. 8/CNW/ – There is no truth to the serious accusations that CARP had inside information about Minister Ralph Goodale's announcement regarding Income Trusts ... The record must be set straight! At no time was CARP given an indication by the Minister's office of when the announcement would be made or what it would say.[14]

The Conservatives, who surely would have received the CARP clarification at the same time as the other political war rooms (and journalists), nevertheless went forward with a call for Goodale's resignation. The release of the story by CP reporter Lorraine

Turchansky, filed from the campaign trail in North Bay, Ontario, quotes Stephen Harper:

> NORTH BAY, Ont. (CP) – Ralph Goodale should resign as finance minister in light of allegations that a leak from his department allowed insiders to profit from a change in tax rules, Conservative Leader Stephen Harper said Thursday.
>
> Harper was commenting on a report that an official of CARP, Canada Association for the 50 Plus, got a warning call several hours before Goodale announced that he was dropping the tax on dividends from income trusts ... "It's very disturbing, it's very troubling," Harper said.
>
> "I would say, given the information we now know, that in any other advanced democratic country where we have a government that operated according to normal ethical standards, the finance minister would have already resigned, rather than continuing to deny and stonewall information."[15]

Turchansky was careful to cite the CARP news release in the following paragraph, offering her readers the opportunity to question the "information" that formed the basis for Harper's attack on Goodale. "CARP has denied the accusations as 'absurd,'" wrote Turchansky. "'There is no truth to the serious accusations that CARP had inside information about Minister Ralph Goodale's announcement regarding Income Trusts,' the organization said in a release Thursday."[16]

NDP strategists (who the previous week had been searching for a reason to call for Goodale's resignation) at this point became uncharacteristically silent. With the CARP denial in hand and time-stamped as a matter of record, the NDP ran the risk of being called on its own ethical standards should it follow the Conservative lead and demand the minister's resignation. On the other hand, Stephen Harper was on the record firmly calling Goodale's ethical standards into question based on "information we now know" (inferring it is information we know *to be true*). For the NDP it was a win-win situation. The attack on Goodale would continue (even if it came from the Conservative camp), but the questionable nature of the "information we now know" cited in the Turchansky report on Harper helped to undermine public confidence in the judgment of the Conservatives, the other major player in this rush to define Liberal credibility.

That the NDP had been in possession of the CARP release for several hours (indeed, since 2:40 that afternoon) and had not publicly questioned the integrity of the CTV report or made any other effort to set the record straight, speaks volumes about the strategic and tactical priorities at work here.

In fact, the NDP war room's decision to remain silent on the CARP issue occurred while it was casting about for another avenue of attack on Ralph Goodale's integrity. At 5:46 PM a reason (if not an opportunity) presented itself on the specialty service Report on Business Television (ROBTV). The rapid response team immediately circulated the gist of an interview with an "investor advocate" by the name of Diane Urquhart. The list-serve message described Urquhart as a "validator," less as a comment on her abilities than as an indication of her usefulness as an outside source with certain credentials who would lend credence to the NDP's call for an OSC investigation into income trusts. The last line of the message recapitulated the war room's prime objective:

To: War Room
Date: Dec 8, 2005 5:46 PM
Subject: FW: ROBTV on Investigation of Illegal Insider Trading

One of our validators on the income trust leak was on ROBTV demanding that the OSC should investigate and make it public that they're investigating.
Another excuse to push this story.[17]

In calling for Goodale's resignation, the Conservatives had provided the risk-free fodder for continued NDP attacks. Financial "experts" were now providing televised reasons to pursue the NDP call for an OSC investigation. Momentum was building. And there seemed precious little that Goodale and the Liberals could do, even when the minister of finance took to the airwaves on Newsworld's influential *Politics with Don Newman*.

Buried in the NDP war room's list-serve correspondence is a daily roundup of election-oriented material from various television programs including segment 5 of *Politics with Don Newman* for 8 December. Captured in the "shorthand" of the war room worker charged with transcribing broadcast material is an exchange between Monte Solberg of the Conservatives and Ralph Goodale of the Liberals:

To: War Room, Media Monitoring
Date: Dec 8, 2005 7:38 PM
Subject: Afternoon broadcast scan, 3:30–7:00

Politics with Don Newman, CBC Newsworld, 4:30–6:00
Segment 5:
* Panel: [Monte] Solberg, [Ralph] Goodale
Solberg: clouds over Goodale's office, questions re: his officials;
he should resign
Goodale: CARP has today thrown CTV story into doubt
Solberg: minister doesn't know, he's not an investigator
Goodale: CARP misrepresented by CTV; "I've made all necessary
inquiries, I'm satisfied"; CARP called us that morning
Solberg: impression was it would be a positive announcement:
that's the problem: insiders used that
Goodale: it was speculation only that it would be good news

Tone: no mention of NDP even though we got the ball rolling.[18]

The media monitor, the person transcribing the exchange, eschewed
an assessment of the *tone* of the segment in favour of a partisan
observation. There was "no mention of the NDP," she writes, "even
though we got the ball rolling." From this point forward, the income-
trust file would be all about which party would get the credit for
taking down the finance minister.

The following day, 9 December 2005, CP ran a report (circulated
on the war- room list-serve) that reiterated the Conservative call for
Ralph Goodale's resignation. By now it would be clear to everyone
that CARP had withdrawn any claim to prior knowledge of the
income-trust announcement. Indeed, the lede line of the CP report
includes the information that there was *no evidence* to support the
Conservative position:

Date: Dec 9, 2005 5:26 PM
Subject: MORE: Goodale Moves Business (B) and General (G)
(FedElxn-Goodale-Trust)
To: War Room

OTTAWA (CP) – Conservatives continued to demand Finance
Minister Ralph Goodale's head Friday, accusing his office of

leaking valuable financial information, but observers say they've still seen no evidence to support the charges.[19]

But the point was no longer proving wrongdoing by the finance minister. War-room strategies and tactics were now concentrated on appearances, the optics of casting Goodale in a bad light. To this end, the NDP war room circulated a news release outlining its intention to send a letter to the head of the Ontario Securities Commission, the same body that just a few days previously had indicated it would not investigate the income-trust matter.

To: War Room Media Monitoring
Date: Dec 9, 2005 5:49 PM
Subject: PR NDP: Wasylycia-Leis Asks OSC to Clarify Position on Possible Income Trust

WINNIPEG, MANITOBA – (CCNMatthews – Dec. 9, 2005) – **>NDP<** MP Judy Wasylycia-Leis sent the following letter to the Ontario Securities Commission today.
    The **>NDP<** finance critic is asking for clarification from the OSC about a possible investigation into alleged insider trading in high-dividend stocks and income trusts in the hours leading up to the announcement of November 23, 2005.
    Ms. Wasylycia-Leis is available for comment.[20]

As a helpful addition, the full text of the letter was included with the news release. It called on the OSC to follow its own guidelines and declare an investigation into a matter that the NDP says is clearly "in the public domain," a matter that speaks directly to the confidence of Canadians in the stock market. However, as "evidence" of the public-domain argument that would justify an investigation, the NDP's finance critic cites media reports of questionable accuracy and the RCMP review of 30 November, a preliminary examination of some highly disputed claims about increased trading around the original income-trust announcement. Furthermore, the RCMP's preliminary examination had been motivated in the first place by political players who called for a police investigation in full knowledge that the RCMP would, at the very least, be required to review the case. "It is abundantly clear that these issues are in the public domain," writes Wasylycia-Leis. "I attach a survey of media coverage of this issue. Furthermore, the RCMP has publicly stated that they have begun a review of trading in income trusts and dividend-paying stocks prior to Ottawa's announcement. The matter is clearly in the public domain."[21]

Wasylycia-Leis's letter to the OSC managed to garner some media attention, but not until the following day. In the jargon of the daily parsing of the information flow, the war-room media monitor referenced the 8:00 P.M. election coverage on CBC Newsworld, noting that Wasylycia-Leis was "clipped" in a story by the veteran CBC reporter Paul Hunter. Hunter's story, however, is at pains to note that evidence of a leak on income trusts has still not been forthcoming: "Hunter – income trust scandal is following the PM (clip of him getting questions on it at gun newser), Judy clipped asking for OSC investigation – Hunter standup still no hard evidence of leak by anybody."[22]

This small media "hit," released on a Saturday evening, passed largely unnoticed in the war room. It should also be kept in mind that the war room was preoccupied at this time with the fallout from the second chapter of the Buzz Hargrove affair, the union boss's appearance at Daimler-Chrysler with Paul Martin, and the subsequent tour of "strategic ridings" in the Windsor area. It is less certain why comparatively little excitement was generated over a journalistic offering published that morning in the *National Post*, a column by Andrew Coyne that may well be credited with turning the "income-trust matter" into "the income-trust scandal."

Under the title "It's not about CARP," Coyne leveled a scathing broadside at the Liberals, all but accusing them of systemic corruption while reserving some vitriol for both the RCMP and his colleagues in the Parliamentary Press Gallery: "The mushrooming income trust affair has all the earmarks of past Liberal scandals: well-connected insiders, the incestuous commingling of public and private business, press gallery indifference and RCMP inertia. All that is needed for the picture to be complete is for the government to threaten to sue its critics."[23]

Coyne goes on to build the case that some stock traders had information that permitted them to cash in on the government's impending announcement. He brushes off the CARP denial of insider information and points a finger at the Department of Finance (not Goodale) before backing off on a charge of corruption in his last paragraph and, simultaneously, assigning a possible political motive to the entire episode:

> At any rate, CARP is hardly the issue: it appears that many more people had some knowledge of what was coming – or at least, that something was coming. And the result was, in a word, a scandal. Millions of dollars were made in those hectic few hours of trading on the 23rd, which means millions of dollars were also lost. Those who were buying that afternoon knew something that those who were selling did not. If it turns out that, indeed, they were tipped off by someone at Finance, wittingly or unwittingly, then heads should roll – at a minimum.
>
> No one is suggesting anyone at Finance had corrupt intent. But might someone have gotten a little sloppy – a little too eager to prepare the political ground, perhaps, to ensure the minister's "decisive action" got the desired glowing reviews, and in time for that night's newscasts?
>
> Let's just say it fits a pattern.[24]

For all of the nuances in Coyne's column, it is certain that he did indeed think that something untoward had occurred prior to the minister of finance's 23 November announcement on income trusts. And even if Coyne does not name Goodale specifically, he draws us a road map of ministerial pressure tactics and timed public announcements for political gain. He points to a culture of shady Liberal practices that lead directly to Goodale's office.

In the meantime, the NDP had started a contest of letters with the head of the OSC. On 12 December the head of the commission formally responded to the request for an investigation by politely, if officiously, telling the NDP finance critic to mind her own business. David Wilson's response was circulated on the war room list-serve, including the passages that essentially advise the NDP that it is not the party's responsibility to determine what is "appropriate" for the OSC:

> Please note that the Ontario Securities Commission (OSC) and Market Regulation Services Inc. (RS) routinely monitor trading and review instances of unusual trading. In conjunction with

other market regulators, we determine the appropriate course of action including whether an investigation is warranted.

The osc practice is neither to confirm nor deny the existence of investigations. Under osc Guidelines for Staff Disclosure of Investigations, the Commission does not generally comment publicly as to the existence, status, or nature of an investigation until the matter becomes one of public record.[25]

The NDP response was to draft and send yet *another* letter to the osc demanding an investigation. The re-response from the chair of the osc was short, to the point, and entirely non-committal:

Thank you for your letter dated December 14, 2005 regarding the osc's mandate pertaining to enforcement and public disclosure and your concerns regarding possible conflicts of interest. As Chair of the osc, it is my responsibility to ensure that the Commission's actions are guided by our dual mandate to provide investor protection and to ensure the integrity of our capital markets.

I assure you that we are doing our job.[26]

Judging by the half-hearted response from the war room to yet another rejection by the commission, it is clear that this line of attack was on the verge of playing out:

Sent: Tuesday, December 20, 2005 1:06 AM
Subject: osc response to Dec 14 letter

Please find attached the scanned text of the osc response faxed to the Ottawa office today.

To: War Room
Date: Dec 20, 2005 7:23 AM
Subject: FW: osc response to Dec 14 letter

Gives new meaning to "brush off."[27]

There are two possible explanations for this list-serve equivalent of a shrug. First, the campaign was a day or two away from shutting down for the Christmas break.[28] Secondly, the OSC's line of attack had already been superseded by one of the more bizarre gambits of the campaign. Buried in the email correspondence between Wasylycia-Leis's office and the NDP war room (and dated 15 December 15) is evidence of a new tactic in the symbolic battle over the income-trust affair:

To: War Room
Date: Dec 15, 2005 6:52 PM
Subject: MP update re: OSC/SEC Letters

FYI

Subject: Letters

OSC letter faxed, will go in the mail tomorrow
SEC letter ready, signed and formatted. Will fax from here and email as well, then mail (as soon as I can find appropriate denomination of stamps or a post office)
Do you care which email address it goes from?
Should it go from the MP or campaign account?[29]

"SEC" refers to the Securities and Exchange Commission, the federal body that regulates and investigates stock markets in the United States. The NDP, a Canadian political party, was taking the extraordinary step of asking a foreign regulatory body to intervene in a highly politicized Canadian controversy over possible financial irregularities during an election campaign, a controversy that was implying wrongdoing by a minister of the Crown. When the war room issued a news release on 18 December, worded and composed in every respect like a news story, a new voice was added to the discussion: that of Paul Summerville, a former economist with a major Canadian bank. The inclusion of Summerville in the news release (he was an NDP candidate) was an obvious attempt to trade on his banking credentials in order to lend substance to the new NDP request for an investigation:

FOR IMMEDIATE RELEASE
DECEMBER 18, 2005

WASYLYCIA-LEIS AND SUMMERVILLE
ASK FOR SEC INVESTIGATION
Pattern of suspicious trading prior to income trust announcement
also present on New York Stock Exchange

WINNIPEG and TORONTO – NDP Finance Critic Judy Wasylycia-
Leis and Paul Summerville, the NDP Candidate in St. Paul's have
asked the Securities Exchange Commission [sic] (SEC) to investigate the unusual pattern of stock and income trust trading on
November 23, 2005. Paul Summerville is a former chief
economist with RBC Dominion Securities.[30]

There was little immediate journalistic response to the NDP's SEC
overture. It was, after all, a bit of a "Hail Mary" pass in strategic-
communication circles. The political campaigns were now criss-
crossing the country, with their respective leaders concentrating on
rolling out as much platform detail as possible prior to the holiday
break. Journalists were either caught up with summarizing the campaigns or looking forward to expectations when the campaign
resumed in the new year. The NDP call for an SEC investigation
seemed like just another bit of political theatre. Worse, considering
the continual rebuffs by the OSC, it smacked of desperation. As war
room workers and journalists drifted into the holiday hiatus, no one
expected that they would be returning to a dramatically different
election campaign, one where the competition for credibility would
be of defining importance.

It is one of the stranger ironies of the 2005–06 campaign that
having invested so much in cajoling various investigative bodies to
examine the income-trust affair, the NDP very nearly missed its own
moment in the sun. On 23 December, RCMP Commissioner Giuliano
Zaccardelli sent a letter by fax to the Parliament Hill office of Judy
Wasylycia-Leis. The letter contained a short official announcement:
"Based on the information obtained during the review [of the income-
trust allegations], the RCMP will be commencing a criminal investigation."[31] But because the letter was sent two days before Christmas,
nobody was in the finance critic's office to receive it and pass it along
to the war room.[32] Not until 28 December did Wasylycia-Leis's
office forward the announcement to the war room and, simultaneously, to the Canadian Press. The wire service issued an immediate

advisory citing the NDP as its source and scrambled to get the story to its subscribers:

> CP NewsAlert (Income-Trust-Investig)
> OTTAWA (CP) – The whiff of scandal was pumped into the federal election campaign Wednesday with confirmation that the RCMP has begun a criminal investigation into the possibility of a leak from the Liberal government prior to an announcement on taxation of income trusts. "There's sufficient information for us to launch a criminal investigation," said RCMP Sgt. Nathalie Deschenes.
> The investigation will determine whether there's enough evidence to warrant criminal charges. The Mounties aren't sure how long their probe will take.[33]

The RCMP announcement, framed as a validation of the possibility, even the *probability* of wrongdoing by Liberal insiders, is still credited (certainly in media circles) with changing the course of the 2005–06 campaign. In terms of the competition for credibility, this was the equivalent of winning the lottery. The NDP could now take credit for pressuring the national police force into launching an investigation into the actions of a department under the direction of a senior Liberal minister who, for all intents and purposes, appeared to have acted against the public interest for partisan purposes.

Canada's major newspapers, which had remained largely mute on the income-trust issue throughout December, exploded with the news of the RCMP investigation. The *Globe and Mail*, *National Post*, *Ottawa Citizen*, and *Toronto Star* all ran similar banner headlines with their 29 December editions. "RCMP CONFIRMS TRUST PROBE," blasted the *National Post* headline, followed by a lede line affirming that "Finance Minister Ralph Goodale has rejected opposition calls for his resignation."[34] "RCMP launch trusts probe," trumpeted the *Globe and Mail*, with a convoluted lede that framed the income-trust issue *and* included the call for Goodale's resignation. "RCMP probes suspected leak at Finance," said the *Ottawa Citizen*, its sub-headline reading, "Goodale rebuffs calls to resign over alleged early release of tax policy on dividends, income trusts." *Globe* columnist John Ibbitson was first out of the gate with an opinion piece declaring, "Ralph Goodale may have cost the Liberals this election."[35] In the days to follow, various pundits would echo the sentiment.

Only the *National Post*, in an editorial in its 30 December edition entitled, "Let the RCMP decide," defended Goodale, declaring calls for his resignation to be premature while demanding his full cooperation with the police and suggesting that this was an RCMP matter and should not be politicized.[36]

Sensing an opportunity, the Conservatives returned to their demand for Goodale's resignation. Conservative Leader Stephen Harper cut short his Christmas break to take a shot at the increasingly beleaguered minister of finance. The Conservative communication strategy at this point – reflected in the suggested ledes to radio stories offered by CP – was to heap contempt on Goodale and "his government":

(FedElxn-Goodale-Harper)
VANCOUVER. x–16s. Conservative Leader Stephen Harper says Finance Minister Ralph Goodale should resign, even though Goodale says he has done nothing wrong in connection with the income trust scandal. Harper says Goodale and his government don't deserve the benefit of the doubt.[37]

Paul Martin was left to defend Goodale and, as best as possible, try to deflect the damage:

(BIZ-Income-Trust-Investigation)
WINNIPEG. x–22s. Prime Minister Paul Martin says Finance Minister Ralph Goodale will not resign his post despite an R-C-M-P probe. Goodale has come under fire after the Mounties launched a criminal probe into allegations a Finance Department announcement was leaked to Bay Street.[38]

The major newspapers picked up on the unusual spectacle of a prime minister going public during an election campaign in an apparently desperate attempt to restore the credibility of a key member of his government. "Martin defends Goodale in RCMP trusts probe," shouted the *Globe and Mail* headline of 31 December. "Goodale is 'good, honest,' Martin says," declared the *Ottawa Citizen*. But the inevitable endgame to the assault on Liberal credibility began with CP's New Year's Eve announcement that Goodale had an appointment with the police: "Finance Minister Ralph Goodale says he will be interviewed next week by the R-C-M-P. It's part of the Mounties' criminal investigation into whether the government's plans for income trusts were leaked. The Mounties say that so far, 'there's no evidence of wrongdoing or illegal activity' by Goodale or anyone else."[39]

From this point forward, journalists would document Goodale's every move with respect to the RCMP. The man who had cockily stepped outside of the House of Commons to challenge his political opponents to prove his complicity in a set of circumstances he claimed had never happened was suddenly reduced to remarking (through a communication manager) on how "constructive" his meeting with the police had been. As CP reported, "Finance Minister Ralph Goodale met Tuesday with RCMP investigators probing allegations that Liberal government insiders may have leaked market-moving information related to tax policy on income trusts. Goodale met in Regina with police for a little over one hour and later described the session as 'a good and constructive meeting,' said his press secretary Pat Breton."[40] We are left to wonder how "good and constructive" Goodale would have found his meeting to be had he known what was about to transpire.

On 6 January, three days after the RCMP interviewed the finance minister on his role in the income-trust matter, the NDP's "Hail Mary" pass connected. Against all odds, the US Securities and Exchange Commission announced in a letter to NDP finance critic Judy Wasylycia-Leis that it would undertake an investigation into the possibility of irregularities with respect to Canadian income trusts in trading on the New York Stock Exchange. The NDP war room immediately released the SEC decision to journalists. In light of the RCMP investigation, and no doubt influenced by its American counterpart, the Ontario Securities Commission indicated that it would now begin its own investigation:

OTTAWA (CP) – The American securities regulator is taking "very seriously" complaints of insider trading involving Finance Minister Ralph Goodale's November announcement on income trusts. There is also a signal that the Ontario Securities Commission may be doing the same.

The U.S. Securities and Exchange Commission revealed it is reviewing the matter in an e-mail Thursday to Judy Wasylycia-Leis, the New Democratic Party's finance critic who filed a complaint with the market watchdog last month. "We are taking your complaint very seriously and have referred it to the appropriate

people within the SEC," the market watchdog's legal counsel,
Ann H. Sulzberg wrote.[41]

Both regulators made it clear that their investigations would not
be conducted in public and the results would be released in due
course; that is, both the SEC and OSC went to great pains to distance
themselves from the political haymaking that was sure to follow
their respective announcements.

For the political operatives in the NDP war room, the alphabet-
soup string of announcements from the RCMP, SEC, and OSC would
be taken as a vindication. The exact war-room list-serve traffic from
this time is unavailable. My email address had been swept from the
system over the holiday break, consigned to the electronic dustbin
by zealous party computer-police who suspected a spy. By this time,
too, my chair and desk space in the war room had been "reassigned"
to another party worker. And while nobody had asked me to leave
the premises, it was becoming increasingly clear that some people
were uncomfortable with my presence. In short, the SEC and OSC
announcements came out of the blue, and I was not present in the
war room to experience the reaction among party workers. But I
could imagine the elation, so I asked campaign co-chair Brian Topp
to recollect the moment. "Certainly we thought it was helpful validation – it suggested there really was an issue here," Topp said. "As
indeed there was, since a senior finance official was ultimately termi-
nated and prosecuted for this matter, despite the finance minister's
insistence that no one in his ministry could possibly have done
anything wrong."[42]

There's that word again: "validation." And yes, as Topp puts it
"there really was an issue here." But was it really the issue that competing political camps claimed it to be? As the 2005–06 campaign
wound down to its inevitable close, *nobody knew the outcome of an
RCMP investigation that would take a full year and a half to complete.*
What had been validated was a suspicion.

With the RCMP investigation underway, open season was declared
on the Liberals. The *Globe and Mail* of 6 January carried a story
about possible Liberal wrongdoing from the political and journalistic
equivalent of ancient history. The *Globe* story alleged that money
had been given to Quebec federalists by the governing Liberals in the
days leading up to the 1995 Quebec referendum, ostensibly as a
means to bolster the anti-sovereignty campaign in the province. The

RCMP, said the *Globe*, was "looking into" the matter. Nevertheless, the report managed to generate a spin-off story in the Canadian Press that kept the Liberal/RCMP connection alive: "Paul Martin could be forgiven for feeling these days as though he's running against an undeclared but powerful rival: the RCMP," wrote CP's Michelle MacAfee. "Martin's daily news conference was dominated by questions about a published report in the *Globe and Mail* that the RCMP is looking into a controversial $4.8-million grant awarded to a federalist group at the time of the 1995 sovereignty referendum."[43]

The *Globe* story, written around the *possibility* of an investigation into *possible* practices by a *former* Liberal government, does not point a smoking gun at anyone. It merely asks us to consider a possible pattern of suspicious Liberal activity. Questionable cash for Quebec federalists, the sponsorship scandal, suspicious activities surrounding insider information and income trusts – taken together these incidents surely had to point to a political party too long in power and too arrogant with the public trust to deserve another term in government? This was the message delivered by Jack Layton in the second English-language debate, a message in response to a question raised by the moderator of the Montreal forum and transcribed and posted verbatim by CP on 9 January 2006, the night of the debate:

MODERATOR: One of the major stories brewing over the week is the RCMP investigation into whether there was an improper leak from the government on how it would handle the issue of income trusts. You have demanded the resignation of the finance minister, Ralph Goodale. What evidence do you have, if any, that there was, in fact a leak of information?

JACK LAYTON: First of all, let me say that we're in a very sad time in Canadian politics because of the ethical standards that have not been set properly by the government. First we had the Gomery Commission, and now we have the income trust issue, and most recently the Options Canada story. It's time that we had a real focus on change, and that's why we have emphasized the need for new legislation and new electoral reforms so that we can sweep the Parliament clean of this ethics strategy. Now, it's not for us to show whether there's a particular scandal that the RCMP has begun to investigate. We simply noticed what happened to people's savings, and some people benefited. We drew it to the attention of the RCMP.

You know, actually, the finance minister should have done this
or the prime minister, and it's sad that they chose not to do so.
It shows they don't understand the concept of ministerial responsibility in parliamentary democracy. The RCMP says there's
something worth looking into.
We'll respect their decision.[44]

Layton, speaking directly to the Canadian people in the televised
debate, laid out a chain of logic that credited the NDP with blowing
the whistle on the income-trust affair. The NDP, said Layton, would
be a "clean" alternative to ethically challenged Liberals. There was a
pattern of scandal. The NDP would clean up Parliament. It was not
the NDP's job to prove its accusations. It was the NDP's job to notice
when Canadians were not being treated fairly and to act accord-
ingly. The top Liberals in charge of the income-trust case had not
acknowledged that there was a problem. As ministers of the Crown
they should take responsibility (resign) but, intimated Layton, let's
leave it to the RCMP.

On 15 February 2007, more than a year after it announced its
investigation, the RCMP charged a bureaucrat in the Department of
Finance with benefiting criminally from inside information respecting
income trusts. CP broke the story:

OTTAWA (CP) – The RCMP have charged a senior Finance
Department official with criminal breach of trust in connection
with the income trust decision of November 2005.
   The Mounties say Serge Nadeau, director general, analysis, at
the tax policy branch of the department, used confidential information in the purchase of securities for his personal benefit ...
The announcement of the investigation, which came in the
middle of an election campaign, sparked a political furor.
   The RCMP say the investigation is finished, with Nadeau the
only person charged.[45]

In May 2010, more than four years after the initial income trust
"scandal" broke, Serge Nadeau pleaded guilty to a charge of breach
of trust by a public official. He was handed a $14,000 fine (double
the amount he had gleaned from his part in the income-trust affair)
and a ten-month conditional sentence. Prosecutors found "no evidence
his actions were the source of the 'heavy market activity' that day."[46]

Are publics taken in by the intentional, often nasty distortions of political communication that are used in the fierce competition for credibility? And how do the perceived attitudes of publics play into the systematic distortions and manipulations of communication that increasingly appear to characterize election campaigns? As the following chapter suggests, in spite of the moralizing, the "pit hits," and even a legitimate commitment to matters of pressing concern, it might come as a surprise to partisan players that publics are far less willing to buy the war-room line than strategic communicators would have us believe.

6

The War Room, Journalism, and Public Discourse

At the midpoint of the second week of the 2005–06 federal election campaign, *Toronto Star* media columnist Antonia Zerbisias posted a paragraph on her weblog, *azerbic,* entitled "Blogopalooza!" It was an acknowledgment of something new in election coverage: in Zerbisias's words, "a blogging 'community'" set up by the CTV television network, "made up of its own correspondents' blogs."[1] Here was the so-called mainstream media reaching into a domain that had largely been the bailiwick of individuals with computers working mainly from home, constructing and maintaining sites on the World Wide Web for the dissemination of their personal viewpoints on all manner of issues and concerns. Now, big corporations like CTV and Torstar (the corporate entity behind Zerbisias's column) seemed to be signalling that they were moving into the blogosphere and things were about to change.

The reality for strategic political communicators was a bit different. Of course the NDP and the other political parties had constructed their own websites, but these were used mainly as clearing houses for party news releases and other official material such as rapid responses and the party platform: anything that needed to be on the record for the duration of the campaign. For the NDP, the business of operating in the blogosphere was mainly left to a site known as *The Blogging Dippers*, a place where individual bloggers of a left-leaning bent could voice their opinion on anything pertaining to the NDP, the election campaign, or the state of the world in general. The site (now dismantled) was a loose electronic clearing house administered by three bloggers who, the site declared, were "elected annually by the members of The Blogging Dippers." The website was adamant that it was "neither affiliated with nor endorsed by the New Democratic Party of Canada." The NDP election website provided a link to the Dippers, but there was no direct evidence during the campaign that the war room was using it to circulate strategic political communication. All of the major parties had (and have) similar communities of bloggers – the Blogging Tories and the Liblogs, for example – although the organizational structure of these groups varies. During the campaign, each of these websites provided a list of links to individual weblogs. Often these lists were more than a hundred entries long.

The individual addresses in the lists usually represented those computer-savvy individuals mentioned above. They are, in essence, computer network-enabled citizens from all walks of life who choose to engage cyberspace on their own terms. Most are simply interested in posting their personal thoughts, logging a kind of stream-of-consciousness worldview for anyone to follow if they are so inclined. But some independent-minded individual bloggers are specifically interested in politics and form a kind of network within a network. They consume the news of the day as presented by the mainstream media. They pick up on tips that are generated by colleagues in their own blogger circles and communities. They comment on decisions made and circulated in the political field and invite comments from anyone who is circulating discourse in the cyber-world. Many provide a "comments section" for discussions around issues that have been raised. By any account, these nodes of communication, enabled by accessible computers linked to the Internet, offer appeals for anyone to process and ideas that may be copied and circulated as far as the technology and human interest will carry them. They are places where publics collide and congregate, discuss and deplore, accept and reject, reside awhile and move on.[2] They are spaces where the invisible communicative circuits of publics operating in the field of power are, for a moment, made visible by the wide and flexible practice of computer networks.

Weblogs would appear to offer a goldmine for the dissemination of politically motivated communication, a direct channel to the real people behind a massive electronic network, people who (in the manifestation of the politically interested blogger) generally self-identify as having a predisposition to a particular political stance. It is immaterial whether those blogging individuals (and the publics that form around their sites) are converts to a political cause or in need of conversion: for political war rooms, they are a potential direct line into circuits of communication that were largely opaque until one-to-many and many-to-many electronic communication became widely accessible. The flexibility of cyber-messaging makes it theoretically simple to tailor strategic intentions. The corporate media understood this and adopted elements of the blogosphere into its election coverage for the 2005–06 campaign. Growing communities of independent bloggers and their individual contributors certainly understood this. But the NDP war room seemed reluctant to invest significantly in this brave new blogging world.

The reasons are both obvious and complex. For Brian Topp, the co-chair and chief strategist for the NDP campaign, the sheer number of voices operating in the blogosphere militates against any direct and concerted participation by the war room. In Topp's words, "the payoff of investing in researching and responding in a blog is low." This is not to say that the NDP's political communicators ignored discussions in cyberspace during the 2005–06 campaign. Indeed, interventions were made on occasion when individual discussions warranted clarification from a war-room perspective, but always with an eye to the verifiable record – the stock-in-trade of opposition research. "Basically," says Topp, "my philosophy is to let the facts talk. The fewer words and more facts in a war-room intervention the better. So every once in a while, we drop facts into blog discussions."[3]

There is also the overriding concern for message control and the strategies that inform the central function of the war room. As we have seen, it is difficult enough to keep political messages on track amid the sound and fury of competing argument strategies, posturing, and language games aimed at distinguishing one political competitor from another. Add another layer of intentional distortion, contextual manipulation, legitimate misunderstanding, confusion, and even responsible analysis once those messages enter the free-wheeling world of the blogosphere, and the dream of a goldmine of message dissemination turns into a potential nightmare. There is simply no way for political operatives to control their finely crafted messages once they enter a sphere of public communication where the practitioners are largely anonymous, potentially limitless, and sometimes predatory, and where it is impossible to recall information or negotiate its use. This reality runs contrary to every instinct in the political-strategy handbook where issues are positioned and registers applied according to the delicate balance between distinction and credibility.

For this reason, political strategists such as Brian Topp have made the decision to deal in "wholesale" messages. "If the topic is important enough to talk about during a campaign," says Topp, "we will generally do so with a statement in some form that goes to all media, on the Internet to our whole list, and onto our website. It will then find its way onto blogs (plural) quoting us. So in other words, look after wholesale and the retail will look after itself."4 For political parties, then (and certainly for the NDP), there are two compelling reasons to keep the blogosphere at arm's length: a practical reason that assigns a limited number of war-room communicators to more value-added tasks than discussing political minutiae with a potentially limitless number of correspondents; and a strategic motivation that seeks to maintain message control by keeping the party's position on issues upstream from the potential fracture and dislocation of the blogosphere.

The same concerns apply to information and attitudes circulating within the blogosphere itself. While it might seem that such material would offer a direct window onto those elusive debates among real people in real time from which political decisions rightly flow, debates that would surely offer political strategists an opportunity to generate credibility by appearing to get behind popular political sentiments, the very nature of communication on blogs makes this a dangerous prospect. Publics are fickle. Yesterday's passing appeal, duly processed and extended, is today's vilified position. Once again, the expending of time and energy on trying to discern the movement of public attitudes through cyberspace is seen to have greater value when applied to "wholesale" communication. But the simplest reason to steer clear of too close an association with the blogosphere has to do with identity and prudence. There is still no way of knowing for certain the true identity of contacts made on the web. War-room operatives were necessarily reluctant to embrace an uncontrollable electronic space where *everybody* is potentially a political opponent masquerading as someone else. Related to this concern is the matter of credit.

A great part of the practice of strategic political communication, after all, is supposed to be based on the advantageous placement of opposition research, the use of the facts in a political opponent's record to undermine current oppositional truth claims. To get a full measure of credit for challenging such truth claims, the party making the challenge must identify itself and *take* the credit. Yet the very power (as well as the frustration) of the blogosphere lies in its anonymity, the exchange of the widest possible range of views from the safety of identities that are impossible to prove even if they are openly declared. In these conditions, political parties face a conundrum: they can identify themselves, declare the origin of their messages, and attract a thousand negative nibbles from anonymous sources, many of them possibly originating from opposition war rooms. Alternatively, they can disseminate their messages anonymously, try to covertly influence the public discourse, and forego all credit – or, worse, be identified as the source of communicative manipulation and lose all credibility.

For good reason, then, the traditional methods of gathering and assessing public attitudes still largely hold sway. Public opinion polls remain the backbone of any election campaign. War rooms closely monitor the work of journalists – reporters, political columnists, contributing editors, ad hoc contributors – for any strategic content worth appropriating and for any indication of useful public response. The traditional forums provided by media outlets for public feedback to stories are assessed, albeit gingerly, for indications of trends in public attitudes or good ideas worth assuming and promoting. By this measure, much if not most of the work of the war room is concerned with taking the public pulse through an assessment of these relatively safe and established indexical sources. This material, the traceable footprint left by traditional media or garnered through qualitative measures such as polls, is particularly important for political players, just as the inherent instability of cyber-indexes, with their seeming penchant for disappearing at will, or forever reappearing in unwanted contexts, is highly problematic.

Like most political organizations, then, the NDP has decided to take a conservative approach to the online world. But the pressure is growing for more active involvement. This is especially the case given the comparatively recent rise of widely used social media such as Facebook and Twitter and self-selecting media sites such as YouTube. In the meantime, the corporate media continue to bet heavily on investment on the World Wide Web and many politically oriented independent weblogs have inevitably gained in credibility through the rough and tumble of successive election campaigns (just as others have disappeared without a trace). Some weblogs have acquired considerable influence, and some of those responsible for forming and posting content on these sites have become opinion leaders in their own special way. A few perform journalistic functions that are indistinguishable from those of their counterparts in the so-called mainstream media. Certain weblogs have assumed a particular political stance and because of this are positioned to engage the thoughts and attitudes that contribute to the force of opinion operating in the all-important field of power and publics. No political war room can long afford to ignore such entities.

The explosion in the use of social media is in the process of shifting the game once again. Politicians in all parties now find it difficult to operate without a Facebook page or Twitter account, though some, such as Conservative minister Tony Clement, are more comfortable with the technology than others. Journalists such as Andrew Coyne and Paul Wells have dedicated Twitter followings. Yet here too the advantages of direct contact with a following public are muted, at least for the political classes, by the need for political strategists to control the message. The last thing a war room needs during an election campaign is for a candidate to go "off message" in cyberspace, where everything is accessible to all and where the genie is truly out of the bottle.

Yet as political war rooms assess the enticements and dangers of the blogosphere and the "Twitterverse," the concerns of partisan strategists point the way to a rich terrain for scholarly investigation. In the 2005–06 election campaign, it was certainly possible to informally observe the flow of information on selected weblogs to test certain aspects of war-room communication at work. And it is worth noting that many of the political blogs in operation in 2005–06 are still operating. They have acquired their own symbolic capital, their own credibility.

They also have accessible archive pages. For this reason, the public processing of appeals posted in the comments sections on some established weblogs offers an opportunity to examine and re-examine how the many of the strategies and tactics of war rooms (specifically the NDP war room) worked with respect to the wholesale truth claims put forward by the party. Does "retail" partisan communication really "look after itself?" The short answer is yes, but in ways that may not be entirely in keeping with the overarching objectives of political strategists.

Another reason to consider the research value of selected weblogs has to do with issues of control, accessibility, and accuracy that apply to more traditional methods of gathering public opinion. The "safe indexical sources" of information currently employed by war rooms may or may not be widely disseminated. For example, average people rarely see how political organizations use internal polling data because the information is considered to be proprietary. To be fair, most regular workers in the NDP war room did not have ready access to it either, except when party strategists chose to release certain results that reflected positively on the campaign. These releases were generally taken as morale boosters.

Indeed, party workers often assigned more credence (and greater prominence on the list-serve) to polls circulated in the media – sometimes commissioned by news organizations but usually provided by the various polling companies, who were themselves in a heated competition for credibility. To accurately "call" the election is, after all, money in the bank for companies that deal in the measure of public opinion, since many depend on contracts with political parties for their economic wellbeing. During the 2005–06 election campaign, as many as twenty-four separate companies participated in some form of overnight polling for public release. The results, collected and presented daily, formed a coarse benchmark indicator of public opinion, usually around a variation on a single question: "If an election were held today, which political party would you vote for?" However, such polls were and remain a very blunt instrument. At best they offer a general aggregate response to the broadest of questions.

Against a backdrop of perpetual polling, forms of journalistic production and the responses to that production remain key measures of public receptiveness to campaign issues. Thus fully three-quarters of the daily circulation of material on the NDP war room list-serve was taken up with forwarding breaking news reports or synopses of recent issues in the news. In spite of the importance of this material, however, political operatives always treated it with a measure of suspicion. Journalism is, after all, considered an adversarial practice, constructed by individuals and filtered and disseminated through organizations that employ standards and methods normally in opposition to the objectives of political communicators. It is also the reason why mediated *public* space – opinions published in the op-ed pages of newspapers, the "Letters" sections of magazines, open-line radio programs, or the talk-back portions of radio and television news programs – seldom gets much quality attention from war-room operatives. While the opinions expressed in these forums might well come from average readers, listeners, and viewers, there is no guarantee that such opinions have not been planted by competing political organizations or otherwise manipulated.[5]

It is commonly held that the editorial filters of the news organizations are applied to reader mail. Comments are selected according to an editorial judgment; they may be trimmed for space/time and edited for content on the basis of that judgment. And while most journalistic organizations make every effort to retain the core substance of letters to the editor and other publicly generated material, many of the control mechanisms that apply to general reportage also apply here.[6] For war-room operators, then, the emergence of "useful" material in the journalistic field is always tempered by the constraints that come with attempting to appropriate heavily mediated cultural production – produced in an organizational culture suspected to be the polar opposite of one's own.

Public space that is not subject to the same filters is another matter and the reason why the content of certain politically oriented weblogs has appeared on the radar of war-room communicators, even if direct participation in the blogosphere remains problematic. A few of these sites became part of the subtle ritual of daily media surveillance in the NDP war room during the 2005–06 campaign. From time to time, references to particular weblogs were posted on the war-room listserve, especially when a third party with a substantial following acknowledged a strategic or tactical gambit favourable to the NDP. Sites such as the Alberta-based *calgarygrit* (Liberal), a site out of Saskatchewan with the taste-challenged title *smalldeadanimals* (Independent Conservative), and especially the Ontario-based *Stephen Taylor Conservative Party of Canada Pundit* (since renamed *Stephen Taylor – a blog on Canadian politics*) were regularly viewed. Also on the viewing list were media-generated sites such as Antonia Zerbisias's *azerbic*, and columnist Paul Wells's weblog *Inkless Wells*, generated under the *Maclean's* magazine web banner.

The development and expression of publicly held attitudes in the field of power and their dissemination through the constellation of interconnected weblogs deserve a major separate study. However, we may obtain certain important insights pertaining to war rooms and the Internet by plotting the public discussions posted in the comments sections of prominent political blogs against the emergence and re-emergence of certain strategic issues of special relevance to the NDP. In other words, it is possible to broadly gauge the resonance in a form of public space to prominent wholesale messages deployed by the NDP and other war rooms and taken up by certain blogs that have acquired their own measure of credibility with a public or publics.

Stephen Taylor's *Conservative Party of Canada Pundit* is just such an entity, as is Dan Arnold's *calgarygrit*. Taylor and his blog are partly funded by the Manning Institute, a Conservative think tank; Arnold is a former president of the Alberta Young Liberals and at the time of the 2005–06 election a graduate student in statistics at the University of Alberta. He was also doing work for the Pollara polling and marketing company.[7] The weblogs operated by Taylor and Arnold, two experienced and politically motivated (even partisan) bloggers, represent nodes of orientation on different sides of the Canadian political debate. Each provided a forum during the 2005–06 campaign for a potentially full and frank discussion of matters of public concern. Both (as might be expected) were the primary voices on their respective sites, but much of their credibility derived from the free and open access to their respective public-comment spaces enjoyed by voices from across the political spectrum.

This openness and willingness to engage diverse points of view was certainly the case with respect to the income-trust affair. While Taylor branded it a "scandal" from the beginning, many of the voices that entered the debate on his blog counselled against jumping to conclusions. Arnold's take on the affair did not discount the probability of insider trading, but public responses to his postings generally supported the view that it was not a Liberal Party scandal but the work of an opportunist within the Department of Finance. The discursive space delineated by the parameters of these two weblogs and the expertise of participants who commented on the income trust affair – the bloggers running the sites as well as the people who responded to their postings – can provide a small case study to illustrate how participation in web-based media is shifting the stakes around political discourse. Unsurprisingly, political war rooms are struggling with decisions on how to handle this emerging dynamic in partisan political communication, one where the lines between wholesale and retail messages become increasingly blurred.

Throughout much of the first half of the election campaign, the NDP seemed to be operating behind the scenes on the matter of income trusts. The party struggled to find a way to use the appearance of insider trading as a means to gain traction with its main strategic objective: to maintain and extend the general finding of the Gomery Commission of Inquiry by reaffirming the governing Liberals as systemically corrupt and therefore without integrity, without credence, and undeserving of further public trust. To reiterate a previous point, the difficulty in making a case against Ralph Goodale came primarily from the finance minister's decision to challenge the accusations against him outside the bounds of parliamentary privilege, thus throwing a libel chill over the whole matter. This chill effectively (if temporarily) removed the issue from the traditional, mainstream circuits of public discussion. Of course Goodale had no reason to think that the RCMP would take the unprecedented step of launching a criminal investigation against him in the middle of an election campaign. Neither did the NDP. It is possible that Goodale and the Liberals were lulled into a sense of security by both the low-key treatment of the matter in the mainstream media and the initial public sensibilities at play in the blogosphere. At any rate, voices of reason in virtually every weblog treatment of the income-trust affair seemed to counsel against a full frontal attack by Goodale's political opponents, including the NDP.

It is of interest to note, then, that the income-trust affair largely became a child of the blogosphere. Once mainstream media sources finished with their initial reporting on the matter, it all but disappeared from the traditional journalistic agenda. Debate around the issue, with a few notable exceptions, circulated largely in non-mainstream space until the RCMP declared its criminal investigation late in the first half of the campaign. Web-based journalists employed by media companies were also involved, but in a more constrained way. "Crossover" media practitioners such as Antonia Zerbisias and Kathy Tomlinson of "Whistleblower" (*CTV.ca*) were instrumental in disseminating some essential details of the income-trust affair both in the blogosphere and across mainstream media outlets, but always within the strict parameters of source confirmation and fair comment that universally apply to mainstream journalistic practice. In the general blogosphere, however, the issue was picked up, reworked, revitalized, and circulated among dozens of individual weblogs, inviting comments from hundreds of interested individuals. The issue was especially prominent on Arnold's *calgarygrit* and Taylor's *Conservative Party of Canada Pundit*.

Arnold's *calgarygrit* of 6 December (speculating on the fallout from CTV's initial story on the CARP/income trust connection) was among the first to set out the credibility stakes for the Liberals. In a posting entitled "Trouble, with a Capital T, and that Stands for Trusts!" Arnold all but drew the conclusion that the RCMP *would* investigate and that, strategically, it would be better for the Liberals to get the matter resolved quickly: "The real question is what kind of timeline the RCMP has for this investigation, and if we can expect to learn anything else (one way or the other) between now and the end of the campaign. It might almost be better for the Grits to have this resolved because, while I find it exceedingly difficult to believe someone in Ralph Goodale's office leaked this, the rumours and accusations are going to continue to grow."[8]

The respondents to Arnold's posting were almost unanimous in their support for Goodale. Most agreed that he could not possibly be behind a prior leak of information on income trusts. However, most also agreed that there was good reason for suspicion. As a voice identified as "two cents" put it: "I have no doubt that Ralph Goodale is a man of utmost integrity. However, the Liberals will not be able to dismiss this so easily if it can be demonstrated that someone in his office felt 'entitled' to provide a little investment advice to his/her friends."[9]

Indeed, most voices in the 6 December comments section had no trouble accepting that someone in Goodale's office had probably leaked information on income trusts. There was very little discussion (two responses out of thirty-five) around the possibility that market forces had led to the appearance of untoward activity. One anonymous respondent, with apparent prescience and claiming his or her own sort of insider knowledge, even seemed to confirm that a leak had come from the civil service: "I know with some certainty that indeed the info was leaked (unintentionally) by a senior civil servant the DAY before the announcement. Having said that the individual that received this info did nothing and told no one. So it is possible that other senior civil servants or this one told others as well."[10] Speculation went no further until four days later.

By 10 December, income trusts were back on the mainstream-media radar. CARP's claims to an income-trust tipoff from the finance minister's office had been roundly debated. The morning's *National Post* carried Andrew Coyne's column, "It's Not about CARP," in which he speculated about the origins of and reasons behind a

Finance Department leak. And Arnold in *calgarygrit* drew attention
to a spike in the volume of trading around a company named
Medisys, offering a quote and a link to another weblog that seemed
to expose a connection between this management company for private health clinics and Paul Martin. In his posting, Arnold made a
point that many others would make over the days and weeks to
come: "If there was a leak (and it looks like there was), I always
assumed it was because of negligence, or because some low level
staffer was trying to make a few bucks. To assume that this was part
of some massive Liberal conspiracy or that Martin was involved
seems a little bit rich."[11]

Arnold freely admitted in this posting that he is not an expert on
trading stocks. His admission opened the floodgates for comments
around the circumstances of the income-trust affair and the market
activity of 23 November. While the culpability of Ralph Goodale (or
those in his office) continued to dominate the discussion – including
a series of nasty attacks from clearly anti-Liberal voices – a significant stream of discussion focused on dissecting the trading activity
just prior to the income-trust announcement.

For the first time, a number of voices entered the discourse apparently unencumbered by the politics of income trusts; instead, they
began to offer a more dispassionate market analysis, including alternate theories of why the market acted as it did on 23 November.
Some remained convinced that the numbers represented evidence of
insider trading. Others such as "annextraitor" made the case that
"this is not the way to take advantage of insider information. You do
it using several different brokers in offshore financial centres over a
number of days."[12] This shifting away from the political meaning of
income trusts to an analysis of underlying market mechanisms (as
well as a thoughtful primer on how to conduct an inside trade)
would be taken up with more alacrity on *Conservative Party of
Canada Pundit*.

Stephen Taylor describes himself as a former Conservative nomi-
nee for the candidacy of Kingston and the Islands (he lost the 2004
nomination). During the lead-up to the 2005–06 campaign, he characterized his weblog in journalistic terms: "During the 2005–2006
campaign, this blog broke many election related stories which got
significant play in the mainstream media." Taylor, according to
Taylor, was at the time of the election completing a graduate degree
in biochemistry and working in Ottawa. He did not specify what

kind of job he held with any political party. And while he still maintains his political blog, he has also been appointed the Ottawa director for the National Citizens' Coalition, a right-wing lobbying concern and think tank.

During the 2005–06 election campaign, Taylor certainly played a significant part in circulating "evidence" about the income-trust affair. Like most media watchers, he picked up on initial reports of unusual market activity in the week following the announcement by the Department of Finance that income trusts would not be taxed. "If this scandal turns out to be insider trading," wrote Taylor on 30 November, "then this may end up plaguing the Liberals during most of the campaign."[13]

Taylor seemed unsure of what to do with the initial income-trust story and moved on to other interests. As with *calgarygrit*, Antonia Zerbisias, and other bloggers, his later interest in the income-trust affair came from web-posted mainstream sources, notably Kathy Tomlinson's "Whistleblower" column and a CTV.ca staff-written story that quoted an OSC source's suspicions about the income-trust file. The same story prompted the NDP war room to suggest a elease calling for Goodale to step aside until the matter was cleared up.[14]

Taylor's weblog remained more or less mute on the issue of income trusts until 11 December, four days after CTV and CP circulated their respective CARP reports and one day after Coyne's column appeared in the *National Post*. Taylor was to take an interesting tack, assembling a series of charts based on information supplied by various sources in the "Conservative blogging community" that appeared to show spikes in trading activity across nine market entities "prior to the Goodale announcement on 23 November at 6:00 pm."[15] This was much more information than any of the mainstream media outlets had assembled (or dared to publish), and it appeared to show a pattern of investment buying suggesting prior knowledge of the Finance Department's decision. Whether these charts actually proved insider trading was highly debatable, but they did invite a cascade of responses among Taylor's Internet publics.

It is worth examining these responses if only to note how few thoughtless and purely partisan comments are posted. While some voices offer conspiracy theories and clearly speak from the position of absolute mistrust of Liberal intentions, most probe Taylor's methodology or question the conclusions he draws from the "evidence" presented in the charts. Many of the voices appear to have more than a passing understanding of the way the stock market works, of how to interpret spikes in trading activity and whether the evidence supports the charge of insider trading. Furthermore, there seems to be an unwritten code among these bloggers to permit other bloggers to have their say, even those who come from a declared contrary political point of view.

Part of a discussion on *Conservative Party of Canada Pundit* was initiated by a blogger self-identified as "Paul": "While insider connections between any of these trusts and the Liberal power structure would be interesting, of more direct imporatance [sic] of course would be any connections between the specific individuals who made these trades (or the individuals who recommended them) and those same Liberal power structures. But having the research at the ready is a handy thing to have. Let's not just ourselves fall into the pit on this one."[16]

His comment was answered by Arnold ("calgarygrit"), who had clearly been following the discussion: "I'm not an expert on stocks, but the connection between these trusts and the LPC isn't really that relevant to the leak, is it? I mean, can't we assume these income trusts would have spiked the day after the announcement regardless? Like Paul said, the real people you want to find are the ones who made these trades. They'd be the ones who were tiped [sic] early and who profited. If you could tie any of them to Goodale's office, or the LPC, then you'd have a stronger case."[17]

Later, another voice, self-identified as "nbob," calls for caution: "I don't want to rain on your parade – because I think something smells and it's sure worth a closer look – but you'll need to expand your methodology if you really want to come up with a valid study.[18] He or she then presents a detailed account of publicly available material about one of the investment vehicles that had a trading spike prior to the income-trust announcement, the company called Medysis that was so prominently featured for its ostensible connection to Paul Martin. The information "nbob" provides seems to confirm that the company had good reason to expect a spike in trading because it had just announced a payout to shareholders, as had four of the other companies cited by Taylor. "I think," writes "nbob," "that you can safely remove those 5 from the list."[19]

This comment was the final one in the initial discussion around trading activity as presented on Taylor's 11 December weblog. It reflects a line of reasoned argument presented by several voices, some with obvious market expertise, against jumping to conclusions based on the appearance of suspicious trading activity. To be sure, there were other voices more crudely inclined to see Liberal skullduggery at every turn. One even suggested that the Liberals might be using insider knowledge to buy into the market before the trust announcement, then sell high in order to top up their election war chest! But for the most part the "expert" voices prevailed.

Therefore, within more-or-less parallel discussions on the same topic, one conducted on the Liberal-leaning *calgarygrit* and the other on the Conservative-leaning *Conservative Party of Canada Pundit*, interested publics essentially took control of the logic of the income-trust affair. On the one hand, Liberal-oriented voices conceded that someone (though not Ralph Goodale) had leaked confidential information; on the other, Conservative-oriented voices rejected the argument that the appearance of market activity proved insider trading.

Since the activity on both weblogs appeared to directly address strategic issues that the NDP was then working on, I mentioned it to two war-room workers. At this time the party was pushing the OSC to launch an investigation. Both workers were aware of Taylor's posting (but not Arnold's) and of the discussion around it. Neither was inclined to talk with me about whether the NDP, for its part, should do some of its own forensic work around the companies that appeared to benefit from information released prior to the official announcement. As it turns out, this was precisely when the NDP was ramping up the communication offensive that would culminate in a request for an investigation by the US Securities and Exchange Commission, when Andrew Coyne's CARP column was in circulation, when the Conservatives had called for Goodale's resignation based on the CARP story, and when a number of weblogs, including Taylor's, were discussing what appeared to be a pattern of insider activity in the markets – though none supplied specific "evidence" in the manner of Taylor's "trade spike" charts. On top of this, the circulation in the blogosphere of a purported connection between Paul Martin and the head of the Medisys Health Group Income Fund offered a potential opportunity to draw a direct connection between income trusts and the issue of private medical clinics, opening the door to a direct challenge of Martin's position on either file. This synergy of strategic opportunities would seem to be an especially rich one, since in addition to investing heavily in its income-trust offensive, the NDP was

about to present its Shirley Douglas stump speech in Regina. Yet the
NDP war room, aware of these connected opportunities, failed to
bring them to public attention.

The NDP's restraint can be explained in a number of ways. All
have to do with issues of message control and credibility. First, there
was nobody in the New Democrat family of bloggers with the same
willingness as Stephen Taylor to post "proof" of unusual trading
activity around income trusts. To publicly recognize Taylor's "information" and the discourse around it would therefore lend credence
to the work of someone sympathetic to a competing political camp.
Even if the blogger in question were not an official employee of the
Conservative Party (and there's no guarantee that this was not the
case), the fact that Taylor is a self-declared Conservative would be
problematic for the NDP. Journalists also read weblogs, so to appropriate material from a Conservative-oriented site and use it publicly
would invite questions from journalists about the source of the
information. To reveal the source would give credence to the Conservatives; to not reveal the source (or claim the information as the
NDP's own) would cause questions to be asked about the party's
own integrity and credibility.

Second, the dominant public discourse carried on Taylor's weblog
was both thoughtful and cautious. The voices willing to jump to
conclusions, to see a Liberal conspiracy in the income-trust affair,
were vastly outnumbered (by about five to one) by those who seemed
genuinely interested in developing alternate explanations for the
apparent spikes in trading or, most significantly, in cautioning that
much more work needed to be done in order to prove a causal link
between the finance minister's office and pre-announcement activity
on the stock market. This causal link was precisely what the NDP
was hoping to accomplish by calling for, variously, OSC, SEC, and
RCMP investigative involvement. The difference is that the party was
interested in using the credibility of the investigative bodies to further its own ends and knew full well that a proper investigation
could not possibly be conducted before the end of the election campaign. The weblog respondents, on the other hand, seemed to want
to get quickly to the bottom of the income-trust trading activity.
These are two very different, even contrary, objectives. It would not
serve anyone in the NDP war room to have a thoughtful discussion
(generated by a blogger with ties to the Conservatives, no less) on
income trusts if that discussion were to lead to an exoneration of the

Liberals. Even entering into such a discussion would detract from the main NDP strategic intention by introducing elements of doubt into the primary objective: to cast the income-trust affair as one more (perhaps definitive) example of shady Liberal dealing.

However, the biggest impediment to jumping on the Stephen Taylor bandwagon may have had to do with institutional culture. While most war-room workers are relatively young, certainly under forty, the senior party brass comes from a generation that is more comfortable with traditional mass media. A guest column in the 13 December issue of the *National Post* situated the issue of income trusts vis-á-vis the "Internet's most rabid political junkies" – code for non-journalists – in a manner that would be in keeping with such a generational divide. In his column, John Moore, host of a Toronto talk-radio program, went to great lengths to discount chatter in the blogosphere around the income-trust affair by making the case that there are perfectly logical reasons why trading in trusts should increase prior to the government's announcement. Many of those reasons echoed the dominant discussion on Taylor's weblog. However, Moore also indulged in some questionable assumptions about the media's role: "The fact that the media have largely ignored this alleged scandal might be taken as further evidence that it amounts to little more than campaign chicanery – except that in the new Internet age, when a story is ignored by the mainstream media ... that's just further proof of its veracity." [20]

Of course, this was very much a confirmation by a practitioner of mass media that the mass media are in charge of determining what is and is not true, or what does or does not warrant further investigation. This was exactly the embedded position of the NDP's communication strategists: that information in circulation does not exist until it is confirmed by journalists and published or broadcast by so-called mainstream media. This is the safe zone of political communication. Everything else is just a conspiracy theory. And while such a position may seem to be unduly risk-averse (especially to younger political communicators), a small but significant incident in the blogosphere seemed to lend support to the more cautious position.

On 15 December 2005, just two days after Moore's column appeared, the NDP was provided with a number of opportunities and a cautionary tale. Among them was a posting on a weblog known as *Captain's Quarters* (no longer in operation) operated by a blogger identified as Ed Morrissey out of the Twin Cities area of

Minnesota. Morrissey has since moved on to become a commentator on mainstream media in the US Midwest and operates a right-of-centre blog called *Hot Air*. Among his postings for 15 December was a rehash of the income-trust affair that ended with some encouragement for the NDP: "The Conservatives and the NDP should continue to press for a federal, independent investigation into the 23 November trading activity."[21] The NDP war room circulated the posting on its internal list-serve. The voices that responded in the *Captain's Quarters* comments section included three anonymous offerings representing three distinct points of view:

> ANONYMOUS 1: The Conservatives and the NDP should continue to press for a federal, independent investigation into the November 23rd trading activity.

> ANONYMOUS 2: Maybe there hasn't been an investigation because the people who really know something about the market haven't seen anything out of the ordinary.

> ANONYMOUS 3: The RCMP and the OSC are not the only two groups capable of investigating this issue. In 2003 the Liberals themselves passed Bill C-46 which gives the Solicitor General the authority to conduct a concurrent investigation into insider trading activity. So in other words, these are the choices ...

> 1 We can have a Liberal controlled police force investigate.
> 2 We can have a securities regulator that is headed by someone who has contributed at lease [sic] $1,000 to the Liberal Party in each of the last five years.
> 3 Or we can have the Liberal Party investigate themselves.[22]

The first two comments are indicative of the manner in which the general discourse around income trusts was becoming polarized. The first point of view supports Morrissey's position, and also the NDP's, that there is good reason to proceed with an investigation by an unspecified "federal [and] independent" authority. The second maintains that there is nothing out of the ordinary. The third introduces something different. It has all the earmarks of a well-informed partisan comment. It introduces elements to the discussion that insinuate a breadth and depth of Liberal corruption that is breathtaking.

It accuses the RCMP of being in thrall to the Liberals. It accuses the head of the Ontario Securities Commission of being a Liberal toady, a cash contributor to the party, with the inference that he is supporting his Liberal chums by blocking an investigation into income trusts. Finally, it points out that the solicitor general – an appointment of the party in power – is empowered to investigate matters such as the income-trust affair, but that a Liberal investigating Liberals would inevitably result in a whitewash. The subtext to this entire line of reasoning is that the whole system is corrupt and only a new government, with a new solicitor general who is not a Liberal, would be able to get to the bottom of the "scandal."

This is precisely the kind of planted information that might originate in a war room, crafted to introduce new elements of doubt into an ongoing public discourse with the intention of leading voters to a conclusion. The tactic has a clear strategic intention: to shift the discussion into a trust/integrity register, to "cut through" with a distinct position in order to induce a general sense of mistrust in the entire apparatus of any Liberal government. The comment likely did not originate with the NDP (although nobody in the party would confirm or deny involvement) because its message is at odds with the NDP's objectives. Indeed, it is unlikely that a solid source could ever be ascertained, given the anonymous nature of the blogosphere.

Should it come as a surprise that war rooms may have infiltrated the blogosphere? Probably not. While strategic political communicators seem to have concluded that information posted on weblogs is best treated with caution – that it is expensive and time-consuming to confirm, and dangerous to appropriate without some kind of independent verification – they are apparently beginning to realize that basic party positions, widely held strategic partisan messages, may be *added* to the ongoing "public" discourse with relative impunity. So much the better if a competing war room unwittingly circulates the message.

These well-crafted messages, however, speak to a new level of communicative manipulation and distortion, one that conceals an intention to deceive by assuming the identity of a public voice, just another citizen, a representative of a public introducing his or her thoughts into the debate on a matter of public concern. This is dangerous ground. Given the flow of discussion in cyber forums, these windows onto the circuits of discourse among diverse participants that are reflexive of the field of power and publics, such an insertion of intentionally distorted material is simply a lie, a crossing of the line that separates strategic persuasion through opposition research from the out-and-out intention to mislead.

At this juncture there is no way to know whether such interventions are mere mischief or indicative of something more insidious. For the reasons cited above, the NDP war room was reluctant to enter into anonymous blogging, choosing instead, on the rare occasions when it posted mainly fact-based material in weblog comment sections, to identify itself openly. However, it is almost certain that this kind of "placement" of the nastier strains of "oppo" will increase, at least until bloggers obtain the electronic resources, develop the skills, and invest the time to track and identify the sources of postings.

Such tracking is not without its rewards. On a related theme, bloggers were largely responsible for identifying fake political ads commissioned by the Liberals and posted to the party's website on 5 December, a story that was picked up and circulated among mainstream media outlets and on competing political websites.[23] These ads featured members of the Young Liberals posing as "ordinary Canadians" lauding the government of Paul Martin on a number of files. While there is some dispute over who first revealed the subterfuge (the NDP gleefully posted the fake ads to its party website and chided the Liberals for their dishonesty), the incident is indicative of a wider, emerging practice, a kind of surveillance system of mainstream journalists, competing political operators, and bloggers acting as independent checks on misleading political communication and blowing the whistle in their own interests.

Therefore, while elements of strategic-communicative action may have already moved to the Internet, war rooms still see the pitfalls of jumping into cyberspace with both feet as greatly outweighing the advantages. For the moment, the effect has been to reserve large areas of weblog discourse for publics most willing to invest the time to process passing appeals on important matters of public concern. In the meantime, most political-communication strategists find themselves restricted mainly to party websites, essentially passive spaces mainly of interest to those publics who are invested enough to find the sites and spend the time navigating their offerings.

As Tamara Small has pointed out in her analysis of the political uses of the Internet in the 2004 general election, all parties at that time were experimenting with some form of web interactivity. All political parties created a limited forum on their official pages for interaction with "the leader." But even here, control of the message took precedence over true interactivity. For example, the Conservative "weblog," associated with that party's site and meant to personalize a connection with Stephen Harper, did not include a comments section. Indeed, says Small, "the blog was not even written in the first person, but was written about Harper by an anonymous staffer."[24] It was not really a weblog at all. The NDP "weblog feature" developed on the party's site for the 2004 election purported to carry comments from Jack Layton, but here too the site did not provide for an interactive comments section. This remained the case for the 2005–06 campaign.

Such a unidirectional flow of communication runs contrary to the central strength of the Internet: its ability to facilitate a wide range of discourse around multiple issues engaged by anyone willing to process the passing appeals on offer. Is it surprising, however, that highly sophisticated communication specialists view this as a disadvantage during an election campaign? Their job, after all, is to *limit* the discussion around partisan positions even as they seek opportunities to undermine the credibility of their opponents. The blogosphere may be tempting as a platform for the practice of the tactics of dis-credit, but it also undercuts message control by admitting public opinions that may run contrary to the party's stated position. The question for future election campaigns is whether war rooms will embrace such tactics while attempting to maintain the control that comes with the upstream dissemination of wholesale messages. Media such as Facebook and Twitter may be more adaptable to strategic political concerns.

In an odd way, the uncertainty of web-based communication in the 2005–06 campaign produced a set of circumstances that were a mixed blessing for NDP war-room communicators. Individual bloggers kept the income-trust affair alive in the face of general reluctance by the mainstream media to engage the issue fully. But the NDP's strategic-communication people were kept from capitalizing on participation in (or appropriation of) important discourses – discussions of central concern to the NDP's own communication strategy. The party could claim a measure of consolation from the knowledge that Dan Arnold's "Liberal" weblog continued to show concern over Liberal Party exposure to the income-trust affair, a persistent line of discussion that seemed to accept as prima facie the case that something untoward had happened on 23 November. Such consolation was tempered on *calgarygrit* by equal persistence in the belief that Ralph Goodale was not personally responsible, thus detracting from the argument for "ministerial responsibility" that the NDP (and Conservatives) put forward whenever the income-trust affair was mentioned.

Similarly, the dominant public on Stephen Taylor's "Conservative" weblog, through three separate discussions in December, was unwilling to concede a full measure of support for the thesis that insider trading was the only explanation for the flurry of trading activity that had preceded Goodale's income-trust announcement. In spite of this, it was somehow reassuring that Taylor's graphs and charts – and his reluctance to compromise on his insider trading thesis – appeared to show the kind of "evidence" that might prod the OSC into action. The competition between these competing streams of discourse likely, on balance, contributed to the NDP's strategic position, the one that eventually (and surprisingly) came to pass: involvement by the RCMP, a body with the power to subpoena records, conduct interrogations, and apply resources to make sense of the evidence – in short, a body empowered by law to get to the bottom of the matter.

The central importance of the voices, the publics that circulated their opinions on weblogs such as *Conservative Party of Canada Pundit* and *calgarygrit*, lay in the simple fact that they were being circulated of their own accord. To be sure, bloggers such as Arnold and Taylor were able to set topics for discussion: comment sections are, after all, offered as a forum for responses to specific musings by the bloggers. But the discourses that developed over income trusts (especially with respect to Taylor's efforts to "prove" insider trading) illustrate the limits of the blogger's influence. Participants made up their own minds about the meaning of the affair based on the circulation of thoughtfully analyzed data, logical conjecture, knowledge of political strategy, and plain, garden-variety belief. And in each case the conclusion of the participating publics was at odds with the strategic objective of the NDP war room. As for the anonymity of the blogosphere, while it may shield communicative abuses, it also supports a kind of freedom to say what is on one's mind in a manner that is virtually impossible to find in any other public forum. It just might be the case that *the people* are showing us all how democracy is done, how the continuing conversation in the field of power and publics sets its own agenda, creates its own conditions for communicative action, and decides what is important, irrespective of the machinations of political (and journalistic) operators.

7

Political Communication
and the Journalistic Field

NDP leader Jack Layton is going to great lengths to stick to his script and
dodge questions on subjects he doesn't want to address since off-the-cuff
comments on private clinics early this week landed him in hot water.

Steven Chase and Bill Curry[1]

The strategic and tactical communication generated by war rooms of
all stripes is only as good as its effectiveness in out-competing all
other "earned media" on any given day. Furthermore, while political-
communication strategists might be convinced that their messages
are of the utmost importance, those messages, even during the privi-
leged conditions of an election campaign, may be easily overshadowed by news events that have no relationship to the political matters
at hand. Worse, unforeseen consequences may arise from the best-
laid plans of political strategists. For this reason, much political communication at election time is aimed at simply guiding the party's
message through the generalized cacophony thrown up by political
competitors and the world at large, and squeezed through the editorial filters of various journalistic enterprises. If a political party of
any stripe is to connect with the people who will ultimately cast their
ballots on election day, it must contend with messages derailed by
adversaries, acts of God that hijack the front page of every newspaper on any given day, journalistic indifference and/or hyper-vigilance,
and plain dumb luck.

The pressure to "cut through," to get the message out, to compete
well in the field of power and publics by structuring and situating
messages in such a way that they are cleanly admitted into the circuits of discourse that will ultimately bring voters on side, almost
inevitably slams headlong into issues of credibility. In a world of
shifting boundaries that often pit good taste and judgment against

the opportunity to state a legitimate concern, enthusiastic and opportunistic political parties and their leaders often wind up on the wrong
side of a sensitive public issue. A case in point is the Boxing Day
2005 shootout on Toronto's Yonge Street, a senseless, unpredictable
act that wounded seven gang members and killed Jane Creba, a local
high-school student and innocent bystander.[2] All three mainstream
federalist parties used the crime as a hook to restate their respective
positions on gun control and on violent crime in general (and to gain
the attention of voters in the riding-rich Greater Toronto Area). Possibly for good reason, the timely response by politicians to this tragedy was viewed in much of the published public discourse as cynical
opportunism, the attempt by shameless political players to jump into
the media spotlight and turn the tragedy into a political advantage.
While crass opportunism may well have been a motivating factor,
the consequences of *not* wading into the debate were not discussed
with the same intensity, even though they may have been equally valid.

By design or instinct (or both), political players, left with the
choice of being tarred as heartless opportunists or uncaring, unin-
volved automata (and therefore unfit to govern), invariably fall back
on practices that reflect aspects of Bourdieu's notion of the connection between distinction and relations of power, that "distinction
among actors within fields and among fields, and the relations of
power that arise from the competition for recognition, lie behind the
'ongoing struggle that is society.'"[3] This concept is instructive. In the
case of the Toronto shooting and similar potentially no-win situa-
tions, for example, it has become widely accepted that it is better to
be criticized for taking a stance (and receive a measure of distinction
through public exposure that at least permits a discussion of the issue)
than to respectfully maintain a dignified silence only to be criticized
for apparent indifference (and receive a measure of distinction based
negatively on no engagement with the issue).

On a significant level, then, political war rooms are charged with
managing this sharp and constant competition for distinction amid
the glut of occurrences that constitutes daily journalistic production
and its circulation in the field of power. And they do so knowing that
recognition and credibility go hand in hand, that distinction without
credibility is usually not desirable, but distinction that generates credibility on an issue, or that supports and enhances residual credibility,
is the aim and objective of the entire exercise. Much of the work of
war rooms, therefore, lies in framing and driving the issues on which

the party may take a distinct position to places where discourse can be positioned, engaged, and enhanced with an eye to generating or protecting credibility. This process must be accomplished against a nexus of daily competing interests that operates against a range of competing occurrences as small as the last Lindsay Lohan faux pas or as large as a killer tsunami.

War rooms spend considerable time and energy on this idea of "positioning the discourse." To more fully understand what it takes to drive a complex public discussion to a place of "communicative safety," it is therefore helpful to briefly revisit the notion of registers or argument strategies.

Simply put, registers may be used to frame an issue within certain thematic categories that resonate broadly with the value commitments of multiple publics. These categories might include (but are not limited to) matters of law and order, public safety, economic stewardship, employment, and so forth. By their very nature, argument strategies provide a basic communicative frame that may be used by a participant in a debate to advance and/or protect a particular point of view.[4] Such positions are themselves bounded by the requirement to appear credible with respect to the issue at hand and by the requirement to offer a distinct position, one that is somehow creditably different from those on offer from the competition. Because argument strategies demand that the truth claims of political actors are distinct *and* credible, there is always fierce competition for ownership of the ideas that will generate the widest resonance.

The positioning of complex discourses within registers has become a kind of default position for political war rooms, a predictable response to complex issues that emerge from the storm of daily competing interests. The NDP, for example, has long positioned itself on the side of "working people," "average Canadians" and, more recently, the "middle class." Whatever these broad terms may actually mean, they resonate for the NDP along an ideological-cultural division that distinguishes the partisan communication of New Democrats from that of other political parties. The distinction that accrues to the NDP derives from registers positioned within broad conceptual areas of concern that claim a dedication to economic fairness, social justice, protection for the disadvantaged, and so on. For this reason, tracking registers and the ways they are employed offers a means to locate and study some of the basic motivations for war-room communicators. The discourses themselves may not be especially revealing, because most election-time discourses are repetitions of established positions. However, the "ownership" of a particular register *around* a significant discourse (gun control, law and order, health care, the economy, etc.) can be illuminating indeed.

Having constructed a terrain where no political communication occurs without strategic and tactical objectives, and where any gambit is subject to the vagaries of outrageous fortune, political war rooms have opted to generate ever-more political communication that reinforces standard positions. These positions are crafted to avoid engaging, as much as is practically possible, messy public discussions or controversies, even if such discussions might be of great importance to some voters. The positions are intended instead to get the message out.

The requirement to be distinct becomes an ever-more complicated prospect as the urge to position discourses within controllable registers runs into conflict with the need to assume safe and defensible communicative positions. War-room communicators have addressed this tension (either unwittingly or by design) by putting Habermas's notion of communicative action to use in a manner that ultimately stands as a classic example of systematic distortion.

Briefly, the Habermasian notion of the ideal-speech situation, of communication for the express purpose of reaching consensus, is precisely the mask that is adopted by political communicators when they attempt to appeal to publics. It is highly useful because it speaks to the very ideals (including the transparent exchange of information) that are widely understood to be among the core values of liberal democracy, ideals that also mesh nicely with Habermas's notion of a public sphere where the rational and critical discussion of common concerns leads to decisions made in the public good. But war rooms are charged with putting *strategic* communication into practice – the "considered choice" of communicative intent whose sole aim is to influence others.[5] This intentional construction by political communication strategists of a binary of communicative opposites, a kind of "debate and switch," permits political communicators to use the best of democratic ideals and intentions for purely strategic and partisan purposes, and to do so in plain sight.

In this respect, political war rooms have performed the unlikely trick of converting communicative action into a strategy. In the wake of the Boxing Day shooting, for example, the Liberals, Conservatives, and NDP immediately promised stricter gun-control measures if elected. Such a promise spoke directly to a core constituency in each party, but more than this, it pushed the debate over gun control into a realm of ideal absolutes, into the register of public safety, a place where nobody could credibly argue that, in the public good, guns and their criminal use should *not* be more strictly controlled. Each party framed its response to the Toronto shootings from the safe position, the consensus position, that the event was (in the words of Paul Martin) "a senseless and tragic act." But from this safe position, the position of communicative action, the party leaders adopted sub-positions with strategic intentions meant to make their responses distinct from those of the competition, or, in the case of the NDP, from its *own* stated position of regarding gun violence as a symptom of a social ill.

Stephen Harper restated his party's law-and-order hard line, declaring, "I am committed to doing everything necessary to crack down on gun violence." Paul Martin and his minister of justice, Irwin Cotler, took a broader view, seen to be consistent with traditional Liberal themes. "Mainly," said Cotler, "we want to address not only crimes of violence, we want to address the root causes." Jack Layton seemed to borrow from the hard-line Conservative handbook, possibly because he was speaking to a hometown voting audience. "These crimes," said Layton, "remind us that we must get illegal handguns off our streets in Toronto and across Canada. To do that, we need tougher border controls, tougher sentencing for weapons offences, and tougher anti-gang policing, prosecutions and sentencing."[6]

The claim to have the solution, to have the means to protect innocent people in the street, to represent the broad consensus, was used in each case to situate the respective party in a protected (credible) space, the position of "something must be done" for the good of everyone. But once the position was established and credibility assured, each party sought to make its position distinct. In the case of the NDP, distinction came from temporarily abandoning the party's traditional support for prevention programs and anti-poverty measures and adopting a strong stance within the law-and-order/ public safety register, the register with the greatest credibility in that place and at that moment.

While the political response to the Boxing Day shooting appears to illustrate a reaction to unique and unpredictable circumstances, in reality it is typical of the overarching communication strategy preferred by war rooms. Indeed, the communication strategies and tactics deployed in each of the cases cited to this point – the Buzz Hargrove affair, the Newfoundland "pit hit," the Clarity Act announcement, and the income-trust affair – are essentially the same, differing only in the intensity of the issue at hand, the surface details, and the registers employed.

The enforced control of the response to Hargrove's apparent defection to the Liberals spoke to the theme of betrayal. The bloodless affirmation that "Mr Hargrove is entitled to his opinion" was an affirmation of a democratic ideal. The right to speak freely and hold contrary opinions is posed as a "pure" commitment to a greater good. Caught off guard by Hargrove's actions, the party rushed to protect its credibility with unionized workers, a core constituency, by appearing to take the high road in the sure knowledge, the consensus understanding (but also the strategic objective), that the jilted lover is always more sympathetic than the cad who does the jilting. Of course party workers and candidates quietly redoubled their campaign efforts at the constituency level, attempting to delicately repair the damage. At the earliest post-election opportunity, Hargrove was kicked out of the party. And for all of the shock and dismay over Hargrove's actions, for all of the negative distinction that was placed at the NDP's door, the union boss's strange dalliance with Paul Martin also put the party into the headlines of *every major newspaper in the country*, a feat that would not be repeated (with one minor exception) until the RCMP announced its investigation into the income-trust affair. From a political strategist's point of view, it is perhaps not such a bad thing to be in the national spotlight as the (literally) wronged party.

The "pit hit" attacking Paul Martin's pitch for a weather-research station at the defunct Canadian Forces Base in Goose Bay, Labrador was framed around a challenge to Liberal credibility that was itself constructed around an issue on which the NDP had staked a long-term claim (and thus could be used as a register): economic security for working people. Could the same prime minister who stood by for the closing of the Gander weather station – and the subsequent loss of jobs – be trusted to deliver on a promise of an alternate use (and jobs) for the Goose Bay military base? Yet, lost in the brief shuffle of reportage around the NDP attack were, ironically, some bald geographical facts that might easily have caused problems for the New Democrats, had journalists been inclined to dig a little deeper.

Goose Bay in Labrador and Gander on the island of Newfoundland are nowhere near one another, so "new" jobs for Goose Bay would be meaningless for Gander. Weather research on climate change (proposed for Goose Bay) and weather forecasting (lost to Gander) are two very different enterprises. The jobs "lost" in the closure of the Gander weather station had been moved, in the main, to Nova Scotia; that is, they were lost to Newfoundland and Labrador but not entirely to Atlantic Canada. However, by challenging Paul Martin and the Liberals strictly on the issue of jobs, that most precious and enduring of themes in rural Newfoundland and Labrador, the NDP was able to use the appearance of communicative action in the economic register to generate a measure of consensus around the issue of employment, while simultaneously engaging a strategic action initiative around questions of Liberal trustworthiness. This manoeuvre produced a measure of credibility for the NDP's role as defender of working people.

Even the Clarity Act announcement, an apparent about-face on a major party policy position, may be viewed as an act of communicative action that concealed a strategic purpose – albeit a rather awkward one. The requirement to "cut through," to appear distinct, was balanced against the need to set the record straight in order to acquire credibility on a major federal file. The Clarity Act flip-flop, the apparent endorsement of a Liberal-generated law aimed at setting the ground rules for any future referendum on sovereignty in Quebec, was framed by the NDP as an issue within the register of national unity, a (somewhat questionable) acknowledgment by the party of the general acceptance in Canada *and* Quebec of the act's legitimacy.[7] Henceforth, the NDP would stand with the majority including, according to Jack Layton, the former leader of the Parti Québécois, Lucien Bouchard.[8]

Yet the location for Layton's announcement on the Clarity Act, a federal building in Montreal where activities related to an inernational climate conference were in full swing, belies the strategic intentions of war-room communicators. The subtext to Layton's presence in Montreal was to remind Quebec voters, who consistently identify with concerns about the environment, of the New Democrats' claim to guardianship of the green file. For Quebec federalists who were having second thoughts about voting Liberal, the NDP could position itself as the "first party of the environment," the party that owned the file before the Liberals appropriated it (and greenhouse gas emissions increased).

To vote for the NDP, then, would afford a two-for-one bonus: Layton and the NDP would be onside with the Clarity Act, a law protecting federalist sovereign interests, and as an added incentive, the NDP would, symbolically, offer a different environmental option to that of the governing party, even if the details of that option were never categorically stated. For its part, the NDP hoped it might actually succeed in electing a member of Parliament in Quebec, thus addressing a matter of deep anxiety (and credibility) for a national federalist party.

The above examples represent relatively discrete instances of war-room communication at work. However, where this system of political communication becomes most deeply revealing is in its application to the positioning and promotion of areas of interest that have an "ownership" stake for a political party. For the New Democratic Party, health care is the most important piece of political real estate of all.

It is no secret that problems with the Canadian medicare system have been the source of much political haymaking. Indeed, Paul Martin's Liberals formed a minority government in 2004 largely on the promise to "fix medicare for a generation" by injecting tens of billions of dollars into the health-care system.[9] This "solution" to a perceived crisis in universal health care was intended to remove medicare as the possible ballot-box issue in the 2005–06 campaign. The Liberal strategy was to reduce the greater debate to a series of lesser arguments over how Martin's reforms were being implemented. For the NDP, the most important of these lesser arguments was wait times, or, to be precise, whether wait times would be shortened for Canadians seeking health services by paying for services offered by private health providers. With its historic connection to T.C. Douglas, the so-called "father of Canadian medicare," the NDP had an opportunity to profit from the revived debate. Without an ironclad guarantee from the Liberals that private health providers, paid for with public money, would be off the table, the NDP could accuse the governing party of trying to undermine the public health system.

So important is guardianship of publicly funded health care to the NDP that the party began positioning itself to present and exploit a campaign debate on medicare long before an election was called.

Indeed, in October 2005 Layton let it be known that the price for continued support from his party for the Liberal minority government would be a guarantee that private medical clinics would not be permitted to benefit from the billions of dollars in new health care funding that the Liberals had committed to the system.[10] Layton had reason to believe that the Liberals would play ball; they had already committed $4.6 billion toward a package of NDP demands.

By early November, with the Conservatives and the Bloc both signalling non-confidence in the government, Layton, well aware that he held the balance of power, used the issue of private clinics to ramp up pressure on the government.[11] The Liberals would not budge. In the NDP's mind, the matter of private health clinics was fast becoming the issue that would bring down the house and launch the party into an election register that it would "own." By 8 November the game was up: Layton announced that the NDP would no longer support the government. The reason: "There is no meaningful accountability or even a real effort to monitor and track public medicare's decline and private care's rise. And today's Liberal Party is unwilling to attach any conditions to prevent privatization to the funds it currently invests in health."[12] The rules of the house prevented a non-confidence vote from happening before 28 November, but the NDP's withdrawal of support over private clinics was the straw that broke the back of Paul Martin's minority government.

It would be expected, then, that the New Democrats would want to reaffirm their "ownership" of the health-care high ground as soon as possible in the campaign. The party was also prompted into taking a stance by the background rumble of health-care proposals beginning to emanate from competing political camps. The *National Post* and *Ottawa Citizen* of Saturday, 3 December, gave prominent play to the Conservative position on hospital wait times and the role of private-sector options, a position reflected in a *Citizen* article entitled "Private Care Is Right for Ontario, MD Says."[13] A second story advised the reader that the Liberals were on the verge of releasing their own wait-time proposal.[14]

In each of these stories, the NDP is relegated to a response to the Conservative position on private clinics, buried in the story on the original wait-time announcement. Predictably, Layton condemns "the augmentation of two-tier health care" as "contrary to the Canadian philosophy."[15] Layton is treated in a similar manner in the *Globe and Mail*'s coverage of the Harper wait-time announcement: his response is relegated, almost as an afterthought, to the last paragraph of the story. [16] To defend its ownership of the publicly funded health-care register, the party would need to do something dramatic.

To this end, Layton visited the British Columbia lower mainland on the weekend of 3 and 4 December to denounce a Vancouver private-health clinic that, in the view of the party, represented the thin edge of the wedge that would lead to the collapse of universal health care. This was a golden opportunity for the NDP, a chance to revitalize and position its traditional ownership of a major issue while enhancing the considerable residual credibility that the NDP had accumulated around the issue of public health care for, quite literally, generations.

Up to this point, Layton had been repeating the standard core message: the NDP would ensure that "Canadians do not need a credit card to access health care." [17] The war room had used a Conservative pronouncement on wait times to restate its position:

To: War Room
Date: Dec 2, 2005 12:35 PM
Subject: Lines re Harper's health care announcement

We share Mr. Harper's view that waiting lists are a big problem after 12 years of Liberal rule.

He is wrong on how to fix it. We need common-sense solutions to the problem.

Solutions that do not lead to the growth of American-style for-profit medicine.

That's where Stephen Harper is wrong. Just like Paul Martin – whose hidden agenda isn't even hidden after refusing to work with the NDP this fall to stop private care in its tracks. Liberals pose as defenders of health care while allowing the growth of clinics that charge $2,300 per year just for the right to see a doctor. [18]

Reporters would have had little reason to expect any change in this oft-repeated position. It was standard fare, intended to reassure supporters in a region that elects NDP members, while simultane-ously reaffirming the party's health care message to the country. The message would also set the stage to re-distinguish the New Democrats from the Liberals over the issue that had, in the NDP mind, launched the election campaign. As a side benefit, a trip to BC would insulate

Layton from embarrassing questions and permit him to "change the channel" about the new relationship between Buzz Hargrove and Paul Martin, a relationship that was front and centre on the front pages of the Saturday newspapers. Indeed, on 2 December, when Martin and Hargrove were shocking NDP staffers with their televised strategic-voting alliance, the war room was preparing the ground for Layton's BC visit. Martin's response, or non-response, to a question about health care, asked in the heat of the Hargrove moment, elicited a rapid response from the NDP war room:

MARTIN DUCKS CLEAR QUESTION ON HEALTH CARE
OTTAWA – Today in a scrum after his speech to the Canadian
Auto Workers, Paul Martin was asked by a Globe and Mail
reporter whether or not he would close down the first for-profit
hospital in Canada.
   Vancouver's Copeman Clinic began providing services at a cost
of thousands of dollars per year for patients, and has announced
they will be expanding with 37 other clinics across the country.
Faced with a clear question on stopping for-profit health care,
Martin refused to give a clear response.[19]

This release telegraphed the NDP's tactical intentions. Indeed, Layton would specifically target the Copeman Clinic – and by association, Paul Martin – in a news conference scheduled for the following Sunday. But before any of this could go forward, the NDP had to take care of a not-so-small credibility issue of its own, an issue with a name: Svend Robinson.

Robinson had been elected to Parliament seven times in a row, long enough to see his riding change its name twice. Over the course of his political career, he had crafted a reputation as a campaigning social activist, a member of Parliament who would, seemingly, go to any length to advance his left wing social-activist commitments. He remains best known as the first openly gay politician in Canada. His personal web page lists his involvement in numerous human-rights organizations past and present: from committees on gay rights to groups opposing apartheid in South Africa to membership in international organizations opposing the Indonesian occupation of East Timor. In short, Robinson was a vintage political activist who had the unwavering support of his constituents until he pocketed an antique diamond ring that did not belong to him. Then his world came crashing down.

The details of the case of the Robinson ring theft were of little concern to the larger issues of the federal election campaign of 2005–06. But it was still an uncomfortable reality that Robinson was caught stealing and charged with theft; that he pleaded guilty to the charge and received a conditional discharge based on his courtroom "revelation" of a previously undiagnosed psychiatric condition (an admission that seemed to many to be too convenient by half); and that he reluctantly gave up the riding he had represented for a quarter-century in the face of these circumstances, on the eve of the 2004 election which he would surely have lost – only to surface in another Vancouver riding in the following election.[20] Robinson, who had always been considered a bit of a loose cannon in the party, became a *radioactive* loose cannon in an election campaign whose central strategic theme was integrity and credibility.

There could have been no hope or expectation that Layton would dodge the "Svend factor" on his swing through the lower mainland. For this reason, he was prepared when reporters cornered him in Saskatchewan the day before his arrival in BC. They were seeking clarification on Robinson's relationship with the leader and the party. While the *Globe and Mail* of Saturday, 3 December, reserved its front-page headline for coverage of the Martin/Hargrove alliance, the newspaper reserved space for two substantial stories about Robinson later in its A section. The first, by one of the *Globe*'s senior west-coast correspondents, Gary Mason, is basically an opinion column disguised as a news story. It outlines the battle for the Vancouver Centre riding, held by Liberal incumbent Hedy Fry (considered by many to be the Grits' loose cannon) and contested by Conservative also-ran, Tony Fogarassy, and the newly resurrected Svend Robinson of the NDP. Mason's lede line is a good indication of the overall tone of the story: "It's already being dubbed the Battle of the Divas. And early indications are that the race for Vancouver Centre between New Democrat Svend Robinson and Liberal incumbent Hedy Fry could develop into one nasty little cat fight."[21]

Mason provides a short profile of Hedy Fry. He talks about Vancouver Centre's substantial gay and lesbian demographic and speculates on Robinson's strategy, the obvious appeal to voters of like mind and, presumably, similar sexual orientation. He then raises the issue of "the ring":

> Mr. Robinson says he intends to deal with the ring issue head-on if it is raised during the campaign. Know that it will be.

And if not by one of the candidates directly, then by some supporter who is put up to it. Besides, does anyone think Dr. Fry is going to be able to restrain herself at the first all-candidates' meeting where Mr. Robinson delivers a long, stinging soliloquy on Liberal corruption?

"They stole your money," you can hear Mr. Robinson thunder.

"Isn't that a bit rich coming from you, Mr. Robinson?" Dr. Fry says in return.

This short, imagined exchange encapsulated the entire problem faced by the NDP. And as if to telegraph to the party that media dragons would be lining up for a bit of sport at Jack Layton's expense, a story on the following page of the *Globe and Mail* revisited the Robinson theft issue while focusing on Layton's often testy responses to reporters' questions the previous day. The *Globe* story sported the headline "Ethics Appear to Be a Hard Sell with Robinson as Candidate." The accompanying Canadian Press archive photograph showed a weeping Robinson, dabbing his eyes with a handkerchief at his 2004 court appearance.[22]

Strategists in the war room did not directly reveal to me their plans or concerns with respect to the Robinson dilemma, but they are not difficult to divine. After all, the *Globe and Mail* "ethics" story of 3 December had been constructed around the question that was on everyone's mind. Layton's response, however, represented a neat turn of campaign logic:

When asked yesterday how he can accuse the Liberals of having "helped themselves" over the past 12 years when Mr. Robinson was convicted of helping himself to a diamond ring worth more than $50,000, Mr. Layton lauded the former MP's behaviour in the wake of the charges. "What Svend did was take responsibility for his actions," Mr. Layton said yesterday morning in Regina.

"He co-operated. He indicated he had done something terribly wrong. He worked with the court. Taking responsibility in many ways is what this [election] is all about and we haven't seen that from the Liberals, taking responsibility for the issues that [Mr.] Justice [John] Gomery has raised."[23]

Given the time to think through a strategy for the Robinson integrity issue – and the war room had certainly anticipated these questions – Layton was able to turn an embarrassment for the NDP into an attack on Liberal integrity and credibility. It placed the emphasis on Robinson's willingness to accept responsibility for his actions while accusing the Liberals of ducking their own responsibility for the sponsorship scandal! The NDP accomplished this by positioning the discourse in the responsibility register, by distinguishing the party from the Liberals through a reference to restitution, the broad social consensus that contrition goes a long way to assuage wrong-doing. Of course, the strategic action lay in a reference to Liberal unwillingness to take responsibility for *their* actions. By the time Layton delivered his health-care speech in Vancouver on 4 December, the matter of Robinson's ring seemed to have been dealt with. Then Layton was side-swiped.

What Layton actually said in his 4 December speech was, by now, NDP boilerplate. The NDP would be committed to ensuring that public dollars would not go pay for services at private health clinics. He pointed out that Vancouver's privately run Copeman Clinic received some of its funding from the BC government. He charged the Liberals and the Conservatives with failing to protect Canada's health care system while pointing to "the rise of private clinics across the country."[24] Then, during the standard give-and-take with reporters after his speech, Layton was asked whether he would shut down clinics if they were completely private, if they received no public funding at all. Layton replied, correctly, that the Canada Health Act provides for the operation of private clinics and that the NDP's concern, once again, was with the use of public funds to buy services from private operators. It all seemed quite clear.

Indeed, the *Globe and Mail*'s front page headline for Monday, 5 December, made no mention of Layton, concentrating instead on a possible Liberal "surge" in Ontario. The story was based on polling commissioned by the *Globe* and, while it was not good news for the NDP, it was not unexpected, given the Hargrove/Martin reports that had ended the first week of the campaign. There was not much more to grab a reader's eye until well into the first section – page A3, for example, was taken up by an extended obituary. Then, on page A5, a photograph of a somewhat startled-looking Jack Layton looks out at the reader next to a headline that proclaims: "Not Opposed to Private Health Care, Layton Says."[25] And in the photograph, gazing over Layton's shoulder, slightly out of focus but recognizable, is Svend Robinson.

By introducing Robinson into the pictorial representation of the party's identity on the West Coast (candidate Libby Davies also peeks out from the photo from the lower right) and by juxtaposing the photograph with a headline that appeared to signal a major shift in long-standing NDP policy, the *Globe* story conflated two unrelated matters into one large question about NDP credibility. Issues with Robinson's own credibility were literally presented in the photograph as the backdrop to Layton's apparent about-face on the file that was used to trigger the election. Between Robinson's lack of credibility on the ring issue and the leader's apparent new stance on health care, the party and its leader could be considered incompetent or, worse, callous, calculating, and unprincipled. It did not matter that the text of the *Globe* story was clearly focused on a process, suggested by Layton, for denying public money to private-health clinics, that the issue of completely private health providers was a different issue altogether, and that Layton was certainly *not* endorsing private clinics. The damage was done.

When the *Globe* published its story inferring that Layton had abandoned the very heart and soul of the NDP position on health care, it threatened both the distinctness of the party's position and the credibility of its claim to be the true defender of universal health care. It is thus scarcely surprising that when I entered the NDP war room in Ottawa on Monday, 5 December, the place was in full damage control. The campaign press secretary was on the telephone "clarifying" the party's position to a *Globe* reporter and angling for a follow-up report to set the record straight. An exchange of messages between the campaign co-chair, Brian Topp, and *Globe*'s managing editor, Edward Greenspon, was in wide circulation on the internal list-serve. Greenspon had asked for the NDP's position in writing. He was provided with the following detailed synopsis:

Cc: War Room
Date: Dec 5, 2005 3:26 PM
Subject: Health Argument

Layton is saying this:
(1) Supreme court may have opened the door to the breakdown in the single-payer system.
(2) Provinces have put ottawa [sic] on notice they're looking into going through that door after the election.
(3) Federal government can help prevent this by more clearly conditioning its transfer – no subsidies to such system. Seems likely that without subsidies, private-pay systems will die in the cradle.

(4) This was the issue we were debating with martin [sic]. They flatly refused to consider point 3 and that, basically, provoked our caucus into withdrawing support.

(5) With regard to private clinics, layton [sic] is noting that there are private clinics in the system now, have been for a very long time, and that it likely doesn't make sense to set out to shut them all down.

(6) He is also noting enthusiasm for an aggressive expansion of this kind of facility – driven in part by the greenlight [sic] apparently given by the court.

(7) He wants the federal government to be out in front to prevent this – a significant further expansion – on the case that health dollars should go to health services – not dividends for shareholders.[26]

The *Globe* of 6 December made no mention of the NDP's "clarification" of its position. The newspaper chose to stand by its story.

In fact, the *Globe* of 6 December makes no mention of health care at all. Its front page is dominated by a now-famous photograph of Saddam Hussein, arm raised and face contorted in anger, taken in a Baghdad courtroom where the former dictator was on trial for ordering the death of fellow Iraqis opposed to his regime.[27] The Canadian political news of the day, also on the *Globe*'s front page (but subordinated to the photo of Hussein), was devoted to the announcement by the Conservatives of a national child-care program that would provide an allowance paid to the parents of preschool-aged children.[28] In the discussion surrounding the Conservative "cut through" and positioning of the discourse on this major policy initiative, the *Globe* ran a comparison between the Conservative option and the national day-care plan the Liberals had introduced in the previous session of Parliament.[29] The NDP is not mentioned. Indeed, the only mention of the New Democrats in the 6 December *Globe* – aside from a paragraph by Jane Taber entitled "Avoiding Svend" that lightly detailed Layton's weekend on the West Coast vis-à-vis Mr Robinson – was a report outlining the party's somewhat ambiguous position on taxes.[30]

The NDP fared slightly better in the *National Post* of the same day. While the newspaper gave the Conservative child-care proposal top billing on the front page, the New Democrats were featured prominently on the inside pages. In a bit of successful spin, the party's hold-the-line position on taxes was actually reported as support for a tax cut.[31] The inevitable comparison between Conservative and Liberal child-care options incorporated a quote by Layton, unlike the treatment in the *Globe*, and there was a short, staff-written story on how Muslims were being encouraged to vote for the NDP rather than the Liberals.

But that's where the good news ended. The only full-length report dedicated to the NDP, on page A5, resurrected the small Vancouver nightmare introduced by the previous day's *Globe*. It was a "catch-up" story, meant to refresh for *National Post* readers the *Globe*'s "scoop" of the previous day. And its lede line undercut every effort of the war room to put the policy-shift genie back in its bottle: "A surprising comment from NDP leader Jack Layton," wrote reporter Tom Blackwell, "may have signaled a potentially far-reaching shift in Canada's health care debate and its emotional focus on two-tier medicine."[32] To make matters worse, to freshen up the story the *National Post* quoted the Ontario head of the Canadian Union of Public Employees who said of Layton's "new position: "It caught me unawares, no question." On the heels of one union boss getting into bed with the Liberals, of one national newspaper publishing a disputed report about a basic shift in NDP policy, of a second national newspaper picking up on the "shift" and bringing a second union chief into the fray, the war room quietly let the matter drop.

The *Globe and Mail* of 7 December made no direct mention of health care, though the *National Post* and its sister paper the *Ottawa Citizen* each published a front-page story on a poll identifying health care as the default concern for Canadians in a campaign that seemed to lack any dominant issue.[33] However, the NDP figured prominently on the inside pages of both the *Globe* and the *National Post*. Each paper offered a very different profile of Jack Layton (with the same Canadian Press photograph of him, head cocked and hand to ear as if listening to a softly spoken question). The *Globe*'s profile was entitled, "Layton Bobs and Weaves, Keeps to NDP Script" and is less about Layton the politician than the NDP's communication strategy. In fact, the *Globe* story focused primarily on a series of gaffes attributed to Layton during the opening days and weeks of the campaign *and* during the previous election in 2004. The key paragraph was almost a word-for-word description of the NDP (or any) war room's basic communication intentions, and the description comes in Layton's own words: "Mr. Layton says he's trying to stay on message. 'There's [sic] several hundred issues we could talk about on any given day – on an almost random basis. We're trying to make sure people understand what our key priorities are.'"[34]

The bulk of the *Globe*'s "profile" then goes on to describe, once again, the "gaffe" over private clinics from the previous Sunday's ill-fated Vancouver news conference. To be fair, the story does offer clarification on the NDP's stance on private health care by quoting a "left-leaning" health expert to tell the reader "the best way to phase out for-profit clinics is to starve them of public cash," because to do otherwise would invite a Supreme Court challenge. And none other than Alexa McDonough, a former leader of the party, is mobilized in defence of Layton, claiming, "Mr. Layton has not changed his position 'one iota' on private clinics." However, these "validators" are shuffled to the last half of the story, their comments coming just before a recap (wedged into the final two paragraphs) of the Buzz Hargrove affair! The overall impression left by the story is that Layton has been tripping metaphorically over his communication shoelaces and now intends to tie them tightly and walk a straight line.

The profile in the *National Post* by the veteran Parliament Hill reporter and columnist Don Martin is based on a one-on-one interview with Layton. It focuses on the prospects of the NDP's return to Parliament as the party wielding the balance of power in a minority government. However, Martin also paints Layton as a coy political player, unwilling to speak in detail about a raft of NDP demands that would emerge in the horse-trading of a government propped up by the New Democrats.

Buried in the subtext of Martin's profile is an indirect but over-arching interrogation of Layton's credibility. "He won't rule out supporting the Liberals," writes Martin, "despite many angry denunciations of Paul Martin's ethical deviations and policy shortcomings." Martin then suggests that Layton would consider getting into bed with the Conservatives if it would help the NDP cause. And buried in the text is a reference to the issue that will not die: "His health care policy took a weird turn this week when he agreed to tolerate totally private clinics as long as they were not milking a profit from the public system. Sounds almost like a Harper position."[35] But the most stinging moment for Layton comes over the NDP's position on the environment and Don Martin's placement of this major policy plank into the economic register: "The Layton plan sounds mighty Utopian on paper – drinking water for all, air scrubbed of greenhouse gases to a level 25% below what they were back in 1990, a chemical crackdown and an energy retrofit on one in every four houses within seven years. The cost? Not much, he says. How little? No idea, he adds."[36]

By raising the issue of the public cost of NDP proposals and promises, Martin put his finger on a sensitive point. Having never been in power at the federal level, the NDP has no experience in administering policies and programs. Yet this election would likely put the New Democrats into a position of significant influence in Parliament. Are Canadians ready, asks Martin, to buy into a shopping list of demands without seeing a price tag that could run to billions of dollars? The question speaks directly to matters of credibility in the classical sense of Bourdieu's meaning, that "symbolic capital is credit ... a kind of advance, a credence, that only the group's belief can grant those who give it the best material and symbolic guarantees."[37] In this respect, Martin is asking the "group" – Canadians – whether the "material and symbolic guarantees" are good enough to sign a blank cheque over to Jack Layton.

The *National Post* and *Globe* profiles of Layton were not discussed openly in the NDP war room. I did informally ask one war-room worker what he thought of the treatment that each paper had published. He indicated (somewhat surprisingly) the sense that it would be foolish to expect more from the news media in general, from the *Globe and Mail* in particular, and especially from the self-declared right-of-centre *National Post*. Then, with a grin, he pointed out that "It *is* December 7th, after all" – a reference to the anniversary date of the attack on Pearl Harbor.

Of greater concern to war-room strategists was the party's apparent inability to get any of its messages out in a significant way. From Saddam Hussein's day in court, to duelling child-care plans, to a surprise headline on the first page of the 7 December *Globe*, "U.S. slashes softwood duties," a partial resolution to a major trade dispute affecting thousands of Canadian forestry workers (symbolic territory for the New Democrats), the NDP simply could not get its core messages into prominent play in the major newspapers. In the days to follow, the Liberals would propose an outright ban on handguns (8 December); Svend Robinson would make a return visit to the front page of the *National Post,* sharing space with an analysis of the meaning of a handgun ban in an uncanny foreshadowing of the Boxing Day shooting debates (9 December); and former US President Bill Clinton would make the front page alongside Paul Martin at the United Nations climate-change conference in Montreal, following the second get-together in Windsor between the prime minister and Buzz Hargrove (10 December). Clearly, the New Democrats were struggling to find an opening. After the largely unsuccessful Clarity Act flip-flop news conference of 7 December, intended to "cut through" but relegated to minor status by the national newspapers, the party went on the hunt for an issue and an event that it could control, an event that could help to reset its campaign. That issue, once again, would be health care.

When Shirley Douglas stepped before the cameras in Regina on 13 December, the timing could not have been better, and worse, for the NDP. In the days leading up to Douglas's "stump speech" at Regina's Tommy Douglas House, home of the provincial NDP political machine in Saskatchewan, news reports and analyses had continued to trickle out on the state of health care in Canada. Most of this journalistic production framed the issue by questioning whether anything had changed in the system since the Liberals had promised to "fix medicare for a generation." Then on 12 December the *National Post* ran a front-page story announcing that the provinces had adopted "national standards for medical wait times," a major concern for Canadians awaiting a number of high-demand treatments such as hip replacements and cardiac-bypass surgery. The wait-time announcement was immediately claimed by the Liberals as proof of their commitment to repair the health-care system, with the federal minister of health, Ujjal Dosanjh, characterizing the news as a major shift. "It is, in fact, a revolutionary process for our health care system," said Dosanjh, "It is the first time we are imposing standards on ourselves as a society."[38] The *National Post* story is based on an intentional leak of inside information. It attributes the information to "health ministers" who are expected to make their official wait-time announcement later in the day (meaning the *National Post* story had actually been written the night before). By an unlikely coincidence, Ujjal Dosanjh just happened to be standing by with a comment on the issue that had been identified days earlier as the prime concern for Canadians.

Not to be outdone, the *Globe and Mail* picked up the wait-time story on 13 December, running the details of provincial commitments on its front page under the headline: "Targets Set for Faster Health Care."[39] The *Globe* report deals mainly with responses from provincial health ministers, although Dosanjh is referenced in the text as the federal representative on the health file. Neither the Conservatives nor the NDP are mentioned in either the *National Post* or *Globe* reports. But by blind luck or stellar planning, Shirley Douglas appeared before a national audience riding the wave of two days' worth of front-page stories on health care, thus permitting the NDP to step into the spotlight on its oldest, most cherished, and most symbolically valuable policy issue. Every moment of the Douglas stump speech was crafted to position the NDP as the defender of single-tier, universally accessible public health care in Canada. Every criticism of Paul Martin and Stephen Harper was meant to challenge the credibility of the political opposition and deliver control of the health-care discourse to the NDP, *especially* in the face of reports that would seem to suggest that the wait-time issue, a major hurdle in health-care reform, had been solved.

Douglas's speech positioned this all-important discourse within a web of symbolic elements, each of which would stand as a meta-language signifier with its genesis in a founding political myth. These elements, powerful registers in their own right, are the source of the NDP's most basic symbolic capital, its credibility on the party's defining issues. In large part, the founding political myth *is* Tommy Douglas who, as the leader of the Saskatchewan Cooperative Commonwealth Federation, led what many believe to be the continent's first quiet revolution, a revolution distinguished by the assumption of public responsibility for a raft of socio-economic concerns including socialized insurance, cooperative electrification of rural Saskatchewan and the creation of a state-owned power corporation, a state-run bus company, and the first state-sponsored and funded Arts Board.

But the CCF's defining act under Douglas was North America's first comprehensive system of public medical insurance: the Medical Care Insurance Act. Furthermore, Tommy Douglas was the founding leader of the *federal* New Democratic Party. Therefore, Jack Layton was the holder in trust of a position that reaches in direct succession back to its most eminent (and politically successful) founding personality.

It is a testament to the war room's belief in the power of its symbols that Shirley Douglas, an actor, was flown in to deliver a speech on medicare in a city that she had not lived in for decades. Here, too, was Layton, a former Toronto city councillor, laying claim to the Douglas legacy in a province where the party had failed to elect a single member in the previous election. The two were positioned at

Tommy Douglas House, headquarters of one of the most successful political organizations in the country, but an organization that had never regarded itself as joined at the hip to the federal party and had largely sidestepped the needs of its counterpart in the federal campaign. In short, the Douglas stump speech of 13 December was artifice through and through, meant to transfer the literal connection of the Douglas DNA to the symbolic DNA of the party via that most resonant of NDP areas of political ownership: health care. To put Jack Layton together with Shirley Douglas, rallying the troops, repositioning the party, setting the record straight yet again within the social-justice register on private versus public health care, was to control the message at last. At least this was the party's intention.

The *Globe and Mail* of 14 December gives play to Layton and Douglas, but not until well into the paper's first section. The photograph accompanying the story frames the duo on a "set" with the NDP logo in the background. To the right, perched on an easel, is a portrait of Tommy Douglas, the "third party" in this bit of theatre.[40] The text of the *Globe* story, written by veteran reporter Bill Curry, begins with Layton's main message on health care, an attempt to situate the NDP's position, once again, on private health-care clinics, but now directing responsibility to the *provinces*: "Ottawa should take a hard line with premiers over private health care, slashing federal cash to provinces that refuse to pass laws banning doctors from working in both the public and private systems, NDP Leader Jack Layton said yesterday."[41]

Curry's story devotes a single paragraph to Shirley Douglas, describing her speech as a "tirade against Liberal Leader Paul Martin for failing … to act in the face of increasing for-profit activity in the health system." The report goes on to position the NDP in opposition to the both the Liberals and the premiers of Quebec, Alberta, and British Columbia. It quotes Layton's call for a federal crackdown on these provinces and any others considering private clinics. But Layton stumbles when prodded on the details of such a crackdown. He cannot say exactly how the NDP would bring the provinces into line without meddling in a well-defined provincial jurisdiction. It does not help that Quebec's minister of health, Philippe Couillard, is quoted in the *Globe* report essentially telling Layton to mind his own business.

This was pure poison to the NDP's position. Couillard, an MD and well-respected MNA, had been dealing since the previous June with his own health-care headache. It arose from a Supreme Court decision in the case of Jacques Chaoulli and George Zeliotis. The two had successfully argued that a prohibition on private health insurance in the province of Quebec and, therefore, reasonable access to private health care, was endangering lives. The "Chaoulli case" had arisen directly from the issue of wait times in the publicly funded system. The high court agreed that denial of access to insured private health services when the public system was unable to deliver timely care was a charter issue. In the court's words, "The right to life and to personal inviolability is therefore affected by the waiting times."[42] Quebec had been ordered to permit private health options. The province had asked for time to get its house in order.

For Layton to suggest that a federal government led by him would cut off funding to provinces exploring private care options was deeply offensive to Couillard, whose government was trying to figure out how to fix the public system. It was doubly irksome because Layton appeared to be unfamiliar with the Chaoulli case and the Supreme Court's decision.

Perhaps surprisingly, the NDP fared better in the *National Post* of 14 December, with a report that actually began on the newspaper's front page. A cascade of interrelated registers – Liberal *and* Conservative unwillingness to stop private clinics (trust); the NDP's traditional defence of public health care (fairness); the "'stealth' campaign" to "Americanize" the system (national distinction) – are all represented in the introductory paragraphs.[43] The use of the term "stealth campaign" was particularly resonant for the NDP, because it simultaneously spoke to issues of Liberal credibility while playing off the issue of a Conservative "hidden agenda," the lingering suspicion (generated largely by war rooms) that the Harper Conservatives would veer to the hard right if they were to gain a parliamentary majority.

However, the story changes after the jump to page A6, when it begins, as the *Globe* report did, to question Layton on his lack of detail on how the federal government should stop the proliferation of private clinics supported by public dollars. The same credibility issues arise when the *Post*, like the *Globe*, introduces Quebec Health Minister Couillard, who points out, rather tersely, that the provinces have jurisdiction over health care. The NDP's attempt to carve out a distinct position on its most important file again becomes tangled in issues of substance, of credibility.

The NDP's health-care position, so carefully crafted in Ottawa and performed in Regina that 13 December, was destined to fall flat. Both the *National Post* and the *Globe* of 14 December (and all other media

outlets) would become preoccupied with the spectacle of David
Wilkins, the US ambassador to Canada, scolding Canadian politicians
for making the United States an object of criticism for political gain
during an election campaign. Newspapers across the country would
run a photograph of Wilkins, finger seeming to point to a Canadian
flag (with the US flag to the ambassador's left) in a purposeful pose,
a reaction to comments by Paul Martin the previous week on the US
role in the climate-change debate. For the record, the *National Post*
did report on the NDP's health-care position, so enthusiastically
delivered by Jack Layton and Shirley Douglas the previous day. But
the story was pushed to a slim side column beneath the front-page
fold, balanced on the opposite side by a piece with the intriguing
headline: "Polar Bears Can Skate If They Have the Right Boots."[44]

For all of this, the NDP's health-care gambit was not a dead loss.
Don Martin, the *National Post* journalist who had "profiled" Layton
the week before, turned his guns on the prime minister in his
15 December column. The writer picked up on a fact, circulated by
competing war rooms, concerning Paul Martin's personal physician
and a connection to a private health clinic. The effect was to offer a
less-than-flattering explanation for Liberal reticence in addressing
the issue of private clinics: "This national trend has been greeted with
stoney [sic] silence from the same prime minister who swore to defend
a pure single tier of treatment, even while his personal physician
runs a private clinic on the side."[45]

Not to be outdone, the NDP war room immediately issued a so-
called "prebuttal," a list of anti–Paul Martin positions anticipated
for the first of the televised debates in the campaign:

> Tonight, Paul Martin may present himself as the defender of
> Canada's public health care system. What he will not say is that:
> He was responsible for the growth in private health care clinics
> under 12 years of Liberal government in five provinces: British
> Columbia, Alberta, Manitoba, Ontario, and Quebec, and that his
> personal doctor runs a private for-profit clinic. After years of
> neglect and rhetoric, when push came to shove, he was unable to
> work with other parties in the House of Commons to safeguard
> Canada's public health care system.[46]

That last line is, of course, a reference to the NDP's role in bringing
down Paul Martin's minority government.

Layton would return to the NDP's health-care position time and again during the first (French-language) debate, and there would at last be a payoff. In a war-room roundup of the media coverage circulated the day after the debate, voices as diverse as the *Gazette* in Montreal, the *Edmonton Journal*, the *Ottawa Citizen*, and Andrew Coyne, speaking on a panel on CBC Television's *The National* would be quoted in praise of Layton's "passionate" defence of health care. But no mention would be made of the health-care issue in the debate coverage in either the *Globe and Mail* or the *National Post*.

The New Democratic Party often claims that it is not well treated by the national media. Several war-room messages circulated on the internal list-serve complained at various times about media bias against the party. Certainly, the spirit of the *Globe and Mail* story of 5 December was at odds with its substance. The headline – "Not Opposed to Private Health Care, Layton Says" – is technically true, but it attempts to infer that a long-held position on fully private health services is, in fact, a major policy shift. The actual substance of the story does not support this inference. The use of a photograph portraying Jack Layton and Svend Robinson in the same frame seems both out of context and unnecessarily rough. It is a low blow, an attempt to attach Layton to Robinson's credibility issues. The paper could have done a better job.

However, the NDP was just as often a victim of its own rhetorical positioning. Its attempt to frame itself as the only credible defender of publicly funded health care failed to gain traction, not because of media bias but because war-room strategists circulated messages that did not stand up to journalistic scrutiny. *How* would the NDP bring the provinces into line over public support of private clinics? *How* would the party deal with the Supreme Court decision in the Chaoulli case? In this respect, the NDP's experience is perhaps a cautionary tale about the limits to strategic political communication. At least, it is a good lesson in the real value of doing one's homework, a particularly valuable form of cultural capital.

Conclusion: Adjusting the Grand Narrative

This book began by proposing an inquiry into the nature of an organizational entity devoted to originating and disseminating partisan political communication at election time. The practices of political war rooms, it argued, could be used to examine some key assumptions about deliberative democracy in our time – specifically, whether strategic political communication effectively excludes everyday people from the open debates that are intended to inform participation in a democracy such as ours. After examining the practices of a war room in action during an election campaign, looking at examples of war-room tactics and strategies applied to election-time concerns, it is fair to say that aspects of strategic political communication often and intentionally mask the true aims and objectives of political actors. It is also fair to say that the relations of power between the fields of politics, journalism, and power make it virtually impossible for those masked aims and objectives to remain concealed for any length of time. However, in politics as in comedy, timing is everything.

The strength of the war room as an organizational entity lies in the conditions of its practical origination: the election campaign. Even if we think they should be deeply considered, the conditions of an election campaign, notably the fast and furious competition to get ahead and stay ahead in the public mind, do not often support a long and thoughtful consideration of the issues and concerns that are brought forward by partisan political players. Senior journalists such as Chantal Hébert of the *Toronto Star* live this reality every day and question the role of competitive media – of mediatization – in the public political debate. "Technological change," Hébert writes, "has brought about a 24/7 news environment in which speed to react and speed to report is often more valued than thoughtful constructive contributions to a debate. That means that rapidity is now more valuable than knowledge and that has translated into a poorer political debate both between parties and in the media. That is especially the case in election campaigns where intelligent debate has been replaced with cheap and often largely irrelevant exchanges via the media proxy between otherwise intelligent men and women."[1]

Hébert's comments recall the political insider's viewpoint, expressed by L. Ian MacDonald, that strategic political communication, notably methods of message control, came about in response to a proliferation of media platforms. In such a hyper-mediatized reality, election campaigns may be thought of as ramped-up versions of the already frenetic practices of everyday political life. They are short, sharp affairs where fortunes may rise and fall on the turn of a phrase. As creatures of this intense and highly competitive democratic moment, political war rooms have been constructed and adapted specifically to address tactical and strategic measures for the benefit of the party that employs them. The people who work in war rooms (at least the one I was admitted to) are well aware of the grand narratives of their party and how those narratives are constructed to play out in the ideological division of political labour. But they also understand on an elemental level that campaigns are about getting members elected to Parliament. Political narratives are meaningless without the elected members to support them.

Especially under the conditions of successive minority governments, war rooms have defaulted to daily responsibility for a number of communicative objectives that do not necessarily play out as they would during an election campaign. One such objective for NDP communication strategists was to craft messages in support of new visionary directives from the strategic brass, directives intended to reflect the "big picture" objectives of the party. This task was in addition to fighting communication skirmishes at the edges of the immediate political reality to support members of Parliament in the daily competition for attention. In short, it has become the job of opposition-research and rapid-response teams to ensure that they guard the advantages earned during successive campaigns, that they prevent the political opposition from gaining an advantage, and that they clear a path for the party to advance when the next election writ is inevitably dropped. The effect has been to create an organization permanently devoted to the accelerated circulation of partisan messages across media.

Yet it has perhaps been slow to dawn on political communicators that none of this matters if publics turn away from partisan messages because those messages are deemed to lack credibility. In an age when social media connect us more than ever before, credible substantiation of political claims has become vitally important, a point that is often strangely lost on some of the more thuggish practitioners of opposition research and rapid response techniques. The bid for credibility based on affirmed claims to a particular vision of the social world is increasingly tested in real time by publics fully capable of separating information dross from politically motivated gambits that run contrary to values, beliefs, understandings, and practices held in the field of power. This testing of truth claims has been supported by the increasing readiness of journalists to talk about the nature of communicative manipulation and the strategic intention behind much that passes for political debate.

While many political pundits predicted that a Conservative majority would bring an end to a constant stream of dirty tricks aimed at political opponents, this did not seem to be the case in the first year of the new government's mandate. The public was treated to stories about a disinformation campaign aimed at a respected long-time Montreal Liberal MP, meant to destabilize his hold on a coveted riding, and an attack ad produced by the National Citizens Coalition (its most famous former president is Stephen Harper) to discredit interim Liberal Leader Bob Rae. An entire public relations tour de force was launched by a former communication specialist in Jason Kenney's ministerial office (Citizenship and Immigration) to rebrand the Alberta tar sands as "ethical oil," the originator of the campaign, Alykhan Velshi, jumping almost immediately to the Prime Minister's Office as director of planning. Nor has the NDP been lily white. When Quebec MP Lise St-Denis crossed the floor to join the Liberals in January 2012, her former party launched a campaign in her riding of anonymous "robo-calls" meant to undermine her credibility.

It is worth bearing in mind that journalists exposed each of these cases to public scrutiny. Journalists such as Frances Russell of the *Winnipeg Free Press* continue to contribute to a growing list of national, regional, and local voices, each speaking to real people in real communities about what they see as a streak of symbolic violence in the strategies and tactics of discredit. And while Russell reserves her ire mainly for the Harper Conservatives, her list of discrediting practices might well apply with equal resonance to previous governments: "Libel chill to stifle public inquiry. Intimidation to turn national institutions into servants of the party in power. Trash talk to destabilize opponents. A 'black book' of procedural dirty tricks to disrupt parliamentary committees. Like former U.S. president Richard Nixon, Prime Minister Stephen Harper wants power 'not to govern the nation but to undermine the government.'"[2]

The *Globe and Mail*'s Jane Taber, a reporter with more than twenty-five years experience on Parliament Hill, distills the concerns of many senior political journalists when she points out, also with respect to the Harper Conservatives, that it is counterproductive for them to alienate the Parliamentary Press Gallery through hyper-control of the political message: "There is too much control from the centre. I understand that discipline is necessary but to clamp down so tightly on individual MPs will end up hurting the party. These MPs have something to say and contribute to the national debate and we aren't hearing their voices."[3]

Taber was writing in 2008 when the Conservatives were seeking yet another majority mandate. So it is more than a bit ironic that by 2011, with a majority in hand, one of the voices cleared by the centre to speak on behalf of the government may have unwittingly called its own bluff over the politics of discredit. It started innocuously enough with a question by the Liberal public safety critic about the government's proposed "Internet snooping" bill, legislation that would give police secret and unprecedented powers to track people online. The minister of public safety, Vic Toews, in the authoritarian tones generated in what one political observer has called the Conservative "anger mill," faced his questioner across the Commons and declared, "He can either stand with us or with the child pornographers."[4]

Such outrageous rhetorical bullying caused a public backlash fed by near universal condemnation from journalists. One anonymous critic – later linked to an Internet address in the House of Commons – lambasted Toews by circulating on Twitter details from court documents outlining aspects of the minister's messy divorce. Typically, the Conservatives trotted out their resident attack dog, John Baird, to accuse the NDP of "sleaze" for secretly releasing Toews's documents, even though the connection to the NDP was far from certain. Indeed, scarcely a week later, Liberal Leader Bob Rae stood in the House of Commons to deliver an unprecedented apology to Toews, revealing that an employee in the Liberal Party's "research bureau" had engineered the campaign.[5]

More ominously for the Conservatives, average Canadians jumped on board a Twitter campaign cheekily entitled "Tell Vic Everything" where message after message detailed the most mundane matters engaging the tweeters at that moment. Journalists reported on this informal campaign, based as it was in a humourous and direct challenge to the credibility of the minister and his government, and originating directly in the field of power. For the first time in its majority mandate, the Harper government opted to "reconsider" legislation it had brought forward.

By this time, however, the party in power was under fire on a different front, one that stood to challenge the very legitimacy of the Harper government. Enterprising reporters had reconstructed a trail of seemingly intentional deceit during the 2011 election campaign in a federal riding in Guelph, Ontario.[6] A campaign of automated telephone calls to Liberal supporters – purportedly originating with Elections Canada – advised that their polling stations had been changed. This caused confusion among voters, possibly causing some to give up in frustration and fail to cast their ballot. The calls were, in fact, fraudulent, a voter-suppression tactic. The initial investigation led to a Conservative Party staffer, who was immediately dismissed. However, as the story entered circulation, opposition MPs claimed to have anecdotal evidence of a widespread campaign of similar calls in dozens of ridings across the country. Amid denials from the Conservatives the matter was handed over to Elections Canada and the RCMP for investigation.[7]

The NDP has also retained and adapted strategic communication measures from successive election campaigns. The party would have us believe, with some merit, that the measures were necessary in order to survive as the fourth party in serial minority Parliaments. Indeed, the actions of the NDP war room in the final days of the 2005–06 campaign do speak to the issue of political survival, but those actions also contain the seeds of a significant, perhaps existential shift in the NDP's vision of its own future on the Canadian political stage.

On a cold winter's day in 2006 with two weeks to go to voting day, I returned to the NDP war room in downtown Ottawa. The grind of the campaign and the tension of the impending 23 January vote were taking a toll. The sense of optimism and possibility that had characterized the first weeks of the campaign were just about gone. The sense of validation arising from the RCMP investigation into income trusts that had set the tone for a return to campaigning in the early New Year was also gone. The mood of the war room was not exactly grim, but the plucky determination to break through, to take the party to the next step as a legitimate force to be reckoned with in Canadian politics, had been overtaken by a more plodding commitment to just get the job done. People were tired. And they were a bit disheartened.

The bald truth is that the NDP had been left behind in the election coverage, and it seemed there was nothing the war room could do to command the attention of journalists or ignite the public imagination. After a passing nod to the New Democrats for their role in motivating the income-trust investigations, the journalistic community had turned its attention to the developing "horse race" between the Conservatives and the Liberals. What was particularly galling for NDP workers was that it appeared that the Conservatives were benefiting from the income-trust affair while the NDP was not. At this stage, the ink and airtime devoted to the NDP was mainly relegated to the concluding paragraphs of stories about other peoples' campaigns, reaction quotes that increasingly gave the New Democrats an "also-ran" aura.

I asked the war-room manager (as I always did) how the NDP "numbers," the internal poll results, were holding up. As always he assured me that they were "stellar." This exchange had become an inside joke in my relationship with the war room. By this point in the campaign I had no expectation of ever seeing the party's poll results, and war-room strategists had no intention of ever sharing them with me, but I continued to inquire indirectly, and they continued to respond in code, and so the game played out. The difference on this day was that the game seemed hollow. There was no energy left. The war room seemed to be struggling to find an issue to get behind, a tactic to exploit, *anything* to distinguish the party from its competitors at this late stage of the contest.

It would take a tactical gimmick to put the wind back in the NDP's sails. In the final week of the campaign, the New Democrats managed to jump back into the public eye with an advertising campaign featuring "real people who used to vote Liberal and are now voting for the NDP."[8] The ad's launch was actually an excuse for Jack

Layton to trot out a new and previously untried appeal to voters. On a swing through Toronto on 16 January, he laid it out: "I'm asking people who have supported the Liberal Party in the past to vote NDP. Lend us your vote while the party you've supported in the past cleans itself up. Vote for us just this once so there's a strong voice in the next Parliament that is standing up for the priorities progressive people believe in."[9]

While the message was clearly tailored to appeal to the disenchanted Liberal crowd, it also contained a subtext in the reference to "progressive people." This was a shot at the Conservatives, the "Harperites," in NDP parlance, who were surely (according to warroom rhetoric) concealing a hidden agenda that would see the dismantling of Canada's social safety net. If voters could see their way through to parking their ballots with the NDP until the dust settled, New Democrats, the "real progressives," would see to it that cherished social programs were protected while Ottawa was cleaned up. Of course, so much the better if the NDP managed to garner enough support to hold the balance of power in a minority government.

There is no question that the "lend me your vote" tactic was a gamble, a hoped-for exploitation of what the NDP saw as enduring weaknesses in both the Conservative and Liberal positions. By now, as intended, concerns over Liberal integrity had become the overarching ballot-box issue, underscored by the very public and heavily reported RCMP investigation into income trusts. The "lend us your votes" gambit was an attempt to regain some of the credit for having motivated the investigation in a bid to cash in on the voter fluidity that seemed to be showing up in public-opinion polls.

In early January, as Ralph Goodale prepared for his "interview" with police investigators, the main polling companies had noted that the gap between Liberal and Conservative numbers was beginning to close. By the time I visited the war room that January day, the Conservatives had pulled into a comfortable ten-point lead, with some pollsters predicting a Harper majority. The NDP needed to get back on track lest the Liberals, who were aware of their own situation and were campaigning hard for every available vote, managed to repeat recent history and shore up support at the expense of the NDP. Conversely, if the New Democrats could continue to hammer away at Liberal integrity while resurrecting oft-cited doubts about a "concealed" Conservative agenda, the party could present itself as the only credible alternative, a place for confused and disheartened Liberals to park their ballots.

The truly breathtaking element of this unusual proposal was that it did not offer any policy options to Canadians. There was no vision of the social world, no sense of a "better way" being offered for thoughtful consideration. The entire strategy was based on discredit arising from a generalized mistrust of the Tories and Liberals, framed by the NDP and extended to Ottawa, the place, and now emerging metonym for big-party political dysfunction.

Considered from another angle, the objective of the "lend us your votes" appeal was to affect a transfer, in trust, of symbolic capital from the field of power and publics *away* from one ideological area of support to another. This transfer is the aim of all competition in the field of politics, but in this case the intent was to effectively reverse the "symbolic and material guarantees" of "the group" by offering a guarantee on the guarantee. The *idea* of the guarantee on offer was of much greater consequence than the offer itself, simply because the NDP was in no position to guarantee anything. However, by placing the idea of a guarantee in wide circulation at the very end of the election campaign when questions about its integrity were less likely to be asked, by convincing journalists that this odd proposal was worthy of a news story or two, by claiming it as a worthy option among competing interests, and by displacing the motivating concern onto the connotation of a "broken Ottawa," the war room thought it could accomplish much more than would have been possible by sticking to the policy script.

This was certainly a distinct position: asking voters from the "natural governing party" for their support in order to obtain a mandate to prove that their support was warranted. But was it credible? The proposal even left Ed Broadbent, a former leader of the NDP, shaking his head in wonder at its apparent audacity. On an edition of the popular CBC Newsworld program *Politics with Don Newman*, Broadbent, speaking as a pundit on a political panel, wondered out loud when the NDP would *return* all of those Liberal votes that had been loaned out? Then fortune turned its fickle head and gave the NDP a toothy grin.

On the day following the launch of Layton's vote-lending appeal, Stephen Harper tried to assuage lingering doubts about a "Conservative hidden agenda." He ruminated that a "Conservative majority government would be kept in check by the judges, senators and federal bureaucrats who owe their jobs to the Liberals."[10] The comment exploded across the front pages and became the lead item on radio and television newscasts across the land. Harper would spend the rest of the week explaining that his words were meant to "reassure those voters who still fear his party may change the Canadian social fabric."[11] But the damage was done. Clearly, some voters were put off by the remark, sensing that rather than be constrained by Liberal appointments, a Conservative majority would begin to purge the courts and bureaucracy of them. The polls showed the Tories slipping into minority-government territory. On 23 January the Conservatives elected 124 members to the Liberals' 103. The Bloc Québécois took 51 seats. One independent member was elected. The New Democratic Party elected 29 members with 17.5 per cent of the popular vote, just shy of the number of seats needed to wield the balance of power.[12]

Of all the statistics from election night, that 17.5 popular-vote percentage is most revealing because it was *statistically identical* to the overnight poll results from every week of the campaign. There was an increase over the 2004 election results when the NDP took 19 seats with 15.7 per cent of the popular vote, but it is fair to say that the efforts of the NDP war room did not significantly influence *general* NDP support across the country from one week to the next over the course of the 2005–06 campaign. There is, however, more to the story.

As party analysts picked over the entrails of the vote distribution, they saw small movements in ridings where the New Democrats were the strong second choice, movements that had given an edge to the NDP candidate. In many cases the second choice for voters was helped into first place by the public profile of the candidate. Olivia Chow, a former Toronto city councillor and wife of Jack Layton, took the Trinity–Spadina riding from Liberal incumbent Tony Ianno by about 3,700 votes. High-profile labour organizer Peggy Nash took the Toronto riding of Parkdale–High Park from Liberal Sarmite (Sam) Bulte by about 2,300 votes. In ridings such as Hamilton East–Stoney Creek, the NDP candidate was able to win the riding largely because of issues with the Liberal incumbent. Voters in Hamilton East–Stoney Creek likely remembered the way long-time representative Sheila Copps (a close supporter of Jean Chrétien) had been treated when the Paul Martin team squeezed her out of the riding nomination in favour of Tony Valeri. NDP candidate Wayne Marston won the riding by 460 votes.[13]

This incremental movement had paid big dividends, as the party's chief strategists had hoped. Going into the campaign, it was thought that if enough close ridings could be enticed into the NDP camp, the party could conceivably regain its position as a legitimate alternative, a party on the rise, a possibility not witnessed since 1988 when the New Democrats under Ed Broadbent took forty-three seats.[14] The "lend us your votes" proposition, then, had been played out less on the grand canvas of the national campaign than at street level in ridings such as Hamilton East–Stoney Creek and Parkdale–High Park, places where the tactics of discredit concerning corrupt Liberals and hidden-agenda Conservatives would have particular resonance. So, why bother to run a national campaign at all? Why invest in the expense of a war room if the real battles were being fought and won in specific closely contested ridings?

The party's political strategists would later reveal that the election of 2005–06 had three connected and subsumed objectives. Each of these objectives seems obvious in hindsight, but they are worth outlining because they tell us much about the long-term strategic intentions of the party, intentions that would eventually help to put the NDP into the offices of the official opposition.

First and foremost, the 2006 election was meant to re-establish the party's core of support, the 17 or 18 per cent of Canadians the NDP can generally depend on for their votes. Secondly, the NDP wanted to regain the ten seats it had lost in 2004, Jack Layton's first federal election campaign. Achieving this would bring the party back to the place it had occupied before the losses of 2004, give the impression of forward momentum, and lend credence to Layton's leadership. Thirdly, there was a good chance that the NDP would hold the balance of power if it could re-establish its numbers in the House of Commons. That did not happen.

What did happen is, faced with another minority government and possibly another after that, the party's inner circle of strategists began implementing a long-term grand strategy based on a new and improved overarching narrative, drawing in part on strategies that had been tested and lessons learned in the 2005–06 contest. This grand strategy would be gradually introduced into the messaging used by the party, incrementally moving the NDP closer to real power.

On an unexpectedly warm winter's day in February 2012, I passed through security and made my way to the opposition party offices in the Centre Block on Parliament Hill. I had an appointment with Brad Lavigne, the principal secretary to the opposition leader. In previous incarnations, Lavigne had served as the director of strategic communications to Jack Layton and, in the 2011 election campaign, as the national campaign director. Lavigne was a member of a tight circle of NDP strategists who followed Layton into the party after he was elected leader in 2003. Other members of the circle include names that are familiar in New Democrat circles, but generally less so outside of the party: former Layton chief of staff Anne McGrath, long-time mentor and supporter Terry Grier, and none other than Brian Topp, who stayed close to the action after being recruited to manage the NDP war room in 2004.[15] Party luminaries such as Ed Broadbent and former Saskatchewan premier Allan Blakeney have been called upon over the years to add their experience and wisdom.

As we sat down to talk, a key point among many that Lavigne wanted to make was that this strategic group was in place, pretty much intact, throughout the Layton years. During that time the Liberals had changed leaders four times and were now working on a fifth; the Conservatives had burned through a half-dozen chiefs of staff and seemingly countless directors of communication. Layton and his hand-picked circle of advisers had remained together. This was the group (give or take a member) that had engineered the 2005–06 campaign in response to the disappointing losses in 2004. And it was the group that, under Layton's leadership, began to retool the party's grand narrative and redesign its messages in order to consciously move the NDP away from its big government, program-for-everything past toward a smaller, more focused, yet more broadly resonant set of aims and objectives. The first objective was to grow the number of people willing to commit their vote to the NDP.

Under the direction of the inner circle, the party had commissioned studies. It had examined polling data and voter preferences. It had identified a profile for a group of voters, says Lavigne, that would bring the NDP its needed boost in numbers: "This next group [beyond the core] was as likely to be men as women. They were slightly older than our base. They were slightly higher on the food chain at work. They were middle management perhaps, they lived in medium-sized cities like Kamloops and Edmonton as opposed to our base that lived in big cities like Toronto or Vancouver ... And so we took this data and we built the campaign around that. It was the most focused we'd ever been."[16] Lavigne did not mention during our conversation that this tranche of voters corresponds nicely with a fairly large chunk of the Liberal base.

However, Brian Topp has written about this demographic in another context, and the possibilities, brought forward at the time by Jack Layton, of using NDP argument strategies to bring them onside. Layton's belief, according to Topp, was that the Liberal Party is "made up of two wings. One – usually small and weak – believes in 'positive liberty,' in an active role for government to make people's lives better ... The other wing – the much stronger and more influential one – believes in 'negative liberty,' in defending people's legal and human rights."[17] Party strategists knew the NDP could benefit, perhaps greatly, if it could persuade the more-or-less marginalized group of "left Liberals" to make their home with the NDP.

For this shift to happen, however, the NDP would have to change. Talk of multi-billion dollar programs such as universal child care would have to be abandoned. There would be no room for taxing inheritances to pay for social programs. Money for programs would come from taxing corporations, entities not likely to support the NDP anyway. In the meantime, the party would promise small, meaningful, affordable, and broad-based measures, as Lavigne would characterize them, measures that were common-sensical and easily accomplished:

I'm not going to fix every problem that you have, said the social democrat to the voter. But I can give you a break on your home heating. I'm going to take the GST off. It's reasonable, it's doable, I can do it with one stroke of a pen and you're going to see ten, twenty, thirty bucks a month off your heating bill. So, we shrunk the offer so that it was easily understandable and it would hit right to the heart. Small things. Small business, tax cuts. Easily understandable. That was our jobs strategy. They [the Conservatives] are for the big guys, the foreign-owned big guys who are making billions and usually probably screwing you over in some capacity versus us, the opposite, who are looking out for the small business operator, working hard, playing by the rules, we just want to give them a break. They will create the jobs.

When I suggested to Lavigne that some of these measures sounded downright Liberal, he looked away and changed the subject.

Clearly, the party was walking a delicate line. It could not run the risk of alienating its core supporters, but it had made the decision to seek its future in appeals to a more moderate and centrist voting public, a middle-class public. To credibly accomplish such a feat required not so much a shift in political philosophy (though many would debate this) as a shift in registers. The vast NDP social justice register – with its dedication to universal health care, decent living standards for working families, and protection for the elderly – would have to be simultaneously maintained and tweaked. Social justice would now include "deliverables" such as a monthly tax break and the recognition that small businesses need modest support to create jobs. Middle-class voters would be given assurance that elderly parents would find nursing home spaces without breaking the bank. "When you take a look at our platform it was moderate, quite moderate," says Lavigne: "small business tax cuts, tax credits for jobs, silent on the Middle East, not poking anybody in the eye, talking about middle-class families, purposefully using language that would be inclusive not exclusive."

A second appeal to left-centrist voters was taken directly from the NDP playbook in the closing days of the 2005–06 campaign. The "lend us your votes" gambit had asked voters to see the NDP as stewards, protecting their interests while Ottawa, made dysfunctional by the big parties, got its act together. The "Ottawa is broken" theme was trotted out and repurposed. With some symbolic help from Barak Obama's successful 2008 "Hope and Change" campaign, the NDP set itself up as the party that would "fix" Ottawa. In Lavigne's words, "This place is broken; let's fix it. Nice and tight. And that way any grievance that you have against Ottawa, whether it's the HST, spon-sorship scandal, they take my money, they make too much. Any prob-lem that you've got, gun registry, no gun registry, doesn't matter, became swept up in our Ottawa's-broken-let's-fix-it attitude."

Other strategic measures were adopted and integrated into the larger narrative. In successive campaigns the NDP would all but ignore the Liberals, placing themselves in direct contention with the Conservatives. The party would eschew policy announcements for "colour" events, avoiding the quagmire of drawn-out explanations, removing themselves as a target for journalists and rapid responses from competing camps. By the 2011 campaign, the war room had developed a system. Based on the calendar of Layton's campaign stops, it would deliver a specific "hit" on the most credible local non-NDP candidate. Instead of plotting to undermine Layton, the opposition team would be diverted in the scramble to repair the damage to its own campaign. As opposition research was put into play by war-room operatives, Layton would move on to the next event and the one after that. As Lavigne describes it, the NDP had managed to develop its own "formidable machine" with a not-so-secret weapon: a leader who had grown into an experienced and trusted brand.

Since Layton's death, there has been much speculation about the true state of his health during the spring election campaign of 2011. The visual evidence was obvious: he entered the campaign on crutches, recovering from a broken hip. Was this injury in some way connected to the prostate cancer he had been treated for during the previous year? No one was to know. As the campaign progressed, Layton, who at the beginning had appeared thin and sick and tired, began to take on energy and colour. He looked like he was gaining some weight. He exchanged his crutches for a spiffy black cane and played it as a prop, part Lucien Bouchard and part Charlie Chaplin. It was a plucky performance worthy of a seasoned and canny political actor, and it brought confidence to the thought that his health problems were manageable.

There can be no doubt that it was Jack Layton's choice to throw himself, full bore, into the 2011 contest. But it is also certain that without him, the NDP's grand strategy would have fallen apart. Years of adapting, testing, thinking, and rethinking would have been for naught. The inner circle of advisers and strategists knew from commissioned research that Layton scored highest among the leaders on metrics such as trust and on the fact that average people genuinely liked him. They also knew that Layton was well recognized and regarded in Quebec, much more so than Stephen Harper or Michael Ignatieff. And the party was betting that its new grand narrative would deliver results based on a strategy that placed Layton firmly in the public eye, supported by the knowledge from its internal polls that, behind the Bloc Québécois, the NDP was the *overwhelming second choice of Quebec voters*. What the NDP needed was a credible message that could cut through the Bloc's boilerplate without alienating supporters in the rest of the country.

"We would talk up how Jack 'gets' Quebec," says Lavigne. "We played up his roots in Quebec, and we had a very sophisticated approach not to attack the Bloc. Not to attack its leader. But what we would do is we would attack the ineffectiveness of Ottawa. We would say to a Bloc voter – I am paraphrasing here – You're against Canadian troops being in Afghanistan. So you vote for the Bloc and send a Bloc representative [to Parliament] yet we're still in Afghanistan. You want Canada to take a leadership role in the fight against climate change, so you vote for the Bloc. You send a Bloc representative to Ottawa. You see where I'm going? Nothing happens."

This was the negative message, subtly delivered, resting on the overarching theme of a "broken Ottawa" and meant to get Bloc supporters thinking about the practical effectiveness of the party they had supported for two decades, a party increasingly under scrutiny by its own base. The second message, the positive message, delivered by a man who was increasingly and affectionately embraced by Quebecers as *le bon Jack*, sought to build a bridge of common and credible value concerns that played the same in Quebec as in the rest of the country. As Lavigne puts it, "We would go into Quebec and we would talk about the same things as we were in Winnipeg. Like, we would talk about making ends meet. The notion that all Quebecers want to talk about is language, the constitution and their place in Canada is something that we found not to be true. They want to talk about, 'How do I support my kids? How do I save up for retirement? How do I put my mom in a home where she gets the care she needs?' And we said, 'Well wait a minute, that's exactly what the folks in Winnipeg and the folks in St. John's are talking about.'"

But to make its strategy work, the NDP needed a way to make Bloc voters abandon their party. To go on a full frontal attack against Gilles Duceppe would certainly backfire in much the same way that an attack on Buzz Hargrove would have backfired in 2005–06. So it must have seemed that fortune was again smiling on the NDP when the Bloc leader lit the fuse that would blow up his own campaign and subsequently, the Bloc Québécois itself.

When Gilles Duceppe stepped in front of the Parti Québécois annual convention on 16 and 17 April and, shoulder to shoulder with Pauline Marois, said, "*Et tout redevient encore possible*," he was echoing the separatist slogan of the 1995 referendum, "*Oui, et tout devient possible*."[18] He really had no choice. The PQ membership had endorsed a number of motions intended to give a kick to the sleeping dogs of the language wars. Duceppe's own sovereigntist credentials were on the line. But he could not have anticipated the backlash from so many Quebecers who were simply not prepared to endorse another referendum like the ones that had so divided them in the past. Support for the Bloc, as anticipated by the NDP's inner circle, began to drain away, straight to the New Democrats. And there was Jack Layton with a moderate and "progressive" message, slinging pints at local watering holes, showing up at "colour" events in a Montreal Canadiens' jersey (the Habs were battling Boston in the playoffs at the time), playing up his Quebec roots in imperfect but forgivable French. He would make appearance after appearance in ridings across the province, wielding his black cane, reminding people of that other charismatic Quebecer with a cane, reinforcing the tag line to the closing ads for the NDP campaign, "You know where I stand. You know I'm a fighter. And I won't stop until the job is done!"

It was a masterful performance, the performance of a lifetime.

Where was the NDP war room in all of this? Clearly it was hard at work providing cover for Layton as he made his way across the country, campaign stop by campaign stop. But the war room also kept a low profile. This was Layton's campaign, the messages were clear, the Conservatives (mostly) positioned as the well-defined enemy. Discipline was the order of the day. Opposition research outside of the bounds of the daily campaign grind was mainly reserved for big "hits." One of those hits came during the English-language debate of 12 April 2011 when Layton asked a very simple question of Liberal Leader Michael Ignatieff: "Why do you have the worst attendance record in the House of Commons?" Ignatieff had no answer.

It seemed like a reasonable and spontaneous question. It was anything but. In fact, Lavigne, then national campaign director, had been looking for a way to piggyback on Conservative efforts to characterize Ignatieff as a political opportunist, a man who had spent three decades out of the country, deigning to return only to assume the prime minister's mantle. The Conservatives had spent millions on attack ads with the tag line "He didn't come back for you." So when the matter of Ignatieff's attendance came up in media reports, Lavigne decided to test it in a focus group. "I found this to be interesting because we had a very good track record in the house. So I said, 'Test this, test the attendance thing, just we'll see where it goes. If it doesn't do well, we'll just drop it. [The researcher] calls from the focus group and says, 'This has got something. This has captured people's imagination, the notion that you don't show up for work.

And that's on top of everything they [the focus group] knew about him from the other inputs [the Conservative ads].' And Iggy did not have a reply. That's when the thing went through the roof."

It was a classic attack on Ignatieff's credibility. A man who had spent much of his life away from Canada, who had been targeted in attack ads for this absence, did not appear to think it was all that necessary to show up for work. And when prodded on his record, this former Harvard professor was unable or unwilling to answer a simple question. It was the effective end of Ignatieff's campaign.

By the time the dust had settled on the election of 2011, the NDP had achieved its coveted breakthrough: 103 seats, 59 of them from Quebec. The Bloc was all but wiped out, reduced to four seats. Leader Gilles Duceppe lost his own seat and left politics. The Conservatives would govern with a majority of 167 in the House of Commons. The Liberals were reduced to 34 seats, an historic low. There would be a defection here and there as the Forty-First Parliament readied itself to sit, but the proportions held.

It is not possible to predict the future of the NDP or any political party. If there is one reality that this book underscores, it is that there are too many inputs, too many wild cards that conspire to make folly of the best laid plans of political actors. Jack Layton's death was certainly one of those wild cards. However, it is possible to suggest that certain strategic positions, large and small, will continue to inform the party as it moves forward. For example, the NDP cannot afford to abandon its winning strategy for Quebec, its appeal to those small, incremental, and broadly resonant "deliverables" that were embraced so fully when brought forward by a charismatic leader. And while the party cannot resurrect Jack Layton, it can (and most certainly will) use his memory to help frame and deliver its messages. In this, Tommy Douglas is likely to get some spiritual support on the campaign trail. Hallelujah *encore*!

Indeed, the new NDP narrative, the successful narrative, now seems to be taking firm root within the party mythology. Upon his withdrawal from the race to replace Layton, leadership candidate Romeo Saganash endorsed a political roadmap that broadly underscores many of the registers the party has adopted in support of its new narrative: "Building on the support we have gained in Quebec, reaching out to rural and suburban voters, and engaging the 40 percent of Canadians who did not vote in the last election will all be important steps for the next leader." Saganash's vision for moving the party forward might just as well have been, and likely was, crafted by one of the party's strategic political communicators.

Pierre Bourdieu might argue that the rules governing the competition for recognition are always in flux, especially in the political field where power relations must literally be reproduced and reinforced continuously across divides predicated on ideological distinction.[19] From this elevated theoretical viewpoint, the excesses of partisanship are naturally aimed at describing the social world, then struggling to control a legitimate vision of that world. The conduct of strategic political communicators is therefore meant to reinforce the internal "structure of the social space" of the political party for the benefit of those who share that space. What the strategists often forget is that there *is* such a thing as a collective memory. It is both internal and external to the social space of the party, and journalists are often its most ardent keepers.[20] The tactics of discredit that characterized the income-trust affair of the 2005–06 campaign came back to haunt the NDP. As details emerged, journalists one after another stepped forward to condemn the treatment of Ralph Goodale. Editorialists and columnists from all the major dailies – the *Toronto Star*, the *Globe and Mail,* the *Ottawa Citizen* among them – served notice on the NDP and other parties that an ethical line had been crossed.[21] The 2005–06 campaign tested the ethical centre of the NDP war room and found it wanting.

Did the party take measures to get its house in order? Bourdieu's conceptual position would suggest so. Indeed, it suggests that something quite remarkable and viscerally transformative happened. From the campaign of 2005–06 through the election of 2011, the NDP was able to simultaneously reinvent the internal structure of its own social space while presenting a new narrative in support of a resonant vision of the social world, a vision that was processed and extended, accepted and rewarded as *credible* by diverse publics operating in the field of power. As we have seen, such credibility is the key to the kingdom, the symbolic capital required to put forward a legitimate vision of the social world. It is extraordinarily valuable.

The value attached to credibility, reflected in the NDP's success, may explain why so many political actors seem so ready to go to the barricades when externally applied matters of credibility challenge ideological belief systems. When the divisions that necessarily characterize the distinction between political parties become inflexible, when there is no incentive to admit the legitimacy of an opposing point of view, the default reaction to reasonable debate is to push back, to undermine, to discredit one's legitimate opponents. Under these conditions the divide between ideological positions easily transforms into a barrier. On one side of the barrier are political agents who view themselves very much as practitioners within a field, complete with immanent laws and relations of power that support a narrowly defined vision of their social world. On the other side is everything else including journalists, political opponents, and non-aligned publics. The war-room tactics of extreme discredit and strategies of hyper-control make perfect sense in such a divided vision of the social world. But when everyone is challenged to make a choice – to "stand with us or with the child pornographers" – the legitimate value of policy proposals from political adversaries, publicly generated contrary ideas, and valid journalistic criticism is squaundered.

Given that *all* matters of democratic public concern are granted credibility in the complex sphere of interactions between political actors, journalists, and publics, it is a dangerous game to opt for the tactics of discredit as a standard response to reasonable concerns. Among other consequences, it makes it very difficult for political parties to grow sustainably much beyond their base, since anyone beyond the ideological barrier is suspect, and anyone who questions the party wisdom from within is a heretic. Given the right plan and the right circumstances, reasonable and credible propositions presented and debated in public space can be made to appeal to more voters. The NDP was the net beneficiary of this strategy in 2011. Its war room succeeded largely by sticking to a supporting role, by (mostly) foregoing the darker arts of strategic communication in favour of a tough but supportable program of solid opposition research and rapid response, crafted to transparently challenge the public record of political opponents in their ridings rather than engage in broadly applied smear campaigns.

Political organizations of all stripes now have a decision to make with respect to the nature of the strategic political communication they choose to practice. They can try to increase deniability by using surrogates to cover their tracks, burrowing more deeply into the realm of discredit and toxic intentions; or they can come clean and practice in the open, within the bounds of credible and creditable political purpose.

The first option represents a strategy of declining returns in the competition for credibility. As the strategies and tactics of discredit are inevitably exposed, as patterns of toxic conduct become apparent, it does not matter in the slightest whether evidentiary connections can be made to one party or the other. Instead, we enter a realm of imaginary possibility. Given the patterns of deceit already in circulation, is it possible to imagine in today's Canada that strategists working for a political party would engage in a secret campaign to destabilize the opposition's vote in ridings where it would benefit the party doing the destabilizing? Is it credible to say that such a thing could happen? The answer has the potential to call into question the democratically conferred legitimacy of an entire government.

Nowhere does this suggest that war rooms should be outlawed, even if such a thing were possible. There is still a place in the debates from which political decisions rightly flow for diligent research into the records of political opponents and, indeed, the requirement to put those records *on* the record in the public good. But if Ottawa is indeed "broken," the only self-interested path to fixing it lies in communication practices that bypass the dark arts to take a higher road. Given the growing willingness of individuals to mobilize new communication technologies to confront outrageous behaviour, to breach the communicative barricades when pushed to swallow offensive truth claims or when faced with false ultimatums, and given the increased willingness of journalists to track down the perpetrators of dirty tricks and expose them to public scrutiny, the high road is fast becoming the only sensible and fruitful way forward.

Notes

INTRODUCTION

1 Tonda McCharles, "Tory 'War Room' Primed for Battle," *Toronto Star*, 7 September 2008, http://www.thestar.com/News/Canada/article/492231.
2 Kirsten Shane, "Tories Running Leaner War Room, Focused on Winning Majority," *The Hill Times*, 4 April 2011, http://www.hilltimes.com/news/2011/04/04/tories-running-leaner-war-room-focused-on-winning-majority/25769.
3 Tom Flanagan, *Harper's Team*, 316–17.
4 Chris Hegedus and D.A. Pennebaker, *The War Room*.
5 Bill Nichols, *Newsreel*; Shawn Parry-Giles and Trevor Parry-Giles, "Meta-Imaging, The War Room and the Hyperreality of US Politics," 28–45.
6 Jessica Bruno, "NDP War Room Working 16 Hour Days, Surviving on Caffeine and Adrenaline," *The Hill Times*, 4 April 2011.
7 James Travers, "Harper's Message Leaves Nothing to Chance," *Toronto Star*, 20 May 2010, http://www.thestar.com/news/canada/article/811794--travers-harper-s-message-leaves-nothing-to-chance.
8 Mike Blanchfield and Jim Bronskill, "Harper's Message Event Proposals Reveal Hyper-Extreme Political Control," Canadian Press, 6 June 2010.
9 David Hogarth, "Agency and Structure in Cultural Production"; Barry Dornfeld, *Producing Public Television, Producing Public Culture*; Georgina Born, *Uncertain Vision*; John Van Maanen, *Reframing Organizational Culture*; Ester Reiter, *Making Fast Food*.

CHAPTER ONE

1 T.C. Douglas, "Mouseland," 1944, transcript, Douglas-Coldwell Foundation, http://www.dcf.ca/en/mouseland.htm.

2 Randall Collins, "The Durkheimian Tradition in Conflict Sociology," 115.
3 Nicholas Garnham, *Capitalism and Communication*, 107.
4 William Kaplan, *Belonging: The Meaning and Future of Canadian Citizenship*, 252.
5 Arjun Appadurai, *Modernity at Large: Cultural Dimensions of Globalization*.
6 Robert Jensen, "Has a Free Press Helped to Kill Democracy?," 1–6.
7 Richard Pierce, "It Is Designed That the Country Shall Be Furnished Once a Moneth (or If Any Glut of Occurrences Happen, Oftener) with an Account of Such Considerable Things As Have Arrived unto Our Notice," *Publick Occurrences Both Forreign and Domestick*.
8 Nicholas A. Valentino, "The Impact of Political Advertising on Knowledge, Internet Information Seeking, and Candidate Preference," 337–54; Glenn W. Richardson, "Looking for Meaning in All the Wrong Places," 775–800; Bruce E. Pinkleton, "Effects of Print Comparative Advertising on Political Decision-Making and Participation," 24–36; Doris A. Graber, "Political Communication Faces the 21st Century," 479–507; Lisbeth Lipari, "Polling as Ritual," 83–102; Carsten Reinemann and Marcus Mauer, "Unifying or Polarizing? Short-Term Effects and Postdebate Consequences of Different Rhetorical Strategies in Televised Debates," *Journal of Communcation* 55, no. 4 (2005): 775–94; Carl H. Botan and Maureen Taylor, "The Role of Trust in Channels of Strategic Communication for Building Civil Society," 685–702; Josh Boyd, "The Rhetorical Construction of Trust Online," 392–410; Matthew Mendelsohn, "Television's Frames in the 1988 Canadian Election," 1–17; June Woong Rhee, "Strategy and Issue Frames in Election Campaign Coverage, 26–47; Shawn J. Parry-Giles and Trevor Parry-Giles, "Meta-Imaging, The War Room and the Hyperreality of U.S. Politics," 28–45.
9 Richard Nadeau, Neil Nevitte, Elisabeth Gidengil and André Blais, "Election Campaigns as Information Campaigns: Who Learns What and Does It Matter?," 242–3.
10 Ibid.
11 Neil Nevitte, *The Decline of Deference: Canadian Value Change in Cross-National Perspective*, 63.
12 Ibid., 100.
13 William O. Gilsdorf and Robert Bernier, "Journalistic Practices in Covering Federal Election Campaigns in Canada," 3.
14 Ibid.
15 Nadeau et al., "Election Campaigns," 243.

16 Ibid.

17 L. Ian MacDonald, editor *Policy Options Magazine*, in discussion with the author, March 2008.

18 Jürgen Habermas, *The Structural Transformation of the Public Sphere: An Inquiry into a Category of Bourgeois Society*.

19 Hans-Peter Müller, "Social Structure and Civil Religion: Legitimation Crisis in a Late-Durkheimian Perspective," 129–58.

20 Warren Kinsella, *Kicking Ass in Canadian Politics*; MacDonald, in discussion with the author, 2008.

21 Thomas H. McLeod and Ian McLeod, *Tommy Douglas: The Road to Jerusalem*; Edward Whelan and Pemrose Whelan, *Touched by Tommy*.

22 Randall Collins, "The Durkheimian Tradition in Conflict Sociology," 107–28.

23 Ibid., 226–8.

24 Heine Andersen, "Functionalism," 213–34.

25 Anthony Giddens, *Captialism and Modern Social Theory*, 80.

26 John Rawls, *Political Liberalism*.

CHAPTER TWO

1 Pierre Bourdieu, "The Forms of Capital," 241.

2 Rodney Benson and Erik Neveu, *Bourdieu and the Journalistic Field*; Patrick Champagne, "The 'Double Dependency,'" 48–63; Bourdieu, *On Television*; Bourdieu, *The Logic of Practice*.

3 Bourdieu, *In Other Words*.

4 Bourdieu, "The Political Field, the Social Field, and the Journalistic Field," 29–47.

5 Bourdieu and Jean-Claude Passeron, *Reproduction in Education, Society and Culture*, 3–9.

6 John Lechte, *Fifty Key Contemporary Thinkers*; Franck Poupeau, "Reasons for Domination, Bourdieu versus Habermas," 69–87.

7 Bourdieu, *Outline of a Theory of Practice*; Hans-Peter Müller, "Social Structure and Civil Religion," 129–58.

8 Anthony Giddens, *The Constitution of Society*, 14.

9 Ira Cohen, *Structuration Theory: Anthony Giddens and the Constitution of Social Life*.

10 Giddens, *Constitution of Society*, xxiii; Cohen, *Structuration Theory*, 1989.

11 Derek Layder, *Structure, Interaction and Social Theory*.

12 Giddens, *Constitution of Society*, 17.

13 Michel de Certeau, *The Practice of Everyday Life*.
14 Bourdieu, "The Political Field, the Social Field, and the Journalistic Field," 30.
15 Bourdieu and Loïc J.D. Wacquant, *An Invitation to Reflexive Sociology*.
16 Benson and Neveu, *Bourdieu and the Journalistic Field*, 3.
17 Bourdieu, "Forms of Capital," 188.
18 Bourdieu, *The Logic of Practice*, 120.
19 Bourdieu, 135.
20 Ibid., 137 (my italics).
21 Bourdieu, *Theory of Practice*, 4–6.
22 Bourdieu, *In Other Words*, 128.
23 Patrick Champagne, "Double Dependency," 50.
24 Bourdieu, *On Television*, 70.
25 Champagne, "Double Dependency," 49.
26 Ibid.
27 Bourdieu, *In Other Words*, 135.
28 Raymond Williams, *The Sociology of Culture*.
29 This theoretical application bridges Habermas's historical theorization of the eighteenth century emergence of the bourgeois public sphere and Bourdieu's conceptualization of competing fields. Habermas's ideal public sphere remains the starting point for most discussions of communication in democratic public space (Habermas 1969/1991), even if its shortcomings have been well documented by successive generations of scholars including Fraser (1990), Stallybrass and White (1986), Eley (1987), Felski (1989), Scott (1990), Mansbridge (1996), and Dean (1992). In short, the idea that an emergent class of leisured males, through an abandonment of status and its replacement by rational-critical debate, could arrive at legitimate decisions in the public good (to be leveraged through publicity to obtain political power from a sovereign entity) has been repeatedly challenged by those who see this "public sphere" as a tool of hegemony rather than emancipation. Bourdieu's field of power admits multiple fields of human endeavour in a hierarchy of power relations that depend on self-affirmed status in and among those fields. Warner (2003) comes closest to addressing the most damning critique of Habermas's ideal public sphere: the sense of privilege for a dominant group at the expense of the powerless. He does so by placing appellative power and discernment in the hands of free individuals, irrespective of their social status. In this manner, Bourdieu's fields become subject to forms of external validation, while Habermas's public sphere is reconsidered as a place of wide

communicative action where the power to confer credibility lies with the free choice of individuals.

30 Michael Warner, *Publics and Counterpublics*, 89.

31 Bourdieu, *Practical Reason: On the Theory of Action*.

32 Chantal Hébert, *Toronto Star* political columnist, in discussion with the author, January 2008.

33 Ibid.

34 Tom Parry, national reporter CBC Radio, in discussion with the author, February 2008.

35 Warren Kinsella, *Kicking Ass in Canadian Politics*.

36 Parry, in discussion with the author, February 2008.

37 Ibid.

38 Jürgen Habermas, *The Theory of Communicative Action*, vol. 1, *Reason and the Rationalization of Society*.

39 Bourdieu, *Logic of Practice*.

40 Véronique Rodriguez, "'*Memoire Ardent*' by Gilbert Boyer, or When Politics Penetrates Contemporary Art," 193–227.

41 Shmuel Noah Eisenstadt, *Social Differentiation and Stratification*; Eisenstadt, *Tradition, Change and Modernity*; Paul Colomy, *Neofunctionalist Sociology*, 138.

42 Stanley Deetz, *Democracy in an Age of Corporate Colonization*.

CHAPTER THREE

1 Tony Blair, "Our Nation's Future – Public Life," 14 June 2007, http://ukingermany.fco.gov.uk/en/news/?view=Speech&id=4616100.

2 "Right Sermon, Wrong Preacher," *The Guardian*, 13 June 2007, http://www.guardian.co.uk/commentisfree/2007/jun/13/media. pressandpublishing?INTCMP=SRCH).

3 George Stephanopoulos, *All Too Human: A Political Education*.

4 Bruce Newman, *The Mass Marketing of Politics*, 111.

5 Paul Wells, *Right Side Up: The Fall of Paul Martin and the Rise of Stephen Harper's New Conservatism*.

6 The organizational structure of the NDP campaign has been constructed here from a combination of observations made by the author while observing the war room in action during the 2005–06 campaign and material taken from informal conversations with campaign workers. These workers agreed to speak about matters of organization rather than party policy and asked for confidentiality concerning their identity. Where

matters of organizational structure are clarified by such conversations and confirmed by observation their wishes have been respected.

7 Warren Kinsella, *Kicking Ass in Canadian Politics*.

8 Andrew Mills, "Layton Lashes Out over Dog Blunder," *Toronto Star*, 30 December 2005.

9 Stephen Taylor, "Campaign Secrets," *Conservative Party of Canada Pundit*, 26 January 2006, http://www.stephentaylor.ca/page/112/.

10 Tom Parry, national reporter CBC Radio, in discussion with the author, February 2008.

11 Todd Gitlin, *The Whole World Is Watching: Mass Media in the Making and Unmaking of the Left*, 7.

12 Erving Goffman, *Frame Analysis: An Essay on the Organization of Experience*, 21.

13 Gaye Tuchman, *Making News: A Study in the Construction of Reality*.

14 Michael Parenti, *Inventing Reality: The Politics of News Media*.

15 Matthew Mendelsohn, "Television's Frames in the 1988 Canadian Election," 3.

16 Mark Schulman, "Control Mechanisms inside the Media," 113–24; David Hogarth, "Agency and Structure in Cultural Production: A Case Study of Newswork at Canada's CBC Newsworld."

17 Public Notice, CRTC (1988–142, 1988), http://www.crtc.gc.ca/eng/archive/1988/pb88-142.htm.

18 Meenakshi Gigi Durham, "On the Relevance of Standpoint Epistemology to the Practice of Journalism," 117–40.

19 Mendelsohn, "Television's Frames," 3.

20 David Harvey, *Justice, Nature and the Geography of Difference*, 207–15.

21 Chris Hegedus and D. A. Pennebaker, *The War Room*.

22 Shawn J. Parry-Giles and Trevor Parry-Giles, "Meta-Imaging, The War Room and the Hyperreality of U.S. Politics," 29.

23 Bill Nichols, *Newsreel: Documentary Filmmaking on the American Left*, 170

24 Parry-Giles and Parry-Giles, "Meta-Imaging," 29.

25 Roland Barthes, *Mythologies*.

26 Campbell Clark, Bill Curry, Gloria Galloway, and Daniel Leblanc, "Behind the Scenes," *Globe and Mail*, 20 November 2005.

27 Doug Fischer, "Media Focus on Lobbyists in the War Room," *Ottawa Citizen*, 5 December 2005.

28 Ibid.

29 L. Ian MacDonald, editor of *Policy Options Magazine*, in discussion with the author, March 2008.

CHAPTER FOUR

1 Alan Ferguson, "Union Boss in Bed with the Liberals," *Vancouver Province,* 7 December 2009.

2 NDP war room, email message, 2 December 2005.

3 Keith Leslie, "Bolstered by Hargrove, Martin Poaches New Democrat Support at CAW meeting," Canadian Press, 2 December 2005.

4 Gary Norris, "Liberal Minority with NDP Balance of Power Best Election Outcome: Hargrove," Canadian Press, 2 December 2005.

5 Ibid. (my italics).

6 Campbell Clark and Bill Curry, "Liberals Touted by CAW leader," *Globe and Mail*, 3 December 2005.

7 Ibid.

8 Ibid.

9 Ibid.

10 A riding profile is provided at http://www.cbc.ca/canadavotes/riding/109/. The Liberal candidate, Brent St. Denis, polled 14,276 votes in the 2004 federal election. His NDP contender, Carol Hughes, polled 11,051 for a difference of 3,225. The Conservative Party candidate garnered 8,093 votes. Results may be viewed at: http://www.sfu.ca/~aheard/elections/2004-ONT.html. In the 2006 election, the Liberals polled 14,652 votes (virtually unchanged) and the NDP polled 13,244 for a difference of 1,408. The Conservative candidate received 8,957 votes. Results may be viewed at http://www.sfu.ca/~aheard/elections/2006-ONT.html.

11 "Vote for Brent St. Denis, Friend of Unionized Workers," *Soo Today*, 5 December 2005, http://www.sootoday.com/ .

12 Liberal Party News Release, email message, 5 December 2005.

13 NDP war room, email message, 5 December 2005.

14 Ravi Baichwal, "Martin and Hargrove Campaign in Windsor," CTV Newsnet, 9 December 2005.

15 NDP War Room, email message, 9 December 2005.

16 "FedElxn-Liberals-Hargrove," Broadcast News, 9 December 2005.

17 Alexander Panetta, "Hargrove Continues Flirting with Martin at Auto Sector Event in Windsor, Ont.," Canadian Press, 9 December 2005.

18 Anne Dawson and James Gordon, "Hargrove Stops Just Short of Hugging PM," *National Post,* 10 December 2005.

19 Steven Chase, Jane Taber, and Campbell Clark, "Leaders Storm Key Ontario Battleground," *Globe and Mail,* 10 December 2005.

20 NDP war room, email message, 16 December 2005.

21 "Harper Snipes at Buzz Hargrove, Paul Martin over Bloc Comments," Canadian Press, 19 January 2006.

22 Gloria Galloway, "Harper Vows to Rush Wait-Time Solution," *Globe and Mail,* 3 December 2005.

23 Thanh Ha Tu, "GST Promise Not Swaying Voters: Poll," *Globe and Mail,* 3 December 2005.

24 "Martin Aide Sparks Storm with Claim That Parents Could Blow Child Care Cash on Beer, Popcorn (FedElxn)," Canadian Press, 11 December 2005.

25 Mike Oliveira, "NDP Says It Would Open up 200,000 New Day Care Spaces Next Year If Elected," Canadian Press, 12 December 2005.

26 NDP war room, email message, 11 December 2005.

27 The NDP's website at http://www.ndp.ca/ serves as a clearinghouse for war-room communication during election campaigns. At the conclusion of the election of 2005–06, all rapid response and news release materials were expunged from the site.

28 NDP war room, email message, 15 December 2005.

29 Liberal Party Rapid Response, email message, 16 December 2005.

30 Greg Weston, "The Battle of the Cheques Is Heating Up," *Toronto Sun,* 14 December 2005; Susan Riley, "Contrast and Compare," *Ottawa Citizen,* 14 December 2005.

31 "Atlantic Advisory,"Canadian Press, 2 December 2005.

32 "Martin Pushes for 'Centres of Excellence' in Newfoundland and Labrador," Canadian Press, 5 December 2005.

33 NDP war room, email message, 5 December 2005.

34 "FedElxn roundup (Liberals)," Canadian Press – Broadcast News, 5 December 2005.

35 NDP war room, email message, 5 December 2005.

36 Susan Ormiston, "Layton Says He Would Not Ban Private Clinics," *The National* (CBC), 5 December 2005.

37 Steven Chase and Bill Curry, "Layton Bobs, Weaves, Keeps to NDP Script," *Globe and Mail,* 7 December 2005.

38 "Jack Layton Reverses Course on Clarity Act in Quebec Campaign Stop," Canadian Press, 7 December 2005.

39 NDP war room, email message, 7 December 2005.

CHAPTER FIVE

1 Murray Brewster, "Ottawa Announces New Policy on Popular Income Trusts," Canadian Press, 23 November 2005.

2 "FedElxn Income Trusts Update (Adds Commons)," Canadian Press – Broadcast News, 28 November 2005.

3 Jim Brown, "Tories, NDP Demand Probe into Alleged Leaks to Investors about Tax Policies," Canadian Press, 27 November 2005.

4 Paul Wells, *Right Side Up*, 206.

5 Sandra Cordon, "Opposition Call for Income Trust Probe Just a Political Smear Campaign: Goodale." Canadian Press, 28 November 2005.

6 "RCMP Reviewing Complaint on Income Trust," CTV.ca, 30 November 2005, http://www.ctv.ca/CTVNews/Canada/20051130/rcmp_incometrusts_051130/.

7 Ibid.

8 "RC to Keep Pushing Income Trusts?" NDP war room email message, 30 November 2005.

9 "RE: ON Regulator – No Need To Investigate Income Trust Situation MORE TO COME," NDP war room email message, 1 December 2005.

10 Sandra Cordon, "No Contact with Investigators over Income Trust Issue: Goodale," Canadian Press, 2 December 2005.

11 Kathy Tomlinson, "Online Posts Suggest Leak in Income Trust Case," CTV.ca, 7 December 2005, http://www.ctv.ca/CTVNews/TopStories/20051207/whistleblower_incometrusts_20051207/.

12 "IN CASE YOU MISSED IT: More Evidence of Alleged Goodale Leak," NDP war room email message, 7 December 2005.

13 "CTV-News-Advisory," Canadian Press, 7 December 2005.

14 "NEWS: CARP Income Trust Announcement," NDP war room – Canada News Wire email message, 8 December 2005.

15 Lorraine Turchansky, "Goodale Should Resign over Allegations of Income Trust Leak, Says Harper," Canadian Press, 8 December 2005.

16 Ibid.

17 "FW: ROBTV on Investigation of Illegal Insider Trading," NDP war room email message, 8 December 2005.

18 "Afternoon Broadcast Scan, 3:30–7:00," NDP war room email message, 8 December 2005.

19 "MORE: Goodale Moves Business (B) and General (G)," NDP war room email message, 9 December 2005; Sandra Cordon, "Tories Call for Finance Minister to Resign but Hard to Find Smoking Gun," Canadian Press, 9 December 2005.

20 "Wasylycia-Leis Asks OSC to Clarify Position on Possible Income Trust," NDP war room email message, 9 December 2005.

21 Judy Wasylycia-Leis, NDP war room email message, 9 December 2005.

22 "Hunter Standup," NDP war room email message, 10 December, 2005.

23 Andrew Coyne, "It's Not about CARP," *National Post,* 10 December 2005.

24 Ibid.

25 "Wilson – OSC Response," NDP war room email message, 12 December 2005.

26 "NDP – OSC Response," NDP war room email message, 20 December 2005.

27 "OSC Response to Dec 14 letter," NDP war room email message, 15 December 2005.

28 The 2005–06 election campaign straddled the Christmas/New Year's holiday. By mutual consent, the parties all but shut down their respective war rooms. Many war-room workers left Ottawa to spend the holidays in their home communities. The campaign resumed its "second half" in early January.

29 "MP Update re: OSC/SEC Letters," NDP war room email message, 15 December 2005.

30 "Wasylycia-Leis and Summerville Ask for SEC Investigation," NDP war room email message, 18 December 2005.

31 Robert Russo, "RCMP Probe Puts Whiff of Scandal Back into Campaign Heading for Nasty Phase," Canadian Press, 28 December 2005.

32 Wells, *Right Side Up,* 206.

33 Maria Babbage, "Mounties Launch Criminal Investigation into Income Trust Leak," Canadian Press, 28 December 2005.

34 Melissa Leong, Chris Wattie, and Carrie Tait, "RCMP Confirms Trust Probe," *National Post,* 29 December 2005.

35 John Ibbitson, "For Liberals, It's a Matter of Trust," *Globe and Mail,* 29 December 2005.

36 Editorial, "Let the RCMP Decide," *National Post,* 30 December, 2005.

37 "FedElxn-Goodale-Harper," Canadian Press-Broadcast News, 29 December 2005.

38 Richard Cloutier, "BIZ-Income-Trust-Investigation," Broadcast News, 29 December 2005.

39 "Goodale-RCMP," Canadian Press, 1 January 2006.

40 Sandra Cordon, "Finance Minister Goodale Meets RCMP over Income Trust Investigation," Canadian Press, 1 January 2006.

41 Joan Bryden, "American Securities Watchdog Looking into Income Trust Trading," Canadian Press, 6 January 2006.

42 Brian Topp, in discussion with the author, December 2007.

43 Michelle MacAfee, "RCMP Proving to Be Martin's Undeclared but Powerful Campaign Rival," Canadian Press, 26 January 2006.

44 "FedElxn-Debates-Trans," Canadian Press, 9 January 2006.

45 "CP NewsAlert (Income-Trust-Charge)," *Canadian Press*, 15 February 2007.
46 "Former Finance Department Bureaucrat Pleads Guilty," *Canadian Press*, 7 May 2010.

CHAPTER SIX

1 Antonia Zerbisias, "Blogapalooza!" *azerbic/thestar.ca* (blog), 9 December 2005 (website no longer in service).
2 Michael Warner, *Publics and Counterpublics*.
3 Brian Topp in discussion with the author, March 2008.
4 Ibid.
5 Allan Woods, "Young Liberals Posing as Average Canadians in Letter Campaign," *Ottawa Citizen*, 9 December 2005.
6 Mark Schulman, "Control Mechanisms inside the Media," 113–24.
7 Dan Arnold, blogger, in discussion with the author, March 2008.
8 Dan Arnold, "Trouble, with a Capital T, and That Stands for Trusts!" *calgarygrit*, 6 December 2005, http://calgarygrit.blogspot.com/2005_12_01_archive.html.
9 "two cents," *calgarygrit*, 6 December 2005, http://calgarygrit.blogspot.com/2005_12_01_archive.html.
10 *calgarygrit*, anonymous posting, 6 December 2005.
11 Dan Arnold, "Who Can You Trust," *calgarygrit*, 10 December 2005, http://calgarygrit.blogspot.com/2005_12_01_archive.html.
12 "annextraitor," *calgarygrit*, 10 December 2005, http://calgarygrit.blogspot.com/2005_12_01_archive.html.
13 Stephen Taylor, "Another RCMP Investigation Dogs the Liberals," *Conservative Party of Canada Pundit*, 30 November 2005, http://www.stephentaylor.ca/page/119/).
14 "RCMP Reviewing Complaint on Income Trust," CTV.ca, 30 November 2005, http://www.ctv.ca/CTVNews/Canada/20051130/rcmp_incometrusts_051130/.
15 Stephen Taylor, "Income Trusts: Suspicious Activity Prior to Goodale's Announcement, *Conservative Party of Canada Pundit*, 11 December 2005, http://www.stephentaylor.ca/page/117/.
16 "Paul," *Conservative Party of Canada Pundit*, 11 December 2005, http://www.stephentaylor.ca/page/117/.
17 "calgarygrit," *Conservative Party of Canada Pundit*, 11 December 2005, http://www.stephentaylor.ca/page/117/.
18 "nbob," *Conservative Party of Canada Pundit*, 11 December 2005, http://www.stephentaylor.ca/page/117/.

19 Ibid.
20 John Moore, "Where There's Smoke ... There's More Smoke," *National Post*, 13 December 2005.
21 Ed Morrissey, "Who Will Investigate the Liberal Insider Trading Scandal?" *Captain's Quarters*, 15 December 2005 (website now out of service).
22 "Anonymous posts," *Captain's Quarters*, 15 December 2005.
23 Allan Woods, "Young Liberals Posing as Average Canadians in Letter Campaign," *Ottawa Citizen*, 9 December 2005.
24 Tamara A. Small, "parties@canada: The Internet and the 2004 Cyber-Campaign," 203–34.

CHAPTER SEVEN

1 Steven Chase and Bill Curry, "Layton Bobs, Weaves, Keeps to NDP Script," *Globe and Mail*, 7 December 2005.
2 Oliver Moore and Omar El Akkad, "7 Shot, One Dead on Busy Toronto Street," *Globe and Mail*, 26 December 2005.
3 Rodney Benson and Erik Neveu, *Bourdieu and the Journalistic Field*, 3.
4 Véronique Rodriguez, "'Memoire Ardent' by Gilbert Boyer, or When Politics Penetrates Contemporary Art," 193–227; Nathalie Heinich, *L'art contemporain exposé aux rejets*; Luc Boltanski and Laurent Thévenot, *Les économies de la grandeur*.
5 Jürgen Habermas, *Moral Consciousness and Communicative Action*.
6 Gloria Galloway, Ingrid Peritz, and Michael Den Tandt, "Toronto Tragedy Sparks Federal Outcry," *Globe and Mail*, 28 December 2005.
7 An Act to Give Effect to the Requirement for Clarity as Set Out in the Opinion of the Supreme Court of Canada in the Quebec Secession Reference ("Clarity Act"), SC 2000, c. 26, Parliament of Canada, (assented 29 June 2000), http://laws-lois.justice.gc.ca/eng/acts/C-31.8/FullText.html.
8 "Jack Layton Reverses Course on Clarity Act in Quebec Campaign Stop," Canadian Press, 7 December 2005c.
9 "Reality Check: Fix Medicare for a Generation." *CBC.ca*, 12 December 2005, http://www.cbc.ca/canadavotes2006/realitycheck/wait_times.html.
10 Bill Curry and Campbell Clark, "Tories, Bloc Put Onus on NDP Leader to Bring Down Minority Government," *Globe and Mail*, 8 November 2005.
11 Gloria Galloway, "Harper Vows to Rush Wait-Time Solution," *Globe and Mail*, 3 December 2005.
12 Curry and Clark, "Tories, Bloc Put Onus on NDP Leader."
13 Tom Blackwell, "Private Care OK If No Public Funds Involved, Layton," *National Post*, 6 December 2005.

14 Norma Greenaway, "Liberals to Release Proposal on Wait Times," *Ottawa Citizen*, 3 December 2005.

15 Allan Woods, "Harper Unveils Plan to Guarantee Timely Access to Health Care," *Ottawa Citizen*, 3 December 2005.

16 Galloway, "Harper Vows to Rush Wait-Time Solution," *Globe and Mail*, 3 December 2005.

17 Bill Curry, "Not Opposed to Private Health Care, Layton Says," *Globe and Mail*, 5 December 2005.

18 "Lines Re Harper's Health Care Announcement," NDP war room email message, 2 December 2005.

19 "Martin Ducks Clear Question on Health Care," NDP war room email message, 2 December 2005.

20 Bill Curry, Rod Mickleburgh, and Petti Fong, "Ethics Appear to Be a Hard Sell with Robinson as Candidate," *Globe and Mail*, 3 December 2005.

21 Gary Mason, "Fur Likely to Fly As Robinson, Fry Square Off," *Globe and Mail*, 3 December 2005.

22 Chuck Stoody, "Svend Robinson," Canadian Press (photograph), 3 December 2005.

23 Curry, Mickleburgh, and Fong, "Ethics Appear to Be a Hard Sell."

24 Curry, "Not Opposed to Private Health Care."

25 Andy Clark, "Jack Layton," Reuters/*Globe and Mail* (photograph), 5 December 2005.

26 "Health Argument," NDP war room email message, 5 December 2005.

27 David Furst, "Saddam Hussein: 'If You Want My Neck, You Can Have It,'" AFP/Getty Images/*Globe and Mail* (photograph), 6 December 2005.

28 Campbell Clark and Jane Taber, "Tories Aim Daycare Dollars at Parents," *Globe and Mail*, 6 December 2005.

29 Daniel Leblanc, "Whoa, Baby! Chew on These Child-Care Plans," *Globe and Mail*, 6 December 2005.

30 Steven Chase and Bill Curry, "Layton Bobs, Weaves, Keeps to NDP Script," *Globe and Mail*, 7 December 2005.

31 Paul Vieira, "NDP Rolls out Tax Cut Policy," *National Post*, 6 December 2005.

32 Blackwell, "Private Care OK If No Public Funds Involved, Layton."

33 Chris Wattie, "Gomery Not a Big Issue: Poll," *National Post*, 7 December 2005.

34 Chase and Curry, "Layton Bobs and Weaves."

35 Don Martin, "Election Promises Give Layton Lots to Smile About," *National Post*, 7 December 2005.

36 Ibid.

37 Pierre Bourdieu, *The Logic of Practice*, 120.

38 Tom Blackwell, "The New Standard Wait Times," *National Post*,
    12 December 2005.

39 Karen Howlett and Caroline Alphonso, "Targets Set for Faster Health
    Care," *Globe and Mail*, 13 December 2005.

40 Chuck Stoody, "Shirley Douglas and Jack Layton," Canadian Press
    (photograph), 14 December 2005.

41 Bill Curry, "Take Hard Line with Premiers on Health Care, Layton
    Advises," *Globe and Mail*, 14 December 2005.

42 *Jacques Chaoulli and George Zeliotis v. Attorney General of Quebec and
    Attorney General of Canada*, S.C.R. 791, 2005 SCC 35 (Supreme Court of
    Canada, 2005), http://scc.lexum.org/en/2005/2005scc35/2005scc35.pdf.

43 Mike Blanchfield, "Other Parties Dismantling Medicare 'by Stealth:' NDP,"
    National Post, 12 December 2005.

44 Jorgen Johanssen, "Polar Bears Can Skate If They Have the Right Boots,"
    National Post, 14 December 2005.

45 Don Martin, "Watch Them Miss the Bull's Eye: Opposition Doesn't Lack
    for a Target in Tonight's Debate," *National Post*, 15 December 2005b.

46 "Prebuttal," NDP war room email message, 15 December 2005.

CONCLUSION

1 Chantal Hébert, *Toronto Star* political columnist, in discussion with the
   author, January 2008.

2 Francis Russell, "Conservative Bullying Undermines Democracy,"
   Winnipeg Free Press, 14 May 2008.

3 Jane Taber, *Globe and Mail* political columnist, in discussion with the
   author, January 2008.

4 "Online Surveillance Critics Accused of Supporting Child Pornography,"
   CBC.ca, 13 February 2012, http://www.cbc.ca/news/technology/
   story/2012/02/13/technology-lawful-access-toews-pornographers.html.

5 Gloria Galloway, "Rae Apologizes after Liberal Staffer Admits to
   'Vikileaks' Attack," *Globe and Mail*, 27 February 2012.

6 Stephen Maher and Glen McGregor, "Firm with Tory Links Traced to
   Election Day 'Robocalls' That Tried to Discourage Voters," *National Post*,
   22 February 2012.

7 Allison Cross, "I Made Misleading Election Calls Claiming to Be from the
   Tories: Call Centre Workers Speak Out," *National Post*, 27 February 2012.

8 Bill Curry, "Layton Urges Liberals to 'Lend' NDP Their Vote." *Globe and
   Mail*, 17 January 2006.

9 Ibid.
10 Gloria Galloway, "Sparks Fly as Harper, Martin Enter Final Stretch," *Globe and Mail*, 21 January 2006.
11 Ibid.
12 "Official Voting Results," Elections Canada, 2006, http://www.elections.ca/scripts/OVR2006/default.html.
13 Elections Canada, http://www.elections.ca /scripts/OVR2006/default.html.
14 Andrew Heard, "Canadian Election Results by Party," http://www.sfu.ca/~aheard/elections/1867-2004.html.
15 Brian Topp, *How We Almost Gave the Tories the Boot*, 31.
16 Brad Lavigne, principal secretary to the leader of the official opposition, in discussion with the author, February 2012.
17 Topp, *Tories the Boot*, 62–3.
18 James McLean, "The Red Door et la Porte Orange," 64–8.
19 Pierre Bourdieu, *In Other Words*.
20 Jill Edy, "Journalistic Uses of Collective Memory," 71–85.
21 Editorial, "Taking Goodale's Name in Vain," *Globe and Mail*, 1 April 2008; "RCMP and Politics," editorial, *Toronto Star*, 2 April 2008; "Smear Tactics in Ottawa," editorial, *Toronto Star*, 15 May 2008; James Travers, "A Whiff of Tropics in the Air," *Toronto Star*, 17 April 2008; Lawrence Martin, "The Politics of Destruction Has Run Its Course," *Globe and Mail*, 21 July 2008.

Bibliography

Ackerman, Bruce. "Why Dialogue?" *Journal of Philosophy* 86 (1989): 5–22.

Alexander, Jeffrey C. *Neofunctionalism.* Beverley Hills: Sage 1985.

– *Neofunctionalism and After.* Oxford: Blackwell 1998.

Allen, Stuart. "News from NowHere: Televisual News Discourse and the Construction of Hegemony." In *Approaches to Media Discourse*, edited by Allan Bell and Peter Garrett, 105–41. Oxford: Blackwell 1998.

Andersen, Heine. "Functionalism." In *Classical and Modern Social Theory*, edited by Heine Andersen and Bo Kaspersen, 213–34. Oxford: Blackwell 2000.

Anderson, Benedict. *Imagined Communities: Reflections on the Origin and Spread of Nationalism.* 2nd ed. London: Verso 1991.

Angus Reid Strategies. "Tories Way Ahead in Canada: Hold Double-Digit Lead." *Angus Reid Global Monitor.* Poll results, 3 January 2006.

– "Canada Election 2006: The Numbers." *Angus Reid Global Monitor.* Poll results, 27 January 2006.

Appadurai, Arjun. *Modernity at Large: Cultural Dimensions of Globalization.* Minneapolis: University of Minneapolis Press 1996.

Arendt, Hannah. *Crisis of the Republic: Lying in Politics, Civil Disobedience on Violence, Thoughts on Politics and Revolution.* New York: Harcourt Brace Jovanovich 1972.

– *The Human Condition.* Chicago: University of Chicago Press 1998.

Asen, Robert. "Seeking the 'Counter' in Counterpublics." *Communication Theory* 10, no. 4 (2003): 424–46.

Bagdikian, Ben H. *The New Media Monopoly.* Boston: Beacon Press 2004.

Barthes, Roland. *Mythologies.* Translated by Annette Lavers. New York: Hill and Wang 1984.

Benhabib, Seyla. "Models of Public Space: Hannah Arendt, the Liberal Tradition and Jürgen Habermas." In *Habermas and The Public Sphere,* edited by Craig Calhoun, 73–98. Cambridge, MA: MIT Press 1992.

Benson, Rodney, and Erik Neveu. *Bourdieu and the Journalistic Field.* Cambridge: Polity Press 2005.

Boltanski, Luc, and Laurent Thévenot. *Les économies de la grandeur.* Paris: Gallimard 1991.

Born, Georgina. *Uncertain Vision: Birt, Dyke and the Reinvention of the* BBC. London: Secher and Warburg 2004.

Botan, Carl H., and Maureen Taylor. "The Role of Trust in Channels of Strategic Communication for Building Civil Society." *Journal of Communication* 55, no. 4 (2005): 685–702.

Bourdieu, Pierre. *Outline of a Theory of Practice.* Translated by Richard Nice. Cambridge: Cambridge University Press 1977.

– "The Forms of Capital." In *Soziale ungleichheiten (soziale, welt, sonderheft 2),* edited by Reinhard Krekel and translated by Richard Nice, 241–55. Goettingen: Otto Schwartz 1983.

– *The Logic of Practice.* Translated by Richard Nice. Stanford: Stanford University Press 1990.

– *In Other Words: Essays towards a Reflexive Sociology.* Translated by Matthew Adamson. Oxford: Polity Press 1990.

– *On Television.* Translated by Priscilla Ferguson. New York: New Press 1998.

– *Practical Reason: On the Theory of Action.* Stanford: Stanford University Press 1998.

– "The Political Field, the Social Field, and the Journalistic Field." In *Bourdieu and the Journalistic Field,* edited by Rodney Benson and Erik Neveu, 29–47. Cambridge: Polity Press 2005.

Bourdieu, Pierre, and Jean-Claude Passeron. *Reproduction in Education, Society and Culture.* Translated by Richard Nice. London: Sage 1990.

Bourdieu, Pierre, and Loïc J.D. Wacquant. *An Invitation to Reflexive Sociology.* Chicago: University of Chicago Press 1992.

Boyd, Josh. "The Rhetorical Construction of Trust Online." *Communication Theory* 13, no. 4 (2003): 392–410.

Brown, Lorne. *Saskatchewan Politics from Left to Right, 1944 to 1999.* Regina: Hinterland Publications 1999.

Calhoun, Craig. "Introduction: Habermas and the Public Sphere." In *Habermas and the Public Sphere,* edited by C. Calhoun, 1–50. Boston: MIT Press 1992.

Carey, James W. *Communication as Culture: Essays on Media and Society.* New York: Routledge 1990.

Carlin, Vincent. "No Clear Channel: The Rise and Possible Fall of Media Convergence. In *How Canadians Communicate*, edited by David Taras, Frits Pannekoek, and Maria Bakardjieva, 51–70. Calgary: University of Calgary Press 2003.

Champagne, Patrick. "The 'Double Dependency': The Journalistic Field between Politics and Markets." In *Bourdieu and the Journalistic Field*, edited by Rodney Benson and Erik Neveu, 48–63. Cambridge: Polity Press 2005.

Charney, Evan. "Political Liberalism, Deliberative Democracy, and the Public Sphere." *American Political Science Review* 92 (1998): 97–110.

Cohen, Ira. *Structuration Theory: Anthony Giddens and the Constitution of Social Life*. Hampshire: Macmillan 1989.

Collins, Randall. "The Durkheimian Tradition in Conflict Sociology." In *Durkheimian Sociology: Cultural Studies*, edited by Jeffrey C. Alexander, 107–28. Cambridge: Cambridge University Press 1988.

Colomy, Paul. *Neofunctionalist Sociology*. Brookfield, VT: E. Elgar Publishing 1990.

Compton, James. "Communicative Publics and Public Journalism." *Journalism Studies* 1, no. 3 (2000): 449–67.

Compton, James. *The Integrated News Spectacle: A Political Economy of Cultural Performance*. New York: Peter Lang 2004.

Crossley, Nick, and John Roberts. *After Habermas: New Perspectives on the Public Sphere*. Oxford: Blackwell 2004.

Dahlgren, Peter, and Colin Sparks, eds. *Communication and Citizenship: Journalism and the Public Sphere in the New Media Age*. London: Routledge 1991.

de Certeau, Michel. *The Practice of Everyday Life*. Berkeley: University of California Press 1984.

Deetz, Stanley. *Democracy in an Age of Corporate Colonization: Developments in Communication and the Politics of Everyday Life*. Albany: State University of New York Press 1992.

Desbarats, Peter. *Guide to Canadian News Media*. Toronto: Harcourt, Brace, Jovanovich 1990.

Dornfeld, Barry. *Producing Public Television, Producing Public Culture*. Princeton: Princeton University Press 1998.

Durham, Meenakshi Gigi. "On the Relevance of Standpoint Epistemology to the Practice of Journalism: The Case for Strong Objectivity." *Communication Theory* 8, no. 2 (1998): 117–40.

Durkheim, Emile. *The Division of Labour in Society*. Translated by W.D. Halls. New York: Macmillan 1984.

Dreyfus, Hubert L., and Paul Rabinow. *Michel Foucault: Beyond Structuralism and Hermeneutics*. 2nd ed. Chicago: University of Chicago Press 1983.

Edy, Jill A. "Journalistic Uses of Collective Memory." *Journal of Communication* 49, no. 2 (1999): 71–85.

Eisenstadt, Shmuel Noah. *Social Differentiation and Stratification*. Glenville, IL: Scott Foresman 1971.

– *Tradition, Change and Modernity*. New York: John Wiley 1973.

Eley, G. "Nations, Publics and Political Cultures: Habermas in the Nineteenth Century." In *Habermas and the Public Sphere*, edited by C. Calhoun, 289–339. Cambridge, MA: MIT Press 1992.

Felski, Rita. *Beyond Feminist Aesthetics: Feminism, Literature and Social Change*. Cambridge, MA: Harvard University Press 1989.

Fishkin, James. *The Voice of the People: Public Opinion and Democracy*. New Haven: Yale University Press 1995.

Fiske, John. *Television Culture*. New York: Methuen 1987.

Flanagan, Tom. *Harper's Team: Behind the Scenes in the Conservative Rise to Power*. 2nd ed. Montreal and Kingston: McGill-Queen's University Press 2008.

Fraser, Nancy. "Rethinking the Public Sphere: A Contribution to the Critique of Actually Existing Democracy." In *Habermas and the Public Sphere*, edited by C. Calhoun, 109–42. Cambridge, MA: MIT Press 1992.

Fuss, Peter. "Hannah Arendt's Conception of Political Community." In *The Recovery of the Public World*, edited by Melvyn A. Hill, 157–76. New York: St Martin's Press 1979.

Garnham, Nicholas. *Capitalism and Communication*. Edited by Fred Inglis. London: Sage 1990.

Garnham, Nicholas, and Raymond Williams. "Pierre Bourdieu and the Sociology of Culture: An Introduction." In *Media, Culture and Society*, edited by Richard Collins, 209–23. London: Sage 1986.

Giddens, Anthony. *Captialism and Modern Social Theory: An Analysis of the Writings of Marx, Durkheim and Max Weber*. Cambridge: Cambridge University Press 1971.

– *The Constitution of Society*. Berkeley: University of California Press 1984.

– *The Nation-State and Violence: Volume Two of a Contemporary Critique of Historical Materialism*. Berkeley and Los Angeles: University of California Press 1987.

– "Structuration Theory: Past, Present and Future." In *Giddens' Theory of Structuration: A Critical Appreciation*, edited by Christopher Bryand and David Jary, 201–22. London: Routledge 1991.

Gilsdorf, William O., and Robert Bernier. "Journalistic Practices in Covering Federal Election Campaigns in Canada." In *Reporting the Campaign: Election Coverage in Canada*, edited by Frederick J. Fletcher, 3–38. Toronto: Dundurn Press 1991.

Gitlin, Todd. *The Whole World is Watching: Mass Media in the Making and Unmaking of the Left*. Berkeley: University of California Press 1990.

Goffman, Erving. *Frame Analysis: An Essay on the Organization of Experience*. New York: Harper & Row 1974.

Gomery, John. *Commission of Inquiry into the Sponsorship Program and Advertising Activities*. Ottawa: Government of Canada 2005.

Graber, Doris, A. "Political Communication Faces the 21st Century. *Journal of Communication* 55, no. 3 (2005): 479–507.

Habermas, Jürgen. *The Theory of Communicative Action*. Vol. 1, *Reason and the Rationalization of Society*. Translated by T. McCarthy. Boston: Beacon Press 1984.

– *Moral Consciousness and Communicative Action*. Cambridge: MIT Press 1990.

– *The Structural Transformation of the Public Sphere: An Inquiry into a Category of Bourgeois Society*. Translated by T. Burger. Cambridge, MA: MIT Press 1991.

– "Further Reflections on the Public Sphere." In *Habermas and the Public Sphere*, edited by C. Calhoun, 422–56. Cambridge, MA: MIT Press 1992.

Harvey, David. *Justice, Nature and the Geography of Difference*. Oxford: Blackwell 1996.

Hegedus, Chris, and D.A. Pennebaker. *The War Room*. DVD. Pennebaker Associates and Ettinger Films 1993.

Heinich, Nathalie. *L'art contemporain exposé aux rejets. Études de cas*. Nîmes: Jacquelin Chambon 1998.

Herman, Edward S., and Noam Chomsky. *Manufacturing Consent: The Political Economy of the Mass Media*. New York: Pantheon Books 1988.

Hobsbawm, Eric, and T. Ranger. *The Invention of Tradition*. Cambridge: Cambridge University Press 1983.

Hogarth, David. "Agency and Structure in Cultural Production: A Case Study of Newswork at Canada's CBC Newsworld." PhD diss., Concordia University, 1992.

Honneth, Axel, and Hans Joas. *Social Action and Human Nature*. Translated by Raymond Meyer. Cambridge: University of Cambridge Press 1988.

Jamieson, Kathleen Hall. *Dirty Politics: Deception, Distraction, and Democracy*. New York and Oxford: Oxford University Press 1992.

Jamieson, Kathleen Hall, and Paul Waldman. *The Press Effect: Politicians, Journalists, and the Stories that Shape the Political World*. Oxford: Oxford University Press 2003.

Jensen, Robert. "Has a Free Press Helped to Kill Democracy?" In *Converging Media, Diverging Politics: A Political Economy of News Media in the United States and Canada*, edited by David Skinner, James R. Compton, and Michael Gasher, 1–6. Lanham, MD: Lexington Books 2005.

Kaplan, William. *Belonging: The Meaning and Future of Canadian Citizenship*. Montreal and Kingston: McGill-Queen's University Press 1993.

Keane, John. "Structural Transformations of the Public Sphere." *The Communication Review* 1, no. 1 (1995): 1–22.

Kinsella, Warren. *Kicking Ass in Canadian Politics*. Toronto: Random House 2001.

Layder, Derek. *Structure, Interaction and Social Theory*. London: Routledge and Kegan Paul 1981.

Lechte, John. *Fifty Key Contemporary Thinkers: From Structuralism to Post-Humanism*. 2nd ed. London: Routledge 2008.

Lipari, Lisbeth. "Polling as Ritual." *Journal of Communication* 49, no. 1 (1999): 83–102.

Lorimer, Rowland, and Mike Gasher, eds. *Mass Communication in Canada*. 5th ed. Toronto: Oxford University Press 2004.

Manning, Peter K. *Organizational Communication*. New York: Aldine de Gruyter 1992.

Mansbridge, Jane. "Using Power/Fighting Power: The Polity." In *Democracy and Difference: Contesting the Boundaries of the Political*, edited by Seyla Benhabib, 46–66. Princeton: Princeton University Press 1996.

McLean, James. "When Head Office Was Upstairs: How Corporate Concentration Changed a Television Newsroom." *Canadian Journal of Communication* 30, no. 3 (2005): 325–42.

– "The Messenger Is the Message." *Policy Options* 29, no. 10 (2008): 12–17.

– "The Red Door et la Porte Orange." *Policy Options* 32, no. 6 (2011): 64–8.

McLeod, Thomas H., and Ian McLeod. *Tommy Douglas: The Road to Jerusalem*. Calgary: Fifth House 2004.

Mendelsohn, Matthew. "Television's Frames in the 1988 Canadian Election." *Canadian Journal of Communication* 18, no. 2 (1993): 1–17.

Merton, Robert, Leonard Broom, and Leonard S. Cottrell, eds. *Sociology Today: Problems and Prospects.* New York: Harper & Row 1968.

Mosco, Vincent. *The Digital Sublime: Myth, Power, and Cyberspace.* Cambridge, MA: MIT Press 2004.

Müller, Hans-Peter. "Social Structure and Civil Religion: Legitimation Crisis in a Late-Durkheimian Perspective." In *Durkheimian Sociology: Cultural Studies*, edited by Jeffrey C. Alexander, 129–58. Cambridge: Cambridge University Press 1988.

Nadeau, Richard, Neil Nevitte, Elisabeth Gidengil, and André Blais. "Election Campaigns as Information Campaigns: Who Learns What and Does It Matter?" *Political Communication* 25, no. 3 (2008): 229–48.

Nevitte, Neil. *The Decline of Deference: Canadian Value Change in Cross-National Perspective.* Peterborough, ON: Broadview Press 1996.

Newman, Bruce. *The Mass Marketing of Politics: Democracy in an Age of Manufactured Images.* London: Sage 1999.

Nichols, Bill. *Newsreel: Documentary Filmmaking on the American Left.* New York: Arno Press 1981.

Parenti, Michael. *Inventing Reality: The Politics of News Media.* 2nd ed. New York: St Martin's Press 1993.

Parry-Giles, Shawn J., and Trevor Parry-Giles. "Meta-Imaging, the War Room and the Hyperreality of US Politics." *Journal of Communication* 49, no. 1 (1999): 28–45.

Parsons, Talcott. *Essays in Sociological Theory.* Glencoe, IL: Free Press 1954.

– *Structure and Process in Modern Societies.* New York: Free Press 1960.

– *Action Theory and the Human Condition.* New York: Free Press 1978.

Pateman, C. "The Fraternal Social Contract." In *Civil Society and the State: New European Perspectives*, edited by John Keane, 101–27. London: Verso 1988.

– *The Disorder of Women: Democracy, Feminism and Political Theory.* Stanford: Stanford University Press 1989.

Phillips, Kendall. "The Spaces of Public Dissention: Reconsidering the Public Sphere." *Communication Monographs* 63 (1996): 231–48.

Pierce, Richard. "Publick Occurrences Both Forreign and Domestick." Boston: Richard Pierce Publisher 1690.

Pinkleton, Bruce E. "Effects of Print Comparative Advertising on Political Decision-Making and Participation." *Journal of Communication* 48, no. 4 (1998): 24–36.

Poupeau, Franck. "Reasons for Domination, Bourdieu versus Habermas."
    In *Reading Bourdieu on Society and Culture*, edited by Bridget Fowler,
    69–87. Oxford: Blackwell 2000.
Radway, Janice. "Ethnography among the Elites: Comparing Discourses of
    Power." *Journal of Communication Inquiry* 13, no. 3 (1989): 3–11.
Rawls, John. *Political Liberalism*. New York: Columbia University Press
    1993.
– *Justice as Fairness: A Restatement*. Edited by Erin Kelly. Cambridge,
    MA: Harvard University Press 2001.
Reinemann, Carsten, and Marcus Mauer. "Unifying or Polarizing? Short-
    Term Effects and Postdebate Consequences of Different Rhetorical
    Strategies in Televised Debates." *Journal of Communcation* 55, no. 4
    (2005): 775–94.
Reiter, Ester. *Making Fast Food: From the Frying Pan into the Fryer*.
    Montreal and Kingston: McGill-Queen's University Press 1996.
Richardson, Glenn W. "Looking for Meaning in All the Wrong Places:
    Why Negative Advertising Is a Suspect Category." *Journal of
    Communication* 51, no. 4 (2001): 775–800.
Rodriguez, Véronique. "'*Memoire Ardent*' by Gilbert Boyer, or When
    Politics Penetrates Contemporary Art." In *Public Art in Canada: Critical
    Perspectives*, edited by Annie Gérin and James S. McLean, 193–227.
    Toronto: University of Toronto Press 2009.
Scammell, Margaret. "The Wisdom of the War Room: US Campaigning
    and Americanization." *Media, Culture and Society* 20, no. 2 (1998):
    251–75.
Scammell, Margaret, and Holli Semetco. *The Media, Journalism and
    Democracy*. Aldershot, UK: Ashgate 2000.
Schudson, Michael. "The Limits of Teledemocracy." *American Prospect*,
    11 (1992): 41–5.
Schulman, Mark. "Control Mechanisms inside the Media." In *Questioning
    the Media: A Critical Introduction*, edited by J. Downing, A.
    Muhammad, and A. Sreberny-Muhammadi, 113–24. Newbury Park:
    Sage 1990.
Scott, J.C. *Domination and the Arts of Resistance*. New Haven: Yale
    University Press 1986.
Skinner, David, and Michael Gasher. "So Much by So Few: Media Policy
    and Ownership in Canada." In *Converging Media, Diverging Politics:
    A Political Economy of News Media in the United States and Canada*,
    edited by David Skinner, James R. Compton, and Michael Gasher,
    51–76. Toronto: Rowman and Littlefield 2005.

Slack, Jennifer Daryl. *Rethinking Communication*. Vol. 2, *Paradigm Exemplars*. Beverly Hills: Sage 1989.

Sloan, David. "The Early Party Press." *Journalism History* 9, no. 1 (1982): 76–97.

Small, Tamara A. "parties@canada: The Internet and the 2004 Cyber-Campaign." In *The Canadian General Election of 2004*, edited by John H. Pammett and Christopher Dornan, 203–34. Toronto: Dundurn Group 2004.

Smith, Adam. *An Inquiry into the Nature and Causes of the Wealth of Nations*. Oxford: Clarendon Press 1976.

Stallybrass, P., and A. White. *The Politics and Poetics of Transgression*. Ithaca, NY: Cornell University Press 1986.

Standing Committee on Canadian Heritage. *Our Cultural Sovereignty: The Second Century of Canadian Broadcasting*. Ottawa: Government of Canada 2004.

Standing Senate Committee on Transportation and Communications. *Interim Report on the Canadian News Media*. Ottawa: Government of Canada 2004.

Stephanopoulos, George. *All Too Human: A Political Education*. New York: Little, Brown 1999.

Supreme Court of Canada. *Chaoulli v. Quebec (Attorney General)*, 1 S.C.R 791, 2005.

Taras, David. *Power and Betrayal in the Canadian Media*. 2nd ed. Peterborough: Broadview Press 2001.

Topp, Brian. *How We Almost Gave the Tories the Boot: The Inside Story Behind the Coalition*. Toronto: James Lorimer 2010.

Tuchman, Gaye. *Making News: A Study in the Construction of Reality*. New York: Free Press 1978.

Valentino, Nicholas A. "The Impact of Political Advertising on Knowledge, Internet Information Seeking, and Candidate Preference." *Journal of Communication* 54, no. 2 (2004): 337–54.

Van Maanen, John. *Reframing Organizational Culture*. Edited by P.J. Frost, L. Moore, M. Louis, and J. Martin. Beverly Hills: Sage 1991.

Warner, Michael. *Publics and Counterpublics*. New York: Zone Books 2002.

Warnock, John. *Saskatchewan: The Roots of Discontent and Protest*. Montreal: Black Rose 2004.

Warschauer, Mark. *Technology and Social Inclusion: Rethinking the Digital Divide*. Cambridge, MA: MIT Press 2003.

Wells, Paul. *Right Side Up: The Fall of Paul Martin and the Rise of Stephen Harper's New Conservatism*. Toronto: McClelland & Stewart 2006.

Whelan, Edward and Pemrose Whelan. *Touched by Tommy*. Regina:
    Whelan Publications 1990.
Williams, Raymond. *The Sociology of Culture*. Chicago: University of
    Chicago Press 1984.
Woong Rhee, June. "Strategy and Issue Frames in Election Campaign
    Coverage: A Social Cognitive Account of Framing Effects." *Journal of
    Communication* 47, no. 3 (1997): 26–47.

Index